Provocations for Development

Peter,

I hope you find some
provocations to enjoy!

Best wishes

Robert

May
2012

Praise for this book

'An intoxicating cocktail of thought and practice, people and things, Chambers pokes and provokes us to reflect on the hubris and hypocrisy with which the "development profession" is stuffed. I shall mine this book – like a rich, nutty fruit cake – to help me understand the messy, iterative world of which we're part.'
Camilla Toulmin, Director, International Institute for Environment and Development, London

'May development scholars and practitioners use Chambers' *Provocations* to put the post-World War II era of the "paradigm of things" to rest once and for all ... and to give space for his better way forward. This book is a gift to development scholars and practitioners. Read it, reread it, maybe even read parts aloud, and ponder.'
Robin Broad, Professor, American University, Washington, and co-author of Development Redefined: How the Market Met its Match

'A smorgasbord of delightful provocations: Robert Chambers at his best – irreverent, sharp and illuminating!'
Gita Sen, Professor, Centre for Public Policy, Indian Institute of Management, India

'Prepare to be provoked! This book is serious fun, and should be read, skimmed or otherwise engaged with by anyone with an interest in making a positive difference to international development work.'
David Lewis, Professor of Social Policy and Development, London School of Economics & Political Science, UK

'This book is vintage Chambers: definitely provocative but also insightful, incisive, funny, and deeply ethical – common sense for a world where it's in very short supply and more badly needed than ever.'
Ian Smillie, author of Blood on the Stone: Greed, Corruption and War in the Global Diamond Trade

'Development studies as a field of inquiry and prescription has become becalmed in recent years, stuck in its own truisms and assumptions. Sadly, few people seem to have noticed. For 40 years, Robert Chambers has been challenging complacency and simply-plausible thinking that lacks empirical justification or ethical rigour. His writings are always worth reading and absorbing, especially when he challenges orthodoxy of all sorts. Even if one doesn't always agree with all of his provocations, they should all be considered seriously. I hope that this book will put some strong wind and better direction into the 'sails' of development studies.'
Norman Uphoff, Professor of Government and International Agriculture, Cornell University

Provocations for Development

Robert Chambers

PRACTICAL ACTION
Publishing

Practical Action Publishing Ltd
Schumacher Centre for Technology and Development
Bourton on Dunsmore, Rugby,
Warwickshire CV23 9QZ, UK
www.practicalactionpublishing.org

ISBN 978 1 85339 724 0 Hardback
ISBN 978 1 85339 733 2 Paperback

Since 1974, Practical Action Publishing (formerly Intermediate Technology
Publications and ITDG Publishing) has published and disseminated books
and information in support of international development work throughout
the world. Practical Action Publishing is a trading name of Practical Action
Publishing Ltd (Company Reg. No. 1159018), the wholly owned publishing
company of Practical Action. Practical Action Publishing trades only in
support of its parent charity objectives and any profits are covenanted back
to Practical Action (Charity Reg. No. 247257, Group VAT Registration
No. 880 9924 76).

Hand-drawn illustrations in the book are by the author
Indexed by Andrea Palmer
Typeset by S.J.I. Services, New Delhi
Printed by Hobbs the Printers Ltd, Totton, Hampshire

Contents

Part Three: Aid

Part Four: To provoke: For our future

Tables

Figures

Boxes

About the author

Professor Robert Chambers is a research associate of the Institute of Development Studies, Sussex, UK, which has been his base since 1969 with periods in other countries. His educational background is in natural sciences, history and public administration. His main administrative and research experience in development has been in East Africa and South Asia. Among other work he has been a field administrator and trainer of administrators in Kenya and East Africa, a field researcher in Kenya, India and Sri Lanka, an evaluation officer with UNHCR and a project specialist with the Ford Foundation in India.

Books he has written include *Rural Development: Putting the Last First* (1983), *Challenging the Professions* (1993), *Whose Reality Counts? Putting the First Last* (1997), *Participatory Workshops* (2002), *Ideas for Development* (2005) and *Revolutions in Development Inquiry* (2008). His current work and interests include participatory methodologies; participation, power and complexity; professional perceptions and the realities of poverty and wellbeing; and going to scale with Community-Led Total Sanitation.

Preface

Provoke vb (tr) 1 to anger or infuriate 2 to cause to act or behave in a certain manner, incite or stimulate 3 to promote (certain feelings, esp anger, indignation etc) in a person... [C15 from Latin *provocare* to call forth, from *vocare* to call].

This little book is meant for busy development professionals, students who don't want much to read, teachers who want to give students less to read, parents distracted by young children, and anyone else who likes or needs their reading short and accessible. It is for practitioners, activists and academics. It is for those who work in governments, aid agencies, foundations, NGOs, universities, colleges, research and training institutes, and consultancy organizations; for freelancers, journalists and anyone with an interest in development. It is for all regardless of discipline or profession. Or, dare I say more accurately, these are fond delusions that have helped to keep me going.

It is not for reading cover to cover. Open it at random. Perhaps you can take it on a trip or dip into it before sleep. To call it a cocktail of exploration, heresy and hope, as I did in a draft, was pretentious. But there *are* explorations of neglected topics. There *are* heresies that question convention, seeking to see things differently. And there *is* hope springing from optimism and the belief that development thinking and practice really can change things for the better.

Much is outside what were or are normal professional or disciplinary boundaries. My anger, mischief and whimsy will show through. The aim is to provoke. If nothing stimulates, irritates or disturbs you, or sheds a new light, or makes you laugh, I shall have failed.

I have picked pieces that are short: all are less than 4,000 words. Some originate in the adrenalin of workshops, conferences or other public occasions. That means that some sections were originally spoken. With one exception I have gone for material that has not already appeared in books I have written. I have also favoured things that have been difficult to get hold of. I have only dredged up fossils where I think they may have lessons for today and the future. The oldest – 'Simple is Sophisticated' – goes back to 1978 but most of them are from the past decade. And there is more that is entirely new in this book than I ever intended or expected.

Let me hope that at least some of this is readable and will be read: perhaps as sources that teachers can use, or overnight reading for students, or nightcaps for drowsy development professionals, or support for activists who work to change our world.

The papers cluster into four themes: words and concepts in development; poverty and participation; aid; and the future. Introductory and linking materials are *in italics*. Each theme has an introduction in which the titles of the sections that follow are **in bold**.

Most of my biases and limitations will show through. Let me warn you about a few that I am prepared to admit (or is it to boast about?). I am undisciplined. My livelihood strategy has been nomadic, looking for gaps between normal professional concerns. I tend to criticize and undervalue conventional wisdom and practice. When I think I have found an error in common belief, I cannot hide my glee. I am irremediably excited by participatory methodologies and turning things on their heads. I have often been wrong while sure I was right. I posture as, and to some extent am, a naive optimist. I try to justify this on the grounds that it can be self-fulfilling. There is outrageous cruelty, greed, suffering and selfishness in our world. But these can be and are confronted by billions of unsung champions of common humanity, decency and love. I believe we do better to treat cups as half full than half empty. Seeking and exploring positive potentials is fulfilling. And fun is a human right.

So be warned. You will not find here direct treatment of some of the great issues of our time. Among the negative ones are global warming, illegal invasions, dictatorships, terrorism, currency speculation, obscene incomes and bonuses, grotesque inequalities of power and privilege, the glorification of greed, drugs, the drugs trade, human trafficking, undemocratic electoral systems, patriarchal religious hierarchies, toothless global governance, the depredation and destruction of forests and fish, the spectacular squandering of fossil fuels... Among those with positive potential that I do not cover are the ideals and aspirations of human rights, trade justice, tax justice and climate justice, the regulation of banks and multinational corporations, the abolition of tax havens, the Tobin tax, the taxation of aviation fuels, living lightly on our planet... For these, with few small exceptions, you will have to go elsewhere. You may ask, in that case what is left? The book must be too trivial to deserve even a glance. You may be right. Try a quick scan of the summaries of provocations that introduce each section and at the titles. This may confirm you in a prudent, risk-averse decision not to dip into, read or buy the book. Put it down. Walk away...

If, despite these warnings, you do buy or borrow the book, or tear out or copy bits of it, be provoked. Disagree. Do better. Be more radical. And, if you can, share and enjoy the serious fun I have had in putting it together.

Robert Chambers
June 2011

Acknowledgements

Those whose words, writings, heresies, insights, and arguments have provoked and provided fodder for this book are far too many for me to know, remember or acknowledge. I thank them all, and apologise to any who are plagiarized, misrepresented or unrecognized.

I have a special debt to Jenny for so many of her ideas and for those we have hatched together. Her insights as a psychologist and psychotherapist have been seminal, and without her this book and others would not have come about. I am grateful too with apologies to Fio, Ajit and Chris who suffered, tolerated and made the most of a semi-nomadic life through much of their childhood. At IDS, I have much appreciated suggestions for this book from Rosalind Eyben, Jethro Pettit and others, and valued support over the years from many colleagues. Throughout all the later stages of putting this together, Sulu Mathew played a vital part, not just checking and managing the text with speed and accuracy, seeking permissions, and doing much else, but also giving advice and much-needed encouragement when I was losing confidence in the whole enterprise. Without her sustained support and mastery of detail this book might have been dead in the water: it is hers as well as mine. Toby Milner and Clare Tawney at Practical Action Publishing have made constructive suggestions throughout and have accommodated many of my wishes to do things differently. Toby thought of the cover with its provocative meanings of provoke. I am glad to be able to thank Laura Cornish, no stranger, for her prompt and careful copy editing and Andrea Palmer for compiling the index.

All that said, the usual disclaimers apply. What follows is my responsibility, not that of anyone else or any organization. You know who to take to court.

In a few cases several attempts to contact earlier publishers have been unsuccessful. To them I apologize. We did try. To others I am grateful for the green light they have given. The sources of previously published material are the following.

Part One: Word Play

Simple is sophisticated *Development Forum* for 'Simple is sophisticated', (No. 6, 1979)

The power of words in development British Council for extract from H. Coleman (ed.) *'Words, power and the personal in development' Language and Development: Africa and Beyond*, (2007)

What words count? The Paris declaration on aid effectiveness Practical Action Publishing, Rugby, UK, for the chapter by Naomi Alfini and Robert Chambers, 'Words Count; taking a count of the changing language of British aid', in A. Cornwall and D. Eade (eds) *Deconstructing Development Discourse: Buzzwords and Fuzzwords*, (2010)

Part Two: Poverty and Participation

What is poverty? Who asks? Who answers? UNDP International Poverty Centre for 'What is poverty? Who asks? Who answers?', *Poverty in Focus,* (December, 2006)

Professionals and the powerless: whose reality counts UNDP *Choices: the human development magazine* for 'Professionals and the powerless: whose reality counts?', Vol. 4, no. 1, pp. 14-15, (1995)

Whose Voice? Participatory research and policy change Practical Action Publishing, Rugby, UK, (formerly Intermediate Technology Publications) for the foreword and afterword in J. Holland with J. Blackburn (eds), *Whose Voice? Participatory research and policy change,* (1998)

Integrated: seasonal poverty, season blindness and **Two syndromes of seasonality** Earthscan, London, for the text and diagrams in 'Two syndromes of seasonality', 2012 in S. Devereux, R. Longhurst and R. Sabates-Wheeler (eds), *Seasonality: rural livelihoods and development*

Participation: tyrannical or transformative? *Development in Practice,* Vol. 15, no. 5, (August 2005), for review of *Participation: From Tyranny to Transformation? Exploring New Approaches to Participation in Development,* S. Hickey and G. Mohan (eds), Zed Books, London and New York, (2004)

Negotiated learning: collaborative monitoring in resource management Resources for the Future, Washington DC, for foreword in I. Guijt (ed.) *Negotiated Learning: Collaborative Monitoring in Resource Management,* (2007)

Measuring empowerment? Ask them? A win–win in Bangladesh Sida for the foreword in D. Jupp and Sohel Ibn Ali with contributions from C.E. Barahona, *Measuring Empowerment? Ask Them: quantifying qualitative outcomes from people's own analysis – insights for results-based management from the experience of a social movement in Bangladesh,* (2010)

PRA behaviours: 21 do's: Earthscan, London, for 'PRA behaviours: 21 do's' from *Participatory Workshops: a sourcebook of 21 sets of ideas and activities,* (2002)

Part Three: Aid

How development organizations see each other and relate Earthscan, London, for pp. 112–13 from *Participatory Workshops: a sourcebook of 21 sets of ideas and activities,* (2002)

Imposing Aid Barbara Harrell-Bond for the foreword to her book *Imposing Aid: Emergency Assistance to Refugees,* Oxford University Press, (1986)

ZOPP marries PRA? And whose realities, needs and priorities count? Deutsche Gesellschaft für Technische Zusammenarbeit (GTZ) for extracts on remarks to a GTZ-convened workshop 'ZOPP marries PRA? and whose realities, needs and priorities count?', (1996)

Part Four: To provoke: For our future

Whose priorities? and **Objectives for outsiders** Pearson Education Ltd (formerly Longman Scientific and Technical, Harlow) for extracts from R. Chambers, *Rural Development: Putting the last first,* (1983)

The Myth of Community: gender issues in participatory development: Practical Action Publishing, Rugby, UK, (formerly Intermediate Technology Publications) for the foreword to Irene Guijt and Meera Kaul Shah, *The Myth of Community: Gender issues in participatory development,* (1998)

Transforming power: from zero-sum to win–win: IDS for 'Transforming power: from zero-sum to win–win', from *Exploring Power for Change, IDS Bulletin,* Vol. 37, issue 6, (2006)

Pedagogy for the powerful: IDS for 'A pedagogy for the powerful', from *Exploring Power for Change, IDS Bulletin,* Vol. 37, issue 6, (2006)

Immersions: something is happening: Participatory Learning and Action for 'Immersions: something is happening', from Izzy Birch and Raffaella Catani (eds), *Immersions: learning about poverty face-to-face, Participatory Learning and Action,* issue no. 57, (December 2007)

The World Development Report: concepts, content and a chapter 12: Wiley for extract of 'The World Development Report: concepts, content and a chapter 12', *Journal of International Development* 13: 299-306, (2001)

Development paradigms: neo-Newtonian and adaptive pluralism: IDS for 'Development paradigms: neo-Newtonian and adaptive pluralism', from 'Paradigms, poverty and adaptive pluralism', *IDS working Paper* 334, (July 2010)

Stepping Forward: children and young people's participation in development: Practical Action Publishing, Rugby, UK, (formerly Intermediate Technology Publications) for the foreword in V. Johnson et al. *Stepping Forward: Children and young people's participation in development,* (1998)

Acronyms

AKRSP	Aga Khan Rural Support Programme
CBD	Community-based Development
CDD	Community-driven Development
CGIAR	Consultative Group for International Agricultural Research
CLTS	Community-led Total Sanitation
DFID	Department for International Development (UK)
DP	Displaced Person
EDP	Exposure and Dialogue Programme
FAO	Food and Agriculture Organization of the United Nations
GTZ	Deutsche Gesellschaft für Technische Zusammenarbeit
IDS	Institute of Development Studies, University of Sussex
IIED	International Institute for Environment and Development, London
ILAC	Institutional Learning and Change (an organization in the CGIAR)
INGO	International Non-governmental Organization
LFA	Logical Framework Analysis
LGBT	Lesbian, Gay, Bisexual, Transsexual
LIC	Low-income Country
MIC	Middle-income Country
NGO	Non-governmental Organization
NDDB	National Dairy Development Board (India)
NNGO	National Non-governmental Organization
ODI	Overseas Development Institute, London
P3DM	Participatory 3D Mapping
PCM	Project Cycle Management
PGIS	Participatory Geographic Information Systems
PLA	Participatory Learning and Action
PMQs	Participatory Methods and Methodologies that Quantify
PRA	Participatory Rural Appraisal
PRADAN	Professional Assistance for Development Action, India
SCI	System of Crop Intensification
SDC	Swiss Agency for Development and Cooperation
SEWA	Self-employed Women's Association
SIDA now Sida	Swedish International Development Cooperation Agency
SRI	System of Rice Intensification
UNHCR	United Nations High Commissioner for Refugees
UNICEF	United Nations Children's Fund
WDR	World Development Report
WHO	World Health Organization of the United Nations
WSP	Water and Sanitation Programme of the World Bank

For starters: assertions to tempt you or turn you off

In June 2008 I was invited to talk at Practical Action's headquarters near Rugby in the UK. I listed some statements to provoke. They lead into this book. Here lightly edited are some:

> ➤ The realities of poor people around the globe are changing ever faster
> ➤ Powerful professionals are increasingly out of touch with the realities of poor people
> ➤ Of the many dimensions of deprivation, the least recognized and most neglected is...? (In ten tries you are unlikely to guess my (of course fallible) answer – see next page)[1]
> ➤ Development practice is in perpetual tension between a dominant paradigm of things and a subordinate paradigm of people
> ➤ Theories of complexity and emergence can underpin better practices in development (e.g. beyond the logframe)
> ➤ The time has come for participatory numbers and statistics
> ➤ Participatory methodologies can be major drivers for professional, institutional and personal change
> ➤ Reflexivity and the personal dimension are as central to good ways forward as they are unrecognized and neglected.

Do you agree? If not, why not? And if so, what should we do?

1.   I have forgotten my answer. What did you guess? How do we look for answers
     to such a question? Is it part of good development practice to ask it, again and
     again and puzzle about answers?

PART I

Word Play

Introduction: words and concepts

'When I use a word' Humpty Dumpty said, 'in a rather scornful tone, it means just what I choose it to mean, neither more nor less'

'The question is,' said Alice, 'whether you can make words mean so many different things.'

'The question is,' said Humpty Dumpty, 'which is to be master – that's all.'

Lewis Carroll, *Through the Looking Glass and What Alice Found There, 1871*

Winnie-the-Pooh sat down at the foot of the tree, put his head between his paws, and began to think. First of all he said to himself: 'That buzzing noise means something. You don't get a buzzing noise like that, just buzzing and buzzing, without its meaning something.'

A.A. Milne, *Winnie-the-Pooh,* 1926[1]

The words used in development continuously change. Some do become hardy perennials – poverty, gender, sustainability, livelihood – long-term survivors, year on year. Others influence policy, thinking and practice and then are used less and less, perhaps in part because their job is done – basic needs, for instance, and feminism (somewhat surprisingly). Others like coordination and integration have their day, fade away and then revive. Yet others gestate for years and then their moment comes and they are almost everywhere – sustainable livelihoods, social capital, civil society, good governance.

Words can feed cynicism and at the same time be a source of fun. To mock fashions in the lexicon of development we use expressions like buzz words, development-speak, flavours of the month, and PC (politically correct); and we describe acronyms as alphabet soup. Current development-speak words can be used for *Development Bingo* (aka tombola or housey-housey), a diverting game that can be played by students during lectures on development and more generally by members of the audience in political fora.

Words, bingo and reflexivity introduces the Development Bingo game in which the columns can list the latest and most used fashionable words, including nowadays acronyms such as MDGs (Millennium Development Goals) and RBM (results-based management) and words like harmonization, capacity development, deliverables, social protection, evidence-based,

---

1. I have shamelessly lifted the two quotations at the head of the page from Deborah Eade's Editorial in *Development in Practice* Volume 17 and now also her Preface to the volume *Deconstructing Development Discourse* (Cornwall and Eade, 2010) which is based on the earlier publication. The journal and the book are a wonderful source of insight and entertainment which I enthusiastically recommend to all who enjoy words, reflect on language, and are concerned about the changing fashions of words in Development-speak, the dominance of English, and issues of language and power. To Andrea Cornwall I am indebted for enjoyable conversations on these topics and to both her and Deborah Eade for having written so acutely, provocatively and entertainingly on this subject and put together such a delightful volume.

empowerment, accountability and fragile states. These are ticked as they are mentioned. Development bingo brings triple benefits: it mitigates the ordeal of the listener; it enhances critical awareness; and it startles speakers with suppressed laughter or cries of 'development' when a column is complete. This includes an invitation to list and reflect on your own favourite words.

The Cornwall and Eade book *Deconstructing Development Discourse* is at once entertaining, enlightening and erudite on the subject of words in development and says almost all that needs to be said. For our purposes here let me underline two points. First, the vagueness of the meanings attributed to the same words by different actors – empowerment and participation are notorious cases – can lead to misunderstanding but is not all bad: for it can also sometimes allow action to go ahead, with the word as a Trojan horse. Second, in contrast, defining what you are going to mean by words, in a talk, lecture, or writing, sharpens thinking and helps communication. These two points are in tension, and it is a matter of tactics and judgement, which should be master when and for whom.

For all the cynicism, critiques, whimsy and fun to which development-speak gives rise, words do matter. In my view they matter hugely. They express concepts. They raise issues. Their choice and meanings reveal and express mindsets. *Reflexivity,* meaning critical reflection on one's own mindset, and warning readers about this, is fundamental. Then the usages and meanings of words evolve. Identifying new ones that have come into use can show us how thinking and practice have changed and are changing. *Development Bingo* is in the spirit of serious fun, a source of learning as the listener or reader lists words and checks them off as they are used. Such words and their combinations frame and form our perceptions and thought, structure our mindsets, and influence our actions. As Fritjof Capra (1996: 47) put it:

> As humans, we exist in language and we continually weave the linguistic web in which we are embedded. We coordinate our behaviour in language, and together in language we bring forth our world.

A word or phrase can make us see things and patterns and possibilities that we would otherwise not have seen. *Small is beautiful* introduced and legitimated intermediate technology: if Schumacher's publisher had not suggested such an arresting and memorable title, development would have been poorer, and Schumacher's work less known. **Simple is sophisticated** which follows below is transparently, some might say grossly, derivative. It sought to develop a theme and never took off or had any significant influence. Was it, is it, anything more than a creature of its time (1978)?

Then **The power of words in development** examines words and phrases as instruments of interpersonal and institutional power. They privilege those who are fluent in English and marginalize those who are not. Jargon has its technical uses but is also an instrument of power, and labelling with words like *participatory* can be a camouflage.

Many words and phrases that come to flourish seem to start their wider lives in Washington DC. The World Bank at one time aspired to be the Knowledge Bank (Broad, 2007). A central repository and source of knowledge would dangerously concentrate power and threaten diversity and pluralism, and the World Bank did not achieve that ambition. But it maintains its position as a prime source not just of dominant ideologies but also of **Words of power.**

Appropriation and misuse of *participatory* was once feared when it was applied to GIS. In the event, committed activists seized the initiative and **Participatory GIS** became a vibrant movement empowering many weak communities.

The name of an organization interacts with its *identity*, which in advertising-speak we came to call its *image* and now in corporate-speak we know as its *brand*. The name of an organization influences not just how it is seen but whom it recruits, what it does and even how much influence it has. Sightsavers and WaterAid are international NGOs concerned with much more than saving sight or providing water but their identities, images, brands and authority are focused and enhanced by the specificity of their names. A book with an arresting title sells better and has more impact. **What's in a name?** is of historical interest, referring to the christening of an international organization which later renamed itself, while **Hubris and hypocrisy** sees mediocrity following the proclaiming of a centre of excellence.

Words empower those who can use them with confidence, especially when the words are or appear new. Some of the power of academics over students, and indeed with their colleagues, lies in the mastery and use of technical terms and jargon. **How to impress academic colleagues** and **Advice to students** (in **Academic games**) are excursions into that world.

What words count? presents ways into analysing a text and the mindset and orientation behind it through counting the number of times words are used and also noting words *not* used. When applied to the Paris Declaration on Aid Effectiveness this provides material for an emblematic sentence of its most common words, and another of words that do not appear at all.

The same can be done when listening to a talk, counting the number of times certain key words are used. This has become a practice of some journalists when reporting on major speeches by politicians.

Finally, **What words and aspirations now?** invites you to make your own list of words and phrases you would like to become part of the lexicon of development, and then to compare them with some of those that have frequently scored high in participatory workshops.

Words, bingo and reflexivity

A place to start is with the words and concepts we habitually use, listing these, and asking how they frame, influence and reinforce our thinking and action. I have tried to do this for myself. Here is a matrix of what, with fond delusion, I like to believe are some of my favourite words. When I use them in writing I have to check that what I have already written is not already peppered with them.

Table 1.1 Some of my favourite words (as I like to believe)

Challenge	Well-being	Diverse(ity)	Listen!	Pluralism
Potential	Ill-being	Responsible	Poverty	Participation(ory)
Explore	Fulfilment	Methodology	Agenda	Professional
Frontier	Fun	Transform	Method	Emerge(nce)
Complex(ity)	Power	Relationship	Five	Paradigm

What are yours? Below is a blank, with more rows, since you are probably not as constrained as I am by pentaphilia (the love of fives of a thing).

Table 1.2 Some of your favourite words (as you like to believe)

In Bingo (aka tombola or housey-housey) players have sheets with columns of numbers. As a caller shouts out random numbers, players tick as theirs come up, and shout out 'BINGO!' when they have a complete column. We can do the same with words in development. So here is an invitation for you to pencil in Table 1.3 with words that you consider have become current and much more used in the past 10 to 15 years. You may want to include acronyms, or make out a separate matrix for them.

When someone is talking or lecturing about development, you can then tick the words as they use them. And perhaps, in development studies, shout 'DEVELOPMENT!' when a column is complete. Particularly after lunch, as a wake up.

Table 1.3 Development Bingo

Overleaf is my list of recent Development Bingo words. Please bear in mind that they will soon be dated, if they are not already.

Table 1.4 My selection for Development Bingo

These are some of the words and phrases which I think have become current and much more used in the past 10 to 15 years.

Empowerment	Globalization	Social capital	Voice	Mainstream
Partnership	Liberalization	Sustainable livelihood	Deliver(ables)	Rights-based
Accountability	Security	Civil society	Impact assessment	Chronic poverty
Transparency	Capacity building	Fragile state	Logframe	Vulnerability
Ownership	Pro-poor growth	Terrorism	Stakeholder	Corruption
Harmonization	Budget support	Social protection	Citizen	Results-based
Effective(ness)	Climate change	Human rights	Multi-dimensional	China

Columns could be added for acronyms such as:

CDD = Community-Driven Development

ICTs = Information Communication Technologies

MDG = Millennium Development Goal

PRSP = Poverty Reduction Strategy Paper

PSIA = Poverty and Social Impact Analysis

RBM = Results-Based Management

'Reflexivity' – critical reflection on one's own mindset, predispositions, values, mental frames, and ways of interpreting experience and reality – is not one of the words in Table 1.4.

And yet, is it not fundamentally important? How can we do well in development if we are not self-aware? Nor are 'power', 'relationships' or 'personal' in much use, though more perhaps than in the past. When we reflect on these, and their omission, are they elephants in the room? And if they are, why do we not use them more?

Simple is sophisticated

Simple is Sophisticated was an unsuccessful attempt to coin a phrase that would catch on and make a difference. The article which follows was a creature of its time, the latter 1970s. In the reference to Modern Rice Mills depriving poor women of livelihoods there lurks the fond idea that technology that would put poor people out of work could be prohibited. This was the decade when a member of the Planning Commission in India advocated banning combine harvesters from Northwest India because they would displace hundreds of thousands of seasonal migrant labourers. We are now in 2011 in a new world. Mobile phones have transformed communications and the quality of life for hundreds of millions of poor rural people. But though their technology is complicated, mobile phones are simple to operate[1] and have become part of many livelihood strategies. They embody the sophistication of both technical complexity and user-friendly simplicity. With them, simple is doubly sophisticated.

To achieve rural development in the third world, the time is overdue for a reversal of professional values; ideas of sophistication should be stood on their head; and true professional sophistication is often to be found in simplicity.

In common usage today (1978) 'sophisticated' means refined, cultivated, advanced and complex, the opposites of crude, boorish, primitive and elementary. Almost everywhere, professionals, including engineers, economists, doctors, architects and agronomists, prefer procedures and techniques which are described as sophisticated and which are variously complex, exact and costly. Professionals believe that it is by using such procedures and techniques that they can best prove their abilities and competence. For them, 'sophisticated' technology is more prestigious than intermediate or appropriate technology; 'sophisticated' methods of project appraisal more rewarding than less elaborate methods; 'sophisticated' surgery more challenging and satisfying than simple surgical operations.

But most of these procedures, techniques and values have been conceived and evolved in and for the rich, privileged and industrialized North, not the poor, underprivileged and predominantly rural South. The flow from North to South of textbooks, training, and professional recognition and rewards brainwashes and socializes Third World professionals into accepting these value systems, which, as Carol J. Pierce Colfer has argued in a recent *Development Forum*, draws them away from the poorer rural people. Prestige and recognition go to those who use complicated and costly tools and whose papers are published in hard international journals. Professionals who seek a

---

Written in 1978.

1. I wrote this before I bought a new phone, which I thought would give me better access around the world. I suppose I am a slow learner. But I find it much harder to make a call or to SMS than with my old simpler phone. It does almost everything except what I want. The video facility has filled all its memory with films of my knees and feet.

national or international reputation all too often sense that this can be best be achieved by excelling according to the values of professional establishments of the North.

Much that passes for professional sophistication is inappropriate in the North itself; but it is doubly so in the South. The cult of these forms of sophistication reinforces dependence and impedes development in the South. Elaborate procedures and complex techniques, when transferred from North to South have high costs. They generate an appetite for expensive equipment, for foreign experts, for counterparts, for training in the North, for data collection and for the processing and analysis of data. Resources to meet these demands are diverted from alternative uses. Urban bias is accentuated, dependence sustained or deepened, and national professionals in the countries of the South gain skills, experience and contacts which encourage them to migrate to the North and to international agencies. The rural areas, where most of the poor people live, remain peripheral within peripheral countries, a mine from which data, skills and funds are extracted.

Reaching the poor

But if development means ending poverty and deprivation, and if most of the poor and deprived people live in the rural areas of the South, then true sophistication will be found in those procedures and techniques which most effectively reach and help them. Methods tailored to the needs and situation of people who are poor and scattered in rural agricultural communities where skills are scarce are likely to be radically different from those evolved for people who are relatively rich and concentrated in urban industrial centres in countries where skills are plentiful. What appears professionally sophisticated for the one will often be professionally crass for the other.

Some examples can illustrate the point. One can ask – which is more sophisticated:

- A soils map made over a long period by a highly trained scientist or a similar map made in a much shorter period in collaboration with local farmers?
- A fishing survey by an international expert, taking months, costing thousands of dollars, and culminating in proposals for expensive equipment to be used on a remote lake in an area with poor maintenance facilities; or a two-week survey by a local university student leading to immediately feasible proposals for upgrading and expanding existing fishing methods?
- The introduction of modern rice mills with a potential for destroying the livelihoods of hundreds of poor women; or the improvement of traditional rice hullers which would maintain their employment?

- A computer-based system requiring experts, counterparts and massive field data collection to monitor rural projects; or a weight-for-age chart to enable illiterate mothers to monitor the growth of their babies?
- The work of a doctor who performs open-heart surgery for a few of the privileged; or that of a doctor who trains health workers from villages to provide services for many of the deprived?

In each case, there is room for argument on the basis of detail. But the general point stands out clearly. The second, simpler procedure or technique, closer to the rural people and involving them more, is more cost effective. The lesson is the paradox: that in attacking rural poverty, it is sophisticated to be simple.

This principle, that simple is sophisticated, applies to much of rural development. It applies, first, in the design of rural development projects. Approaches which can be managed by rural people themselves are usually more successful than those which cannot. Approaches which enable them through their own efforts to improve their levels of living are usually more successful than those which require major inputs from outside. Housing, tools, machinery, cropping systems and services which they can maintain, operate and manage are likely to be more cost-effective than those which they cannot. Moreover, in rural development, simple is replicable.

Simple is sophisticated applies also to rural project appraisals. Manuals of social cost–benefit analysis grow fast even if the economies in which they are applied do not. As economists struggle to make the procedures more comprehensive, they conflate more and more criteria into the one measure. As the procedures become more elaborate, they demand more manpower, more training and more experts, and generate more dependence and delay. They may make decision making not better but worse as the decision makers cannot see how the final figures have been arrived at. For large and expensive projects, simple decision matrices with columns for criteria would be clearer than much current practice; and for smaller projects, simple appraisals should suffice.

Field staff woes

Simple is sophisticated, too, with government procedures. Bureaucrats load procedures onto procedures, add reports to reports, modify regulations with further regulations, and pursue one circular with another. Procedures become ever more complicated and demanding in staff time. Moreover, field programmes are added to field programmes, often without considering the demands on the time of field staff who become hopelessly overloaded, and who are tied to their office and forced to invent data to fill up their reports. It may take five minutes for a central official to draft a circular requesting information; it may take field staff thousands of hours to provide it. It is also easier to introduce a new procedure, report or regulation than to abolish an old one. In most bureaucracies, a pruning and simplifying of reports and procedures would release time and energy for more productive work, especially among field staff.

That simple is sophisticated is more and more widely recognized in technology. Each situation is special, but complexity, high cost and capital-intensity often go together. Such techniques are more accessible to those who are already better off and more powerful in rural areas and who are often enabled to use them to appropriate communal resources, to displace labour, and to reinforce their dominance as local elites. But it is not sophisticated to deprive poor people of resources or to put them out of work. Truly sophisticated techniques will be those usually simpler ones the net effect of which is to generate, not destroy, livelihoods.

Simple is sophisticated applies to choices made in research and development. Too often research and development decisions lead to innovations which are unnecessarily large-scale, costly, difficult to maintain, and dependent on spare parts or inputs which have to come from outside the rural environment. If the innovation is profitable, all these factors tend to benefit those rural people who are already better off, rather than the poorer marginal farmers and landless labourers. In contrast, innovations which are small-scale, cheap, easy to maintain and use locally available and renewable materials and inputs are more likely to benefit the poor. Too often research and development has been pointed in the wrong directions and has missed opportunities. Why otherwise was the bamboo tube-well invented not by an engineer but by a farmer? What were the engineers doing all those years? Why also was it that so much rice breeding for so long concentrated so heavily on responses to chemical nitrogen which is often cornered by larger farmers, to the neglect of nitrogen-fixation in the root zone of the rice plant, a biological technology which may be scale-neutral, cheap, renewable and more readily available to many of the smaller farmers? Research and development should be directed towards those simple outcomes to which the poorer rural users will have better access.

Simple is sophisticated also applies to the choice of site for the conduct of research and development. Agricultural research carried out in controlled conditions behind the fences of a research station may enable the researcher to publish a tidy journal article. What matters, though, is whether the outcome fits conditions on farmers' fields. Mechanical research may most conveniently (and congenially for the researchers) be carried out in urban institutes of technology. What matters, though, is whether the techniques developed fit the needs, resources and skills of potential rural users. In practice, much agricultural research leads to advice which is against farmers' interests, and much mechanical research leads to innovation which makes no sense to rural people. Part of the solution is to move research off the research station, out of the urban institute, and into the rural environment. Conducting agricultural research trials on farmers' fields and with farmers and developing mechanical technologies in villages and with rural people may involve losses of precision and of professional respectability; but these will usually be outweighed by large gains in applicability, benefiting both from exposure to field conditions and from the detailed knowledge which rural people have of their needs and of their environment.

We have here a further paradox. Rural people are stereotyped as simple and ignorant, but they usually know much more about their environment than do highly trained and travelled outsiders such as government officials, staff of voluntary agencies, and researchers. Farmers know the soils, the plants, the pests, the seasons, the problems and the risks. Farmers on their fields experience the sequence and conditions of their cultivation as a whole and have an insight not constrained by disciplinary blinkers. Their adaptations are often skilful, sensitive and subtle – in short, sophisticated – and may involve many activities, many crops, many linkages not obvious to outside observers, and many complex choices. It is only when the approaches made by outsiders are themselves simple and adaptable that the knowledge and skills of rural people can be called into play, enabling their sophistication to make its full and fruitful contribution.

Who's sophisticated?

If all this is so, who then are the sophisticated professionals? They are, I suggest, those who see the challenge of simplicity – that it is personally and intellectually demanding, and often more difficult than conventional complexity. They are those whose values and practices are related to the needs and knowledge of rural people and who use their professional training as a means to serve them and not as an end in itself. They are those for whom the primary complexity is that of the rural environment and of human adaptations to it, and not that of the methods developed in and for the rich, urban and industrialized North. They are those who are willing to learn from and work with rural people, gaining insight, relevance and priorities from their knowledge and the needs they express. They are those whose simple lifestyles keep them close to the rural people.

Such true professionals are already at work. They are those economists and planners who rebuff the interests which try to foist on their countries complex technologies which will destroy the livelihood of poor people. They are those officials who abstain from flooding field staff with demands for excessive data and for the instant implementation of impossible programmes. They are those in voluntary agencies and governments who repeatedly expose themselves to rural realities and whose work is sensitively tuned to the needs of the poorer people.

They are engineers who give up conventional careers in order to work with rural people in developing appropriate technologies; doctors who train paramedical staff to do what doctors did before; agricultural scientists who work on farmers' fields in order to make their research more relevant. They are in each case people who have the vision and courage to question their professional indoctrination, to risk their careers, to abandon the interests of their class, and to tailor and trim their work to fit the needs of those who are deprived. They are the true professionals. And it is their work that is truly sophisticated.

They are as yet a minority... often discriminated against in promotion, denied opportunities to publish, and still regarded by many in the professional establishments as a lunatic fringe. They have the satisfaction, though, of knowing that their work matters, not only for what it achieves now but also for the example it sets. For they are not a lunatic fringe but a vanguard, presenting a foretaste of a possible future when professional values will have been reversed and when the nature of true sophistication in trying to eliminate rural poverty will have been better and much more widely understood.

But these changes are kicking against the pricks. A massive conservative inertia in professional and university establishments in both North and South weighs against this reversal of values. Much of the critical reappraisal has to occur in the institutions which are dominant – the international organizations, and organizations in the North – professional associations, universities, training institutes and donor agencies. Awkward and painful questions have to be asked, and answered, about university curricula, about professional recognition, about the criteria adopted by the editorial boards of professional journals, about the content of textbooks, about exchanges of professionals between countries, and about lifestyles. Only in this way, and through an exercise of imagination and will, does it seem possible that we can slough off the archaic and primitive ideas of sophistication which pervert so much professional activity.

The power of words in development

The British Council organizes International Language and Development Conferences. This originates in the 7ᵗʰ such Conference, held in October 2005 in Addis Ababa. It was memorable for an ice-breaker activity in which we were asked to stand in our national groups and decide on something we were proud of and would like to sell to the other national groups. The Brits were nonplussed and embarrassed, unable to think of anything. At last, remembering how the television programme 'Yes Minister' about senior politicians and officials had been an international hit in India and elsewhere, we settled with relief on political satire. The Japanese chose toilets.[1]

What follows draws on a talk and paper I was asked to give.

Introduction

Change in our world and in development appears to be accelerating in many dimensions. Some of these changes are obvious and receive much attention, most notably information technology and communications. At the same time, other key areas of change have been relatively neglected in development practice and discourse. Among these are words – the lexicon of development – and the power which they have and confer.

Words and power are interconnected in many ways. As already cited, in *The Web of Being* (1996: 47) Fritjof Capra wrote:

As humans, we exist in language and we continually weave the linguistic web in which we are embedded. We coordinate our behaviour in language, and together in language we bring forth our world.

Relating language and power raises questions of whose language and whose words count. In whose language do we – or are we – compelled or induced to exist? In whose language do we – or are we – compelled or induced to coordinate our behaviour? And in whose language do we together bring forth our world?

This is edited and shortened with minor additions from 'Words, power and the personal in development' in Coleman (2007).

1. The Japanese had good reason to be proud (see George, 2008: 45 ff). But you need, so to speak, to be on top of the technology. On the first day of my only visit to Japan there were to be formalities so I put on the suit I had brought and after breakfast went through the normal routine that follows a strict upbringing. The loo in the hotel presented a tree-sparing alternative to toilet paper, however: six buttons – deodoriser, stand by, water pressure, bidet, spray and stop. Job done I looked down and saw the bidet button and pressed it. A pregnant pause while a tube came out from the back, and then bingo! generous quantities of warm water in exactly the right place (how did it know?). Good, but it went on, and on, and on and on. Losing my presence of mind I stood up. It was some fatal seconds before I found the STOP button. By then the jet had done its work... and so it was in conspicuously soaking trousers that I set out for a courtesy call on the head of JICA (the Japanese aid agency).

The words and phrases used in development are instruments of power and reflect relationships. In subtle and not so subtle ways, languages can reflect power relations and realities. Social relations can be embedded in a language. An illustration can be found in English where the words for animals – ox, cow, calf, sheep, ewe, ram, pig, sow – are those of the conquered Anglo-Saxon serfs who herded the animals, whereas the words for meat – beef, veal, mutton, pork – are those of the conquering Normans who ate them. And today, invasive and dominating languages which become lingua francas – like English, French, Russian, Spanish, Portuguese, Mandarin, Hindi and Arabic – marginalize and disempower those who do not command them well.

An example: a poor man in Northern Ghana with whom a colleague stayed on an immersion programme was frustrated that he had not been taught English. His own language, Pasali, was spoken by only 30,000 people. He had been arrested in Kumasi for urinating against a wall. He could read, but he did not understand the notice of prohibition against urinating because it was in English.

Another example: in the past, the staff of the International NGO ActionAid estimated that they spent a quarter of the year writing and polishing and correcting reports written in English. They felt, perhaps correctly, that they would be judged on the quality of their written English.

Differential command of languages can lead to mutual disrespect, with perceptions of arrogance on one side and stupidity on the other. Many of us will have experienced this on both sides. I know that I have been insensitive in speaking too fast or using difficult words with people for whom English is their second, third or fourth language. I am also ashamed to confess that I declined to supervise a Japanese student in the first year of a two-year course because his limited grasp of English misled me into underestimating him; but when in his second year, I took him on, he wrote the best thesis of any student I have ever had.

New words, expressions and acronyms, and the realities or processes they represent, are continually being introduced into development and are instruments of power. Many of these words, expressions and acronyms travel and spread round the world through mouths, emails, websites and writings which are based in or originate from Washington DC, most prominently the World Bank.

Six which have become particularly prominent in recent years are 'participation', 'partnership', 'empowerment', 'ownership', 'accountability' and 'transparency'. All refer to power and relationships,[1] and all are used with hypocrisy: there is a gap between how the word is used and what it implies, and then what is done in practice.

---

1. For recent sources on power and relationships see Eyben (2006) and Eyben, Harris and Pettit (2006).

Four ways stand out in which words are used as part of a power play in development:

1. *To legitimize actions* – as with these six power and relationship words, and with *partner* and *partnership* – the most used word in the Paris Declaration of March 2005 (OECD, 2005) (see pp. 31–2 below) with *donor* close behind it. Another example is *community-driven development,* which sounds good but in practice often takes the form of top-down centre-outwards infrastructure programmes which are driven not by communities but by pressures to disburse funds before the end of the financial year (World Bank Operations Evaluation Department, 2005 and pp. 121, 133–4). Such target-driven development inhibits self-help, induces dependence and reduces ownership and sustainability.

2. *To maintain dominance.* People feel disempowered when new words, phrases or acronyms come in, and they neither know what these terms mean nor do they want to show their ignorance by asking; these terms often come as part of the baggage of new required conditions (in the jargon, 'conditionalities'). Many of us will have felt marginalized when a new one comes along.[1]

3. *To camouflage and conceal realities.* A stark example is the last chapter of the *World Development Report 2000–2001* (World Bank, 2000), concerning aid[2] (see page 186) where the words *donor* and *donors* are used over 100 times, but *lender* (which would acknowledge putting countries in debt) never,[3] while loans are camouflaged through the phrases 'donor funds', 'aid money', 'resource flows', 'concessional funds', 'concessional financing' and 'concessional assistance'. More recently, the conditionalities of aid – earlier 'structural adjustment' – have been relabelled 'policy and programme lending'.

4. *To sanitize, stereotype or stigmatize.* CNN stopped calling Gilo, an illegal Israeli settlement on Palestinian land, a 'Jewish settlement' and instead used the comfortable, cosy, friendly term 'Jewish neighbourhood'. Supplies of arms to Palestine are 'arms smuggling' but to Israel they are 'defence supplies'. Another set of examples is the spectrum from 'freedom fighter' and 'martyr' through 'belligerent', 'guerrilla' and 'insurgent' to 'terrorist' and 'murderer'; these terms are used in contemporary conflicts by each side to describe the other, blind to the irony of symmetry.

---

1. This was my experience with *civil society.* At first I did not dare to use the term because I was afraid someone would ask me what it included and did not include. I did not know, and I still do not know, but I no longer fear being asked: it is so widely used now with different understandings that I could simply throw the question back to the person asking it.
2. For a fuller analysis of the cosmetic and dissembling use of language in the *World Development Report* see pp. 186–7.
3. The World Bank is mainly a moneylender but calls itself a donor. It is ironic that anyone in the World Bank who described a moneylender in a developing country as a donor might be met with incomprehension or ridicule.

There are many other examples of such pejorative or positive labelling in development,[1] as Table 1.5 illustrates:

Table 1.5 Pejorative and positive terms in development contexts

Pejorative	Positive
slash-and-burn	fallow farming
squatter	settler
encroacher	pioneer
poacher	commercial hunter
smuggling	cross-border trade
illegal immigrant	refugee

Those who are dominant, or 'uppers' in relationships, have power to name and through language to frame and mould the mindsets of lowers. Parents do this to their children, and teachers to their pupils. Who does this naming in development, and in what circumstances, and who is empowered or disempowered, are areas to explore and analyse. The uppers who introduce and popularize expressions in development include the World Bank, aid agencies, and intellectuals of various hues. Their words express and form their own mindsets and shape their actions and those of others. And this may empower or disempower the lowers, depending on purpose, context and process.

In all this, the effects of the adoption and legitimizing of words are not trivial. 'Globalization' and 'liberalization', when used or assumed as motherhood words, can be used to justify a cluster of often questionable policies. Conversely, the adoption and legitimizing of good governance, and the repeated naming of corruption, have brought into the open issues that were previously hidden and that have needed to be confronted. The power to name and frame, and to mould and orient mindsets, itself has to be named, recognized and consciously used for good purposes.

An agenda?

There will be many ideas about an agenda for analysis and action. Here are six presented rhetorically as questions:

1. *Enhance and celebrate linguistic richness and diversity?*

    The Inuit are said to have at least 63 words or expressions to describe conditions of snow (de Boinod, 2005: 166–7). At a recent party, an Indian and a Nepali identified 18 Hindi words or expressions for different forms of non-violent protest. Somali words for different degrees of

---

1.   For the power of labelling in development practice see Eyben and Moncrieffe (2006).

thirst are said to be numerous. We need to celebrate the richness of perception and discrimination of such diversities. A brilliant example was the front page of the London-based newspaper *The Independent* on 26 July 2006 headed '26 pupils. 26 languages. One lesson for Britain' which showed 26 pupils from the same primary school,[1] and all their 26 different native tongues.

We also need to respect people's priorities for learning English, which increasingly is the language of power, of access, of the market, of employment.

English as the inexorably dominant global lingua franca has adopted many words from other languages. Many concepts in other languages, like 'ubuntu',[2] have much to offer but have not yet been adopted to a significant degree. It is a question whether we should make more effort to enable very young children, at the stage when they can easily learn languages, to be brought up bilingually or multilingually. Should we, development professionals and uppers, generally enhance and celebrate linguistic richness and diversity?

2. *Narrow gaps?*

Much can be done to narrow the hypocrisy gaps between words and actions. This can apply especially to the words associated with power. In international aid, this applies most starkly to *partnership*, repeatedly used to describe manifestly unequal relationships (Eyben, 2006). Should narrowing such gaps – by challenging those with power to define what the words should mean in terms of their relationships with their 'partners' – be at the core of a campaign to improve aid?

3. *Non-verbal and visual communications?*

Should we use video, theatre and other forms of communication, given their potential for enabling weakness to speak truth to power, and for power to learn? Participatory video has shown a big potential here, with local people, literate or non-literate, displaying remarkable capabilities to express themselves through taking videos (Lunch and Lunch, 2006). Theatre, puppetry and mime also enable people who are subordinate to speak truth to power (Abah, 2004; McCarthy with Galvao, 2004). Should we, development professionals, do much more to encourage such creative forms of communication through drawings, diagrams, theatre and video, especially where they can empower and give voice to those who are weak and marginalized?

---

1. The school was Uphall Primary School in Ilford, UK.
2. *Ubuntu* is an African philosophical concept from Xhosa, Zulu and other languages. It refers to human relationships, mutual interdepence and sharing, and to the nature of being as expressed in 'I am what I am because of who we all are' and 'I am because you are'.

3.   Define terms?

Jargon can be useful technical and professional language for some, and unintelligible gibberish to others. Often it empowers some and disempowers others. Should we insist on glossaries of terms in papers and reports as a matter of course and of good professional practice? How many terms have I used in this paper which I should have either omitted or explained?

4.   Introduce and use words proactively?

Expressions like 'social capital' (especially in the World Bank) and 'sustainable livelihoods' (especially in DFID, the UK Department for International Development) have served internal political purposes in power relations, enabling a degree of levelling with dominant economics and economists, and providing an acceptable common ground which is not owned by any one discipline.[3]

Should words, and the language of development, be placed more centre stage? For good change, are the words which we use and the meanings we give them one promising place to start? Can they be Trojan horses in the citadels of development thinking and practice?

---

3.   For a summary of the institutional and power-related functions of the terms 'social capital' in the World Bank and 'sustainable livelihoods' more generally, see Chambers (2005: 200–201) which also gives sources.

Words of power

The lexicon of development is in constant flux and evolution, and those whose livelihoods depend on careers in aid agencies, INGOs, national NGOs and particularly consultancy firms, learn to present themselves parroting the latest.[1] So, mixing the zoological metaphors:

> Consultants with contracts to win
> wear colours they know to be 'in'
>> Chameleons, they
>> fake a fashion display
> Camouflaging for cash is no sin

The most concentrated hilarious irreverence in the English language may be Tom Lehrer's Vatican Rag, sung to one of his piano ragtimes. It never ceases to have me in stitches. It was also appreciated by some nuns who begged me to play it to them. It starts:

> First you get down on your knees
> Fiddle with your rosaries
> Bow your head with great respect
> And genuflect! genuflect! genuflect!

With punchlines

> Ave Maria
> Gee it's good to see her and

> Two, four, six, eight
> Time to transubstantiate

The Washington Rag (see also page 124) is a pale punning parody. It starts:

> First you get your glossary
> Learn PC vocabulary
> Use the words that are correct
> And
> Genderflect! Genderflect! Genderflect![2]

---

1. The Live Aid Project Committee was faced with a very large number of project proposals, most of them hastily cobbled together. Triage was essential. Those which commanded the least confidence were collages of the latest development-speak. They simply rang false. In those days there was a species of development professional whose livelihood was sustained by writing proposals for others. I doubt whether it is yet on the endangered list.
2. Over a beer, or it may have been a second beer, a speech-writer for one of the Presidents of the World Bank told me that when he had a draft he did a word check to see how often he had mentioned women and gender. If it was not enough, he slipped a few more in.

With the punchline

> Two four six eight
> Time to say 'participate'

Many of the words that are now 'in' relate to power relations. They have been widely used by the World Bank and by development professionals more generally, with varying degrees of commitment, unconscious irony or hypocrisy.

> We are the Talking Bank that names
> Words for Development Bingo games
> Masters of illusion we
> Rule through our vocabulary
>
> Ever to maintain our power
> We frame meanings by the hour
> Opposites for you and us
> Yours are minus, ours are plus
>
> *Empowerment* means having voice
> You enjoy the right of choice
> You are free in every way
> To run you country as we say
>
> *Partnership* we all agree
> Reflects the way we want to be
> Fraternally as bigger brothers
> We're more partner than you others
>
> Mutual *transparency*'s a must
> To gain the benefits of trust
> In practice it's a one-way fake
> We see through you while we're opaque
>
> *Accountability* we require
> Of the lower to the higher
> For us as uppers it's a plus
> It means that you account to us
>
> *Ownership* we now bestow
> To countries under us who owe
> The terms of ownership we set –
> Debtors are owners of their debt
>
> One proviso you must meet
> You sit in the *driver's seat*
> (but you must never try to feel
> to find whose hands are on the wheel)

Participation's all the rage
Use the word at every stage
You can all participate
In our planning for your State

Lending and *loans* we never name
Grants and loans we treat the same
Fudging distinctions is professional
Donor funding is *concessional*

Self doubt's strictly for the birds
When power weakens, change the words
We have confidence in our trick
Listening's our new rhetoric

We're now the Listening Bank that cares
Wrenched with anguish, drenched in tears
As we harken more and more
To the Voices of the Poor

On our Empire the sun won't set
We are the Lords of Poverty yet.

Policy Postscript

 'Whatever happens we have got
the Maxim gun, and they have not'
said Belloc's Captain Blood, but we
use words, not bullets, as you see

Our Maxim's rules that we devise
– deregulate and privatize
Empowered you must first agree
To sell your assets and be free

Participatory GIS

Geographers and others at the University of Durham convened a workshop in 1998 on GIS (Geographic Information Systems) and participation. GIS was a powerful technology, and in several ways maps are power. The fear was that it would be used against people who were poor and powerless. Pioneers had been found who were using it in a participatory and empowering mode. They shared their inspiring experiences. But I was pessimistic. The esoteric jargon of GIS and its expensive and technical character seemed to stack the odds in favour of the strong against the weak. So this verse happened.

> Jargon abounds with GIS
> We uppers use it to express
> Superior power and gleeful joy
> With our new technology toy
>
> To keep the ignorant in their place
> A map's a visual interface
> Data topology's software gives
> Locals as spatial primitives
>
> As computerized clever chaps
> ours are digital mental maps
> Optimally sited let us note
> Sensing the poor can be remote
>
> Locals should show respectful deference
> When they have no georeference
> Naturally they're marginalized
> when their maps aren't digitized
>
> Ignore the questions 'who then gains?'
> 'Who owns the map?' and 'Who explains
> whose map to whom?' Just pull the wool
> with unintelligible bull
>
> Build ever higher your Tower of Babel
> Adding 'participatory' as a label
> No word passes as more respectable
> To make your jargon more acceptable
>
> Can words change actions? Let us pray.
> *Participatory* GIS – save the day.

The brilliant news is that the pessimistic cynicism of this verse has been confounded by one of the more remarkable movements of our time. Participatory GIS (PGIS) has indeed gone far to save the day. The Durham workshop was followed by a published summary, almost a manifesto (Abbott et al., 1998) in *PLA Notes*, and the emergence and linking of a connected and committed group of practitioners and champions. The formidable creativity, energy and inspired leadership of Giacomo Rambaldi based at CTA[1] in the Netherlands led to the convening of a landmark international conference in Nairobi in 2005. Edited papers of that conference were published as *PLA 54* with translations in a dozen languages. Many sources are in open access fora.[2] PGIS has had many successes in empowering marginal communities in many parts of the world, enabling them to claim their rights, defend their lands, and better plan and act.

So this was a case where a word was embodied in action and really meant something. The consistent and sustained commitment of champions was crucial. In addition, three other factors were in play. First, PGIS works and is a powerful technology. The very potency we feared would be used against poor communities has repeatedly been reversed to empower them. Second, from the start, practitioners were deeply preoccupied with ethics (see Rambaldi et al., 2006). And third, communication technology and open access have been well deployed to link practitioners and disseminate experience.

---

1. The Tropical Centre for Agriculture and Rural Cooperation, an organization dedicated to sharing knowledge and improving livelihoods especially in ACP (African, Caribbean and Pacific) countries.
2. For example www.ppgis.net and www.iapad.org – sources and materials are available in numerous languages.

What's in a name?

Brand is a word I have tried to resist using but like other business and management speak it has become so commonplace it is hard to avoid. Organizations brand themselves through their names. If their name becomes widely known it cannot be changed. OXFAM is not the Oxford Committee for Famine Relief: it is Oxfam. BRAC is not the Bangladesh Rural Advancement Committee: it is BRAC. Others need to change because their name implies an orientation or focus from which they are moving on. As niches and activities change, they may rename, rebrand and redefine themselves. Thus Action in Distress became ActionAid and then with internationalization, ActionAid International; Foster Parents Plan became Plan International.

Here is an example, a problem of naming, provoked by the process that led to the setting up of the international organization for irrigation in the CGIAR.[1] I was one of a three-person team that made the third attempt to conduct a study and write a report, which could be accepted as a basis for setting up the organization. What it should be called was much debated.

> So we can't have Service
> and Centre's out
> we're feeling nervous
> time's running out
> let's call the brute
> an Institute
> but that won't do
> an institute's too formal too
> Consortium? Consociation?
> Cadre? Cluster? Federation?
> Core? Or Corps? Or Core Corps? No
> it's more like Archipelago
> Headquarters, Focus, Node or Hub
> are too damned central, that's the rub
> Bureau's too office-bound, the field
> is where we find all truth revealed
> and Agency's a private eye
> or CIA, a public spy
> The situation's really grim
> I do not feel my mind's in trim
> INTRIM!? Thanks Freud.[2] You're just in time
> to give the name and one last rhyme
> International Network for Training and Research
> in Irrigation Management

---

1. Consultative Group for International Agricultural Research.
2. The allusion is to Freud's illuminating book *The Psychopathology of Everyday Life* (1901) which establishes that verbal slips or associations have subconscious significance.

Provocations
for Development

Provoke *vb tr.* **1** to anger or infuriate **2** to cause to act or behave in a certain manner, incite or stimulate **3** to promote (certain feelings, esp. anger, indignation etc) in a person...[C15 from Latin *provocare* to call forth, from *vocare* to call.

Development *n.* **1** process of development or being developed **2** a specified state of advancement **3** the process of starting to experience or suffer from an ailment or feeling **4** an event constituting a new stage in a changing situation.

ROBERT CHAMBERS

PROVOCATIONS FOR DEVELOPMENT

Do we use obscure words to impress our colleagues – or fashionable ones to win research proposals? How do poor people define their poverty? How can we use aid budgets most effectively? Are many of our actions against poverty simple, direct... and wrong?

Provocations for Development is an entertaining and unsettling collection of writings that questions concepts, conventions and practices in development. It is made up of short and accessible writings by Robert Chambers, reflecting on the evolution of concepts like participation and of organizations like the World Bank. Besides provocations, there is mischief, verse and serious fun. The book is organized into four sections. The first, 'Word Play', irreverently examines vocabularies of development and how words are instruments of power. The second 'Poverty and Participation' challenges concepts of poverty, presents empowering breakthroughs in the current explosion of participatory methodologies, and concludes with what can be done at the personal level. The third, 'Aid', is critical of past and present procedures and practices in aid and points to feasible changes for doing better. The provocations in the last section 'For our Future' touch on values, ethics, gender and participation, immersions, hypocrisy, and paradigms, and sees hope in children. The final provocation invites readers to find answers to the question 'What would it take to eliminate poverty in the world?'

To receive a 10% discount, order fr[...]

Since 1974, Practical Action Publishing (formerly Intermedia[...] and disseminated books and information in support of interna[...] Publishing is a trading name of Practical Action Publishing L[...] company of Practical Action. Practical Action Publishing trad[...] are covenanted back to Practical Action (Charity Reg. No. 24[...]

...chnology Publications and ITDG Publishing) has published
...al development work throughout the world. Practical Action
...ompany Reg. No. 1159018), the wholly owned publishing
...ly in support of its parent charity objectives and any profits
..., Group VAT Registration No. 880 9924 76).

www.developmentbookshop.com

ISBN 9781853397240 Hardback

ISBN 9781853397332 Paperback

2012 • 240 pages • 234 x 156 mm

Studies, UK.
Associate at the Institute of Development
Professor Robert Chambers is a Research

ABOUT THE AUTHOR

wider public.
staff of international agencies, as well as the
academics, students, NGO workers and the
by development professionals, including
Provocations for Development will be enjoyed

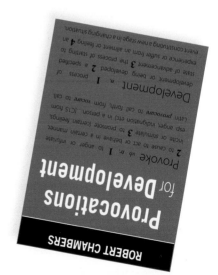

CONTENTS includes...

PRACTICAL ACTION Publishing

Order Form

How to order

To receive a 10% discount, order from www.developmentbookshop.com

☎ **+44 (0) 1926 634501**

✉ complete the order form below and return to:
Practical Action Publishing, Schumacher Centre for Technology and Development, Bourton on Dunsmore, Rugby, Warwickshire, CV23 9QZ, UK.

Postage & Packaging:
UK – allow 4-5 days.
Europe – allow 6-15 days.
Rest of the World Allow – 28 days, or up to 180 days to remote areas.

Payment Details (please tick payment method)

I enclose payment of total cost
(cheques should be made payable to Practical Action Publishing)

Please send me a proforma invoice

Please charge my credit card Mastercard/Visa/Maestro

Card No.

Valid from   Expiry date

Issue number (Maestro only)

Security number (last 3 figures on the security strip)

Signature

Title and ISBN

Title and ISBN	Price	Quantity	Amount
Provocations for Development ISBN 978 1 85339 733 2 paperback	£9.95		
Cost of Postage (see below)			
Grand Total			

Cost of Postage
UK, add 15%, min. £5. **Europe,** add 20%, min. £5.
Rest of the world orders up to £100, standard delivery, add 25%, min. £10. **Rest of the world orders over £100,** standard delivery, add 20%, min. £10.
Rest of the world priority service add 40% min. £10.
Please contact us for a quote on courier of airfreight services

Cardholder's Details

Name	
Address	
Postcode	Country
Telephone	Email

Delivery Address (if different from cardholder's details above)

Name	
Address	
Postcode	Country
Telephone	Email

Any profit supports the work of Practical Action, Reg. Charity No. 247257.   *Thank you for your order!*

For Practical Action Publishing's full catalogue or any other queries please email publishinginfo@practicalaction.org.uk

Publication dates, prices and other details are subject to change without prior notice. 1998 Data Protection Act. Practical Action Publishing will NOT pass your details on to a third party.

1 2 3 4 5 6 7 8 9 10

In the event it was called IIMI, the International Irrigation Management Institute. But it later rebranded to become the International Water Management Institute. The shift from irrigation management to water management must have been profoundly important, for only that can explain the adoption of an acronym (IWMI) so unpronounceable that people still call it immi.

So, acronyms can matter. So too can how we describe ourselves or are described. I cannot account fully for my distaste for the word excellence. But it is sometimes associated with:

Hubris and Hypocrisy

If you indulge in the pretence
Of being a Centre of Excellence
The gods will deal your hand a joker
Making sure you're mediocre
Hubris and hypocrisy curse
So what you do gets worse and worse
Don't tempt the gods, but pass this test
Be modest and you'll do your best

Academic games

I hate marking essays. I have discovered that my criteria differ from those of most other examiners. I avoid it as much as possible. Among other things, and unfair to students, I have hate words and expressions, most of them superfluous fillers or fraudulent, or so it seems to me. So any students who read this, what do you make of:

Advice to Students

When you're stuck and don't know what to write
Choose long words so you seem erudite
Hermeneutic, holistic subtexts
In your discourse will have good effects

If your essay's too short, don't despair
There are words you can add here and there
Specifically, crucial and critical
Problematic, essentially, political

When there's something you don't know about
Start the sentence 'beyond any doubt'
When asserting without evidence
'it is clear that' will give the right sense*

Make your sentences long and obtuse
With subclauses prolific in use.
To avoid any chance of rebuttal
Call themes nuanced, and complex and subtle

Never mind if confusion's endemic
Your community's now epistemic
The truth's neither simple nor pure**
So it's right that your essay's obscure

The examiner's half-open eyes
Will blink as he heavily sighs
And wonders whatever to do
How can he (most are men) take a view?

You laugh last as he finds a way out
It is called 'benefit of the doubt'
So you bask in examiner's praise
As you make it in style with straight As?

---

*   Speech is different. Then apply
       'To be honest' when you lie

**   To be rigorous, footnote your source
       It was Oscar Wilde who said this, of course

That academics play games with one another has been notorious but may be a waning phenomenon. I hear less of it than I used to (but then I do not go to social anthropology seminars). I do not mourn the passing of these games, though there can be a related loss of sharp and critical debate. Nor do I mourn the passing of the obscurantism of some (not all) post-modern writers, sometimes indistinguishable (as I like to believe when I cannot understand them) from thought disorder.[1] But of course we members of university, college and institute faculties believe we need to make careers and get promoted so here is some valuable advice, well grounded in personal experience.

How to Impress Academic Colleagues

If you're slow and none too bright
Don't be put off. See the light.
Play the academic game.
Make it fun and have no shame
The rules are simple, sure and few
To seem to say things wise and new

First, always make your prose obscure,
Never lucid, never pure
The way to get the upper hand
Is say what none can understand
Critics can never vent their spite
If they can't fathom what you write

You will never get it wrong
If your sentences are long
What you write may make no sense
But lay it on, be doubly dense
People will bolster your pretence
To show their own intelligence

Just now and then, for safety's sake
Short sentences and words can make
A good effect. Against rebuttal
Show they're nuanced, deep and subtle,
Disarming any doubting Thomas
By giving words inverted commas

---

1. There is an interesting speculation and research topic here. With ageing, as I can testify, short-term memory does not improve. Do people, as they get older, then write shorter sentences because otherwise they forget the beginnings? Mine have got shorter. And when reading do they find long sentences and complex paragraphs harder to understand because the beginning slips from their memory by the time they reach the end (how did this footnote start? Those who write for the growing grey market might bear this in mind. For wrinklies, write shorter sentences. The older the shorter. Becoming very short. Very.

Don't write of risk when 'risk' implies
Meanings both profound and wise
Readers may have no idea
What they are, but have no fear
No one will ask for that would show
Them as the ones who did not know

--

You think I'm joking? Yes and no
Post-modernists, well, some we know,
Have played these games for years and years
Causing poor students endless tears
Unchallenged because no one dares
They get university chairs

Do they admit to their confessors
How they rose to be professors?
I doubly doubt it. Self-deceit
And muddled thinking when they meet
Combine like treacle to ensnare
I doubt they are so self-aware

It's overdue we call their bluff
Expose their obscurantist stuff
Let's challenge them: 'Friends, please translate
Your texts and subtexts and just state
In simple prose for all to see
Your meaning if meaning there be'.

What words count? The Paris Declaration on Aid Effectiveness

Counting words in documents can be revealing. It is salutary to do this for one's own writing, and to identify favourite words and also words that are not used. In MS Word, the way to do this is CTRL + H and then type in the root of the word. Each tap of ENTER then finds the next. This takes time but has the advantage of showing the context, and also allowing the identification of all words with a common root – like using participat for participate, participating, participatory, participation and so on.

WORDLE is a programme which allows the generation of a word cloud. It can also give a tally of the number of times a word is used. Wordle was first published by Jonathan Feinberg on wordle.net. The clouds give prominence to words according to how frequently they appear in the source text.

If you do this for a report, or a research proposal, or a similar document whose author you do not know, it is intriguing, illuminating and fun to guess their profession or discipline. Engineers are among the easiest to detect. We all become transparent in our different ways when this is done!

A question worth asking is whether word counts of policy documents can reveal more now, in the early 21st century, than in the past. This could be so if there was more attention now to using currently fashionable terms, and where international agreement on content is concerned. Perhaps as donors engage in harmonization of policies, they also harmonize (or standardize) their vocabulary trying to sing in unison from the same hymn sheet. These conjectures are supported by an analysis of the Paris Declaration on Aid Effectiveness, drawn up in Paris at the OECD in February/March 2005 (DAC, 2005). Though a short document, the density of key words is striking. For that document, an emblematic sentence can read:

> To **monitor indicators** of **effective performance** from **aid**, **donors** and **partners** need the **capacity** to **manage** the **mutual harmonization** of **programmes** to **assess**, **measure** and **report** on **results**[1]

Based on the conclusion of Alfini and Chambers (2007) 'Words count: taking a count of the changing language of British aid' in *Development in Practice* 17. The first paragraphs in italics have been added.

1. The number of times I counted the words as used was:
To monitor (18) indicators (30) of effective (38) performance (17) from aid (61), donors (70) and partners (96) need the capacity (20) to manage (17) the mutual (12) harmonization (21) of programmes (22) to assess (16), measure (11) and report (11) on results (20).

Paradigmatically, this is a mechanistic world without people where aid effectiveness is to be achieved through top-down standardized bureaucratic norms, with measurements and upwards reporting.

A shadow sentence can be made up of words never used in the Declaration:

> To **negotiate** and **evolve agreements** that **optimize outcomes** for **poor, vulnerable** and **marginalized people** requires **compromises** and **trade-offs** based on **personal conviction** and **interactions** and **relationships** that **nurture trust**, and **reflective appreciation** of **power** and **conflicts**

Paradigmatically, this is for a world that names and recognizes the realities and significance of power, trust, negotiation and relationships in aid (see for example Eyben, 2006).

Many words, like those in the shadow sentence, are candidates for future use. Not surprisingly, perhaps, much that matters is not mentioned in official documents. The spiritual sides of life are missing. Words like *critical, reflection, professionalism, self-awareness, personal development, fulfilment* and *fun* are not found. Nor, until recently, were negative aspects like conflict and corruption much named or confronted. Deadly sins like the greed that dominates and drives so much 'development' (the bonus-bloated bankers and others we love to hate) do not appear, nor virtues like faith, hope and charity (generosity).

What words and aspirations now?

Words for our future

If Fritjof Capra is right, that together in language we bring forth our world, let me end this section with an invitation. What concepts, concerns, values, aspirations, policies and actions would you wish to be widely used and realized in development, together to bring forth our future world?

And overleaf (don't look yet) you can find some words that others have named.

Table 1.6 Words for our future

Others' words for the future

These include words named and given high scores by participants in workshops when asked for concepts, concerns, values, aspirations, policies and actions they wish to be widely used and made real, together to bring forth our future world. I have added some of my own.

The gap between aspirational words and actual practice will always yawn. The realistic aim is to narrow it, not once, but again and again, to define what the words imply, to expose gaps between meaning and application, to strive to embed them in rules, procedures, norms, declarations and mission statements, to struggle with personal and professional practice and to recognize hypocrisy, and more and more to make such words signposts to follow on paths to a better future.

Table 1.7 Others' words for our future

Critical	Respect	Redistribution	Immersion	Empowerment
Reflexivity	Love	Climate justice	Celebration of diversity	Well-being
Self-awareness	Peace	Taxation justice	Equity	360 degree accountabilities
Empathy	Listen	Participation	Reconciliation	360 degree transparency
Facilitation	Honesty	Rights and duties	Solidarity	Fulfilment and fun
Responsibility	Ethics	Democratic	Non-negotiable principles	Emergence
Reciprocity	Trust	Relationships	Complexity	Edge of chaos

PART II
Poverty and Participation

To provoke: poverty and participation

Professional understandings and definitions of poverty have changed. For economists and planners in the decades of development, poverty was widely taken as poverty of income. The term income-poverty, which implicitly acknowledges other dimensions of poverty, was not to my knowledge used before the mid 1990s and the Social Development Summit of 1995 in Copenhagen. **What is poverty? Who asks? Who answers?** outlines four professional definitions of poverty or deprivation, and a fifth which is how poor people themselves experience and describe ill-being and the bad life. This leads to questions: whose experience, whose reality, counts? Ours, as we construct it with our mindsets and methods and for our purposes, or theirs as they analyse and express it? This was elaborated at the time of the Social Summit in **Professionals and the powerless**. This reflects on ourselves as development professionals, our power, how our convenience and methods affect how we see poverty, and how this can contrast with what poor people experience as bad and what they value, and what would enhance their well-being as they define it.

PPAs (Participatory Poverty Assessments) were a methodological break-through of the 1990s.[1] In a participatory mode they enabled poor people to present and analyse their realities and what would make a difference for them. Many of them used PRA visual methods of analysis. The first, in Ghana in 1993, was initiated and managed by Andy Norton, on secondment from the Overseas Development Administration (now DFID) to the World Bank. Other PPAs followed in Zambia, South Africa and Mozambique and then spread worldwide. **Whose Voice? Participatory research and policy change**, edited by Jeremy Holland with James Blackburn, brought together contributions and insights from some of the main actors, and showed how PPAs had revealed surprises and influenced policy. The **foreword** and **afterword** here give background to the PPAs and examples of significant findings, and the **postscript** describes an innovation in Bangladesh that holds promise to be a wave of the future.

Major insights from the PPAs, broadly taken here to include the Voices of the Poor study in 23 countries (Narayan et al., 2000b), and from other participatory research, were aspects of poverty, deprivation, ill-being and the bad life which had previously been largely overlooked. **Blind spots: hidden, unseen and sensitive dimensions of deprivation** details and describes six of

---

1. For good sources see Holland with Blackburn (1998) *Whose Voice?*, Norton et al. (2001) *A Rough Guide to PPAs*, Robb (2002) *Can the Poor Influence Policy?* and Praxis (2007) *Participatory Poverty Assessments: a guide for critical practitioners*. For comparative analysis and presentations of findings see Narayan et al. (2000a) Voices *of the Poor. Can Anyone Hear Us?* For the findings of a PPA conducted in 23 countries see Narayan et al. (2000b) *Voices of the Poor: Crying Out for Change*.

these: the body; places of the poor; poverty of time and energy; violence; sex work; and open defecation.

However, for combining significance for poor people with professional neglect, seasonality stands alone. In innumerable contexts, local people have made seasonal diagrams which show how significant seasonality is for their lives and livelihoods. **Integrated: seasonal poverty, season blindness** reviews what is not seen and how and why we – outsider professionals – do not see it. It incorporates material from conferences on seasonality in 1978 and 2009. These occasions provoked **To celebrate conferences on seasonality: an ode and a sonnet** (with a footnote for those who wish to become rich beyond the dreams of avarice from the seasonality of financial crises). Again and again the interlocking nature of deprivations, and of dimensions of well-being, is revealed by the lives and livelihoods of people living in poverty. Linear sentences cannot express these linkages. They are best shown in diagrams. Some modest attempts are made in **Poverty in diagrams**, which includes one about the integrated season blindness of professionals.

For professionals, a time to provoke bridges poverty and participation with serious fun at the expense of ourselves and our professionalisms.

In the name of participation, there is much bad practice. Participation can also suit neo-liberals because it can be used to justify shrinking the state, as is widely alleged with David Cameron's Big Society. One test of participation is whether people are better off and feel they are better off as a result of it. A critical and not always well-informed stance was taken in *Participation: The New Tyranny?* (Cooke and Kothari, 2001). This was followed and updated by its more balanced sequel *Participation: From Tyranny to Transformation? Exploring New Approaches to Participation in Development* (Hickey and Mohan, 2004). This **review**, in *Development in Practice*, of **Participation: from tyranny to transformation** gives a personal assessment.

Participatory methodologies have proliferated in recent years. Many of these have been improvised and invented ad hoc, often by consultants who have to move on to other work. All too often important methodological innovations have then been forgotten and lost. Two outstanding exceptions are recognized here. They invite and challenge those in the mainstreams of monitoring and evaluation to adopt new approaches to learning. The **foreword** to the first, **Negotiated Learning: collaborative monitoring in resource management** edited by Irene Guijt (2007) celebrates a new approach to monitoring in which communities and outsiders negotiate and evolve the ways in which they will learn together. This innovation promises applications in monitoring and evaluation in contexts far beyond forestry. The other outstanding exception comes from Bangladesh. A brief overview of **Measuring empowerment? Ask them** describes a remarkable participatory methodology in which members of a large social movement have facilitated and conducted their own analysis. Their assessment of their own social change and empowerment leads them towards further social change and empowerment. It also shows how statistics of social change and empowerment can be generated and aggregated. It is a win–win: those who assess themselves are empowered; and those who support them are informed. But this is exceptional. **Participatory numbers and statistics** asks why the many participatory approaches and methods which can generate numbers remain on the fringes. Despite their accuracy, relevance, ability to quantify the qualitative, and win–win nature they are nowhere the norm. Why not? And what should be done?

This leads to an invitation, an exhortation, really, to **Start, stumble, self-correct, share**. It dates back to 1992 and the early days of PRA. Do its provocative imperatives still apply? It urges us to engage, to make mistakes, to fail forwards, to learn, to correct and to share the experiences. This means being alert, aware and nimble. It means improvising and adapting. It means that in order to learn and change, we have to be daring, as in the **21 do's**. These were listed for those who facilitate participatory workshops. Do they apply more generally? Can they be fun? Can they mean that we get more out of, and put more into, life and living? Can the last word be *enjoy!*?

What is poverty? Who asks? Who answers?

The flood of development rhetoric on poverty, the primacy accorded by lenders and donors to the Millennium Development Goals, of which the reduction of extreme poverty is the first and usually considered the most important, and the frequency with which reducing, alleviating or eliminating poverty is seen as a prime goal and measure of development – these factors make it matter more than ever to know what poverty is. What it is taken to mean depends on who asks the question, how it is understood, and who responds. From this perspective, it has at least five clusters of meanings.

The first is *income-poverty* or its common proxy (because less unreliable to measure) consumption-poverty. This needs no elaboration. When many, especially economists, use the word poverty they are referring to these measures. Poverty is what can be and has been measured, and measurement and comparisons provide endless scope for debate.

The second cluster of meanings is *material lack or want*. Besides income, this includes lack of or little wealth and lack of or low quality of other assets such as shelter, clothing, furniture, personal means of transport, radios or television, and so on. This also tends to include no or poor access to services.

A third cluster of meanings derives from Amartya Sen, and is expressed as *capability deprivation*, referring to what we can or cannot do, can or cannot be. This includes but goes beyond material lack or want to include human capabilities, for example skills and physical abilities, and also self-respect in society.

A fourth cluster takes a yet more broadly *multi-dimensional view of deprivation*, with material lack or want as only one of several mutually reinforcing dimensions.

These four clusters of the meanings of poverty have all been constructed by 'us', by development professionals. They are expressions of 'our' education, training, mindsets, experiences and reflections. They reflect our power, as non-poor people, to make definitions according to our perceptions. And the primacy we accord to poverty alleviation, reduction or elimination implies that these meanings that we give are fundamental to what development should be about.

But they are all abstractions, to varying degrees reductionist, based on our analysis and views. They tend to overlook and ignore the analysis and views of the objects of the definition and description – 'the poor', that is people who are in a bad condition variously described as poor, marginalized, vulnerable, excluded or deprived. There is then a fifth cluster, which is the multiplicity of *their* meanings.

One expression of this has twelve dimensions, each one potentially having an impact on all of the others, and in turn being potentially affected by each

---

Written in 2006.

one of the others, thus emphasizing the interdependence of the dimensions of poverty as we see them. The dimensions are material poverties, physical ill-being, insecurities, places of the poor, seasonal dimensions, poverty of time, poverty of institutions and access, lack of education and capabilities, lack of information, lack of political clout, ascribed and legal inferiority, and bad social relations (see pp. 62–3 for versions of the diagram).

These dimensions have been elicited in many contexts, most extensively perhaps in the World Bank's participatory research programme Voices of the Poor, in which over 20,000 poor women and men from 23 countries were convened in small groups and facilitated to analyse and express their realities.[1] Questions had to be confronted concerning words, translations, languages and concepts. The word poverty translated into other languages carries different connotations. This was one factor in deciding to seek better insights and comparability by inviting the local analysts to use their own words and concepts for ill-being or bad quality of life, and well-being or good quality of life. Even allowing for the pitfalls of analysing and imposing outsiders' categories on their diverse responses, values and realities, it was striking how common and strong the same dimensions were across cultures and contexts.

There were many poverties or deprivations. Dimensions of the bad life included not only income-poverty and material lack, but many others, some of them represented in the web of poverty's disadvantages in Figure 2.4 (page 62), for example poverty of time, living and working in bad places – 'the places of the poor' and bad social, especially gender, relations. Others were the body as the main asset of many poor people, indivisible, uninsured, and vulnerable to flipping from asset to liability; many aspects of insecurity, worry and anxiety; and pervasive powerlessness.

The many ideas of well-being and the good life to which people aspired had striking commonalities – material well-being, having enough; bodily well-being, being and appearing well; many aspects of social well-being including being able to settle children, and being able to help others; security; and freedom of choice and action.

Both these commonalities and local differences make a case for changing language, concepts and measures in development. The case is for the language of ill-being and well-being to be widely used in addition to poverty and wealth, which are only one part of them. It is for repeated participatory processes to enable local people, especially the poorest, most marginalized and most vulnerable, to analyse and monitor the quality of their lives, and for this to be fed back regularly to policy-makers. It is for policymakers to spend time living in poor communities and appreciating their conditions and realities firsthand. If we are seriously pro-poor professionals, the answer to 'What is poverty?' is 'That is the wrong question.' It is our question, not theirs. The question of those who are poor, marginalized and vulnerable is more likely to be, in varied forms and many languages with different nuances:

---

1.   See Narayan et al. (2000b) *Crying Out for Change*

'What can you do to reduce our bad experiences of life and living, and to enable us to achieve more of the good things in life to which we aspire?'

Policies and actions that follow would then be designed to reduce ill-being and enhance well-being in their own terms. The MDGs may help, but are far from enough for this, and may at times even misdirect effort. Direct actions towards their achievement may often not present the best priorities and paths. For they narrow and standardize vision, leave out much that matters, and do not allow for the multifarious ways in which people can be enabled to enjoy a better life. Policies and actions need to be informed much less by top-down targets and much more by the diverse bottom-up realities of the powerless.

The questions are then: whose reality counts? Ours? Or theirs? Or more precisely: ours, as we construct it with our mindsets and for our purposes? Or theirs as we enable them to analyse and express it?

Professionals and the powerless: whose reality counts?

The World Summit on Social Development was held in Copenhagen in 1995.
In the run up to the Conference, UNDP convened a roundtable in Stockholm.
This is an abbreviated version of a paper written for the roundtable.

A key challenge for the Social Summit is to define the 'problems' and seek solutions from the perspective of the poor. If this challenge is not met, we risk plodding along in worthy but well–worn ruts that lead nowhere new.

We are all part of a world system that perpetuates poverty and deprivation. Those who are poor and deprived do not wish to be poor and deprived. We who are well off and have power say that poverty and deprivation are bad, and should be reduced or eliminated. Yet poverty and deprivation prove robustly sustainable. Why?

The usual response is to seek answers by analysing poverty and deprivation rather than ourselves. It is not surprising. We in power do not like to examine ourselves. To salve our consciences we rationalize: *The objects of development are the poor anyway, not us. It is they who are the problem not us.*

But poverty and deprivation are functions of polarization, of power and powerlessness. Any practical analysis has to examine the whole system; 'us' as well as 'them'. One of the most important challenges for the Social Summit, as I see it, is to ask the question: Whose reality counts? The reality of the few in the centres of power, or the reality of the poor, the many at the periphery? As development professionals, our views of the realities of the poor, and of what should be done, are constructed mainly from a distance. We promulgate those views in the words and concepts we use, which then become confused with reality itself. In much professional discourse, for example, the term 'poverty' has been narrowly defined for purposes of measurement and comparison. This narrow, technical definition, which I will call 'income poverty', has overtaken common usage. What is recorded as having been measured – often low consumption – masquerades in speech and prose as a much larger reality. It is then but a short step to treating what has not been measured as not real. Patterns of dominance are reinforced: of the material over the experiential; of the physical over the social; of the measured and measurable over the unmeasured and immeasurable; of economics over disciplines concerned with people as people.

What matters most to poor people often differs from what outsiders assume. Income matters, but sometimes less than other aspects of life – health, security, self-respect, family and social life, access to goods and services. In the early 1980s, for example, N.S. Jodha asked people in two villages in Rajasthan, India

Published in *Choices*, Vol 4, 1995.

to define their own categories and criteria of well-being. He then compared this to data he had collected some 20 years earlier. The 36 households whose incomes had shrunk significantly in real terms, were, on average, better off, according to the criteria they had expressed themselves. While their real per capita income was less, other improvements had, in their eyes, made their lives better: improved housing, wearing shoes regularly, less dependence on patrons and landlords, not having to migrate in search of work.

As this and other research shows, people's own descriptions of well-being and deprivation – of the good and bad life – tend to be multi-dimensional. In recent studies in Asia and sub-Saharan Africa, the factors cited as detracting from well-being included disablement, the lack of land or farming tools, being 'poor in people' (lacking family or other sources of social support), and being forced to accept demeaning work. In contrast to the professional definition of poverty – which tends to be narrow and one-dimensional – the realities of the poor are local, complex, diverse and dynamic.

As with poverty, so it is with the notion of employment. Jobs, unemployment, workplace and workforce are concepts derived from the urban industrial experience of the North. Yet we project them onto the very different realities of the rural and agricultural South, and of the urban informal sector. The majority of the world's families cope by having different members of the household perform different tasks in different places at different times of the year. For the majority of the world's people the challenge is not one of jobs or employment; it is how to make their labour more productive and how to gain more secure, sustainable and adequate livelihoods.

By looking at poverty and employment from this vantage point, we begin to reframe the objectives of development. We are able to move from ideas about reducing income-poverty to enhancing well-being; and from increasing employment to supporting sustainable livelihoods. Yet to identify and implement a truly new agenda for development will also require us to change: to be able to reverse the normal view, to see another reality, to soften and flatten hierarchy and to embrace a new professionalism. As stated in a recent vision paper for the Consultative Group on International Agricultural Research, written by a group chaired by Gordon Conway, the challenge is to 'reverse the chain of logic, starting with the socio-economic demands of poor households' in order to identify appropriate research priorities.

Underlying all of this is the basic right of people to define their own needs and to set their own agenda. In the past few years a number of powerful tools have been developed that have enabled poor people and communities to do just that. Participatory Rural Appraisals (PRA) and Poverty Assessments (PPAs), for example, conducted under the auspices of the World Bank in Ghana, Kenya, Zambia and other countries, have helped people in both urban and rural areas to analyse their own condition, express their own values and define their own priorities.

But to carry these priorities forward will demand deep changes in the way we development professionals think and behave. At the most obvious personal level, this will involve looking at the concepts we use, the language we employ and the actions we take or neglect to take. While we have been quick to grasp the potential of concepts such as 'participation', 'ownership' and 'empowerment', we have been slower to recognize the changes these concepts demand of *us*. We have failed to understand that participation by them means non-ownership by us. Empowerment for them means disempowerment for us.

Much of the challenge has to do with both power and ownership. It requires giving up behaviours that reinforce the dominance of the North, and of whatever is industrial, capital-intensive and 'sophisticated'. It demands handing over the initiative to others, enabling them to do more and to do it in their own way.

If the poor and weak are not to see the Social Summit as a celebration of hypocrisy – signifying sustainable privilege for us, not sustainable well-being for them – the key is to enable them to express their reality, to put that reality first, and to make it count.

Whose voice? Participatory research and policy change: Foreword, Afterword and Postscript

Whose Voice? Participatory research and policy change (1998), edited by Jeremy Holland with James Blackburn, brought together contributions and insights from Participatory Poverty Assessments.[1] In a participatory mode they enabled poor people to present and analyse their realities and what would make a difference for them.

Foreword

Whose Voice? presents a dramatic learning: it is that now, in the last years of the 20th century, we have new ways in which those who are poor and marginalized can present their realities to those in power, and be believed, influence policy and make a difference.

The context

To many readers this will seem improbable. We live, after all, in a world of increasing polarization of power and wealth into North and South, into overclasses and underclasses. Materially, those in the overclasses have more and more, and are increasingly linked by instant communications. At the same time, the numbers in the underclasses of absolute poverty continue to rise. Among them, many millions have less and less, and remain isolated both from the overclass and from each other. Almost by definition, the poor and powerless have no voice. It may be politically correct to say that they should be empowered and their voices heard. But cynical realists will point to inexorable trends, vested interests and pervasive self-interest among the powerful, and argue that little can be changed.

The contributors to this book present evidence of new potentials to the contrary. They confront that cynicism with their own promising experience. They have found that there are new ways to enable those who are poor, marginalized, illiterate and excluded to analyse their realities and express their priorities; that the realities they express of conditions, problems, livelihood strategies and priorities often differ from what development professionals have believed; and that new experiences can put policymakers in closer touch

---

1. For good sources see the contributions to the book introduced here – Holland with Blackburn (1998), Norton et al. (2001), Robb (2002) and Praxis (2007). For comparative analysis and presentations of findings see Narayan et al. (2000a). For the findings of a PPA conducted in 23 countries see Narayan et al. (2000b).

with those realities. These potentials come from participatory research in which the poor themselves are active analysts. This has a long pedigree, not least in the traditions of participatory action research and the inspiration of Paulo Freire and his followers. In the late 1980s and early 1990s a confluence of older streams of research together with new inventions evolved as a family of approaches and methods known as participatory rural appraisal (PRA). This has spread fast and wide. It is now often urban and frequently much more than appraisal. It has been applied in all continents, and many countries and contexts.

PRA stresses changes in the behaviour and attitudes of outsiders, to become not teachers but facilitators, not lecturers but listeners and learners. 'Hand over the stick', 'Use your own best judgement at all times' and 'They can do it' (having confidence in the abilities of local people, whether literate or not) are among its sayings. When well conducted, PRA approaches and methods are often open-ended, visual as well as verbal, and carried out by small groups of local people. They have proved powerful means of enabling local people, including the poor, illiterate, women and the marginalized, themselves to appraise, analyse, plan and act. While some consider that PRA should always be part of an empowering process, others have used the methods for research, to learn more and more accurately about the realities of the poor.

As PRA evolved, it soon became evident that it had applications for policy. Thematic and sectoral studies were carried out and presented as reports to decision-makers, sometimes in only days or weeks from the fieldwork. The World Bank, through trust funds from bilateral donors, initiated participatory poverty assessments (PPAs). Some of these used PRA methods to enable poor people to express their realities themselves. The insights from these thematic studies and PPAs were often striking, convincing and unexpected. A quiet revolution was taking place in parallel in different parts of the world, but it was too scattered for full mutual learning or for its significance to be fully seen.

In reading *Whose Voice?* there is excitement to be found, and a certain exhilaration. For one realizes gradually that there has been a breakthrough. Many questions are raised. Among these, certain insights and issues stand out and deserve comment, among these methods and ethics and the realities revealed.

Methods and ethics

With participatory research, and especially with PRA, methods and ethics are intertwined; issues raised are of time taken, expectations aroused and whose realities are expressed. Several writers agonize over whether the research process is exploitative. Participatory research is time-consuming for local people: PRA methods, especially the visual ones like mapping, diagramming and matrices, tend to be fun and to engage people's full attention, but sometimes for hours; and poor people's time is not costless. Expectations are also liable to be raised. After being helped to analyse their conditions, problems and opportunities, people often expect action, but with facilitators in a policy research mode, and not concerned with planning for action, follow-up may not be feasible.

No solutions can be universal, but two points are widely agreed:

- *Transparency*: facilitators should make clear from the start who they are, what they are doing, and why, and what can and cannot be expected; often, even when nothing can be expected, local people will collaborate, not least because they find the activities interesting and enjoyable, and themselves learn from them.
- *Selection for follow-up*: communities and groups can be chosen where responsible follow-up may be possible through an on-going programme.

A further concern is whose reality is being presented, and whose reality counts. Those most accessible to outsiders in communities are usually men, and those who are less poor, less marginalized, less excluded. Women are often continuously busy. Ensuring that the excluded are included, and that their reality is expressed, can demand patience, persistence, tact and inconvenience. The best times for poor women are, for example, often the worst times for outsiders.

There is then the question of how their reality is analysed, and into whose categories. (Researchers tend to fit material into preconceived concepts.) The Management Committee of the South African PPA set an example of best practice by going to pains not to impose their categories and constructs on the material. Instead, through card sorting, they allowed the categories and constructs to emerge from the material, and then to influence the structure of the report, which they wrote as spokespersons for the poor.

Realities revealed

Much of the power of PRA methods lies in what has been called group-visual synergy. Group activities include: making maps, lists, matrices, causal and linkage diagrams, estimating, comparisons, ranking and scoring, and discussing and debating. Realities are expressed in a cumulative physical and visual form, often democratically, on the ground. Typically, people become committed to the process and lose themselves in it. Visually, more diversity and complexity are expressed than can be put into words. Much in the contributions to this book was first presented visually.

The realities revealed in both the thematic studies and the PPAs are often striking. Once stated they seem obvious, but it is sobering to recognize that for urban-based professionals they have usually been new insights, or understanding presented with new force and credibility. To take examples in turn from the thematic studies:

- In Nepal, in the Tarai (plains) area, the continuous introduction of irrigation and of new crop varieties led to yield increases, but was masking long-term declines in soil fertility. (Gill, 1998)
- In Guinea, contrary to officials' views, indigenous land-tenure systems persisted and were complex and diverse. (Schoonmaker Freudenberger, 1998)
- In The Gambia, 25 per cent of girls of school age were found to be overlooked at the village level because they were pregnant, married or about to be married; girls cared deeply and bitterly about the denial of education. (Kane et al., 1997)
- In Jamaica, poverty and violence are interconnected in complex ways, including area stigma, which hinders those from a neighbourhood with a reputation for violence from getting jobs; interpersonal violence is far more common than political or drug-related violence. (Moser and Holland, 1998)
- In India, local people understood the ecology of a national park better than conservation-minded professionals; excluding buffaloes in the name of conservation both damaged their livelihoods and led to a decrease in bird life in the park.

The PPAs were similarly revealing: in Ghana, infrastructure was found to be a higher priority for rural people than had been recognized (Dogbe, 1998); in Zambia, school fees had to be paid at the worst time of the year, coinciding with high incidence of sickness and hard work, and shortages of money and food (Milimo et al., 1998); in South Africa, seasonal deprivation, urban as well as rural, was more significant than had been supposed (Attwood and May, 1998); in Bangladesh, in a subsequent PPA sponsored by UNDP, enforcement of anti-dowry laws was a surprise priority of poor people (UNDP, 1996). These are illustrative examples from reports rich in policy-relevant detail. The evidence is abundant that these approaches and methods, used well, elicit insights into previously hidden realities of the poor.

Whose Voice? deserves to be read, studied and acted upon by all who are concerned with poverty and policy, in whatever context, country or continent. Its lessons transcend the boundaries of professions, disciplines, sectors and departments. It indicates actions open to NGOs, governments and all agencies concerned with deprivation and with development. It shares seminal experiences, rather than set answers. It is for readers to select from these what makes sense for their purposes, and to go further themselves.

Let me hope that this book will encourage and inspire many others to join the pioneers who write here, to explore more of this new territory, and to share their experiences with the same disarming frankness. It may then be that the voices and realities of those who have been last – the poor, powerless, marginalized and excluded – will come to count and to change policy both in principle and in practice.

Afterword

Making a difference

Empowering poor people to conduct their own appraisal and analysis, and to present their realities, is one thing. Whether their voices are heard, understood and acted on is another. There are two weak links: from voice to policy change (policy-in-principle); and from policy change to practice (policy-in-practice)...

Policy impacts from the cases reported include: priority to rural infrastructure in Ghana; balance between sectors, and influence on health policies in Zambia; the timing of school-fee payments and rules for girls' school uniforms in The Gambia.

From voice to policy

There are practical lessons to be drawn about the link between voice and policy change. These concern ownership, credibility and process.

1. *Ownership* affects likelihood of change. There is no one best approach. Sometimes ownership at first by groups in civil society may be unavoidable: policy-related research may have to be initiated without explicit government support. This can then lead to confronting policymakers with evidence about desirable change. Early changes in policy may, however, be more likely if the research process is owned by policymakers from the start, and especially if they themselves or their colleagues take part in the field. In practice, much participatory policy research to date has been undertaken with donor support, which can have both negative and positive effects. Negative effects can include lack of continuity: the fickle behaviour of USAID in Guinea in abandoning support is a warning to governments to choose stable and reliable donors. More positive in the longer term is for donors to negotiate government partnership and ownership. In South Africa the PPA process was taken over and managed by South Africans, leading to its findings being taken seriously at the cabinet level.

2. *Credibility* is needed to convince policymakers. In practice, credibility has come in three ways: researchers have carried conviction by being transparent and self-critical about their methods and findings; reports and outputs have included 'voices' in the form of what people have said, and visuals in the form of diagrams which they have made; and those presenting to policymakers have variously spoken on behalf of the poor, and/or been officials, and/or local people themselves.

3. *Process* is critical... Process is far more than just presenting a report. Perhaps most important is sensitive tenacity, sometimes waiting, sometimes acting decisively to seize an opportunity. As with conservation policy, a long process may be entailed in local, national and international fora.

From policy to practice

The link between policy-in-principle and policy-in-practice has been less explored. Implementability will vary. Some changes can have potentially big effects for poor people at low cost, for example changing the dates for payment of school expenses, or training health staff to be polite and considerate. Others, for example rural infrastructure, may appeal to some donors; others, which confront vested interests or entrenched custom, may require long campaigns.

Thematic research can play a part through feedback on field realities. In Zambia, contrary to policy, many of the poorest were found being excluded from health and education services. Revisits to communities can indicate changes which are occurring. Perhaps most of all, in the longer run, participatory monitoring and evaluation by communities and groups themselves, with their own baselines, will serve to close the circle, with feedback to policymakers on grassroots developments.

The future

The practical scope for policy-related participatory research is expanding. In most of the experiences reported in this book, teams had initially to be trained in PRA. Now local capabilities are multiplying. CEDEP in Ghana and PAG in Zambia both received their initial training for a PPA and then continued with their teams to provide a national capability for PRA-type policy-related studies. In many countries, initial training and orientation will soon be less lengthy because in-country capabilities will already be there. Participatory research into the realities of the poor will be a widespread, if not universal, option.

The opportunities opened up by this book are, then, immense. They are for new ways in which the powerful can learn from the weak, and in which the weak can express their realities with authority and credibility, and so influence policy and practice. The approaches and methods are continuously being invented and developed. There will never be, and should never be any blueprint for what to do and how to do it. In a spirit of pluralism, lessons can continuously be learnt from experiences like those reported and analysed here. Each is, and should be planned, invented and improvised as a new and unique process. Already, through the diversity this book shows, practical experience is impressive. Readers may agree that these approaches and methods should continue to be developed, adopted and adapted worldwide, by governments, by civil society, and more and more by the poor and powerless themselves through their organizations.

Governments, NGOs and other bodies now have a menu of options to choose between or combine. This includes:

1. *Sectoral research networks*. The Tarai Research Network is a model amenable to widespread adoption and adaptation by governments

which need quick insight into and feedback on local realities, including policy issues and policy-in-practice.

2. *Thematic studies.* These can be on almost any sector or issue...
3. *Participatory poverty assessments.* These can be in a variety of modes, and at a national or local level.
4. *Direct interaction and learning* between decision-makers and poor people. Decision-makers can be involved in the participatory research, as in Guinea or through poor people going to decision-makers and presenting evidence in visual as well as verbal form. The decision of James Wolfensohn, President of the World Bank, that all senior World Bank staff members should spend a week of total immersion in a village or slum sets an example which other donors, and national governments, could follow. The potential here is to transform insight and commitment among policymakers through direct experience of a type they are normally denied (see pp. 171–180).

In making any list, or outlining categories, there is a danger of closure. Participatory research for policy is evolving rapidly. This book cannot and should not set firm patterns. At the same time, good advice is available, drawing on experience to date. The essence of good participatory research is methodological pluralism and improvisation. After initial inventiveness, innovations tend to settle into stable patterns and ritual sequences. The antidote is to invent each process anew, drawing eclectically on past experience, and always experimenting and exploring better ways of doing things.

The experiences reported and analysed here are, then, only a beginning. They point towards a potential the magnitude of which is difficult to grasp: that throughout the world participatory research in a PRA mode could give voice to the unheard, and persuade and change the powerful; that the realities of those who are last could be presented personally and credibly to those who are first; and that the needs and priorities of the last could come more and more to be understood by others and to count.

After *Whose Voice?* one is tempted to say that the world should never be the same again. It will, however, repeat itself in denying the realities of the poor, weak and vulnerable. What cannot now be repeated is any assertion that the poor are incapable of their own analysis, or any assertion that the powerful lack the approaches and methods to enable them to undertake that analysis. Verbally, there have always been ways. Visually, now, there is a new additional repertoire. Behaviourally, too, we now know better how critical are the ways we interact, and how what sort of people we are affects our interactions. There are now fewer excuses than ever before for ignoring the needs and priorities of the poor.

Postcript: what has happened (2010)

Since 1998 hundreds of PPAs have been carried out, at national and increasingly subnational level. *A Rough Guide to PPAs* (Norton et al., 2001) was a landmark. The Uganda Participatory Poverty Assessment Project which continued for years, with several iterations, was outstanding, and had major influences on policy, not least because it was owned and implemented by the Government (Bird and Kakande, 2001). Reviews were conducted and published (Robb, 2002; Praxis, 2007). Immersions as a means of research were pioneered, facilitated by Dee Jupp and her colleagues first with SDC in Tanzania (Jupp, 2003, 2004) and then with annual Reality Checks in Bangladesh initiated by Sida. The Reality Checks focus on primary education and primary health care, two sectors which Sida supports. Some 15 participatory researchers immerse at the same time each year with the same family, and informally learn about what is happening. Reports for 2007, 2008 and 2009 have been published[1] (Sida, 2008, 2009, 2010). These give a vivid, authoritative insight into rapidly changing realities, both urban and rural. Policy implications stand out. The reports indicate that this is a powerful approach for keeping in touch and up-to-date. AusAid has now sponsored a Reality Check on education in Indonesia, facilitated by Dee Jupp, Enamul Huda and others (Australia Indonesia Partnership, 2010) and another is planned for Mozambique. This could and should be an influential wave of the future.

---

1.   See www.sida.se or google Reality Check Bangladesh

Blind spots: hidden, unseen and sensitive dimensions of deprivation

Participatory approaches and methods, creatively evolved and carefully facilitated, have repeatedly opened up aspects of the lives and experiences of poor people that have been hidden, unseen or considered too sensitive.[1] Questionnaires have not been effective in doing this – in part because their questions are framed by outsiders whose ignorance and categories are often precisely the problem – not knowing what one does not know – and in part because of the inhibiting and distorting nature of the interview situation. An early participatory example was wealth or well-being ranking in which members of a community first draw a social map of all households, then list these on cards, and then sort them into piles according to degrees of wealth or more usually some concepts of well-being and ill-being. Middle class urban-based professionals have regarded this as either impossible, or unethical, supposing it will be demeaning and humiliating for those who are worse off. These fears have again and again proved unfounded.

Six of the blind spots that have been identified and illuminated can illustrate:

1. Places of the Poor. A whole chapter in *Voices of the Poor* (Narayan et al., 2000b: 71–88) came to be concerned with places where poor people live and work. This was not foreseen in the planning of the participatory study, but emerged as the findings were collected and sorted. The places where poor people live suffer combinations of isolation, lack of infrastructure, lack of services, crime, pollution, and vulnerability to disasters like drought, floods and landslips. Stigma of urban place can mean that place of residence must be concealed or dissembled when applying for a job. Inordinate amounts of time may be required for obtaining basics like water. The *Chronic Poverty Report 2004–05* devotes a whole chapter (CPRC, 2005: 26–35) to 'Where do Chronically Poor People Live?' and does a service by describing and analysing spatial poverty traps, their ecological characteristics, poor infrastructure, weak institutions and political isolation. Disadvantages of place, whether rural or urban, as a dimension of deprivation, have for long been recognized, especially by social critics and social geographers. The question is whether the multiple interactions of dimensions of disadvantage, which have spatial dimensions, have been adequately appreciated.

2. Poverty of time and energy. Some of the poorest wish they had work. A very poor woman in a Bangladesh village complained:

> These days I have no work. If we had land, I would always be busy – husking rice, grinding lentils, cooking three times a day. You've seen

---

1. For examples and discussions of creativity in evolving participatory methodologies, see Brock and Pettit (2007).

how hard Jolil's wife works, haven't you? I have nothing to do, so I watch the children and worry. What kind of life is that? (Hartmann and Boyce, 1983: 166–7)

There can be poverty of too much time, and poverty of too little. The evidence from the *Voices of the Poor* study suggested that unwelcome surplus time was becoming more common for men with unemployment while poverty of both time and energy were becoming more common for women. Poverty of time and energy was recognized in the South African Participatory Poverty Assessment (PPA) (May et al., 1998: 108–9). It has become more acute for many women as they have become breadwinners in addition to their domestic and reproductive roles (Narayan et al., 2000b: 111–14). When asked what her dream was, a poor rural woman in Zambia said that it was to be able to go to town, spend time with her friends, and come back again.[1]

3. The Body. The importance of the body, and of health and strength, to poor people shouts out from participatory study after study. The categories that emerged from the *Voices of the Poor* led to a whole chapter entitled 'The Body' (Narayan et al., 2000b: 89–108). From their analysis of over 250 life stories of poor people in Asia, Parasuraman and his co-authors devote a whole chapter of *Listening to People Living in Poverty* to 'The Labouring Body' (2003: 274–97). This, they point out, is often the only resource a person living in poverty is able to use:

> the continuous exertion of their bodies in labour that is underpaid and undervalued leaves them exhausted. Their work is hazardous, seasonal and leaves them vulnerable to outside harm. They are forced to use and sell their bodies as an instrument. They rarely have time to recuperate or rest, and are reduced to what their bodies can do. These processes inscribe on their bodies and leave them to diseases, degenerating illnesses and death (ibid.: 293)[2]

The central importance of the body to most poor people has been under-recognized. The slogan at the head of a poster of the trade union SEWA (the Self-Employed Women's Association) in India reads: OUR BODIES ARE OUR WEALTH. The body is more important to people living in poverty than it is to professionals. For many it is their most important asset. But unlike many other assets, like land, small livestock, jewellery, trees, and savings, it combines all of the following. It is:

Vulnerable. It is often exceptionally exposed to hard and dangerous work and accidents, to contamination and pollution, to violence, to sickness, to lack of nutrition, overwork and exhaustion. These affect the whole body and the whole person; and if one part is damaged the whole is affected.

---

1.   The source is a video of PRA training in Zambia in 1993, entitled *The PRA Report*, made by World Vision, Australia.
2.   The authors refer at the end of this paragraph to Scarry (1985), but these conclusions flow too from their own analysis.

Both main asset and indivisible. The poorer a person is, the more the body is their main asset. For the poorest it may be almost all they have. It is also all of a piece. It is indivisible: apart from the exceptional case of sales of blood and organs, and unlike money, crops, and small stock, it cannot be realized in small amounts.

Liable to flip from asset to liability. Combined with vulnerability and indivisibility, this can devastate, and distinguishes the body most sharply from most if not all other assets. With an accident or illness the body suddenly ceases to be an asset or means of earning. Instead, it is a liability, needing care and feeding and treatment. It is a recurrent finding that many people fall into bad conditions of deep poverty because of what has happened to their bodies or those of others in their families.

Uninsured.[1] On top of all this, unlike professionals, poor people's bodies are rarely insured. Outside some middle-income countries, unemployment benefit is unthinkable and unheard of. The health insurance scheme of SEWA in India for its members is exceptional. The importance of medical expenses is underlined, though, by the frequency with which loans are made for them by self-help savings groups.

We can ask whether economists, health professionals, policymakers and bureaucrats, themselves with medical insurance, good access to health services, protected by safe environments and work, with stocks of divisible assets in money, and mostly able to work with their brains even if their bodies are damaged, truly appreciate the vital importance of a strong and secure body to poor people. The vulnerability of this main indivisible asset, and the way it can flip from asset to liability, points sharply to the priority for poor people of quick, effective and affordable treatment. We know too from the work of Anirudh Krishna[2] and others, that ill health and accidents are the most common cause of slides into deeper poverty. In addition to human and ethical aspects, it may cost much less, and be more feasible, to provide good curative services so that poor people avoid becoming poorer in the first place, or if they do, to enable them to claw their way back up again.

4. Gender relations, sexual behaviour and sexual and reproductive well-being. Participatory approaches and methods have proved potent in bringing these into the open, and empowering women to take action. Gender relations, and how they have been changing, were a major theme in the Voices of the Poor study (Narayan et al., 2000b: chapter 6 pp. 109–32). Much was explored and documented as never before in *Realizing Rights: transforming approaches to sexual and reproductive well-being* (Cornwall and Welbourn, 2002). The lives and realities of those who are marginalized, despised, excluded and ignored have been brought out into the light. Sex workers, for example, come to life as people like other people, for whom respect, security and good relations matter

---

1. Since this was written, more programmes of social protection have been introduced, many of them with some success, reducing vulnerability to becoming poorer.
2. See Krishna (2007, 2010)

as much, if not more, than they do for others. Participatory approaches to HIV/AIDS, especially through the group processes known as Stepping Stones (Welbourn, 1991, 2002) have brought what was hidden or unspoken into the open, with frank talk about sex and death, concern for sensitive behaviour and relationships, acceptance of HIV-positive women and men, and counselling and care for the sick and dying. Participatory approaches and methods have also been developed for HIV/AIDS work with drug users (International HIV/AIDS Alliance, 2003). Another area is the sexual behaviours and preferences of adolescents[1] and of prepubescent children (unknown to their parents).

5. *Violence, physical insecurity and social abuses.* Participatory studies of violence in Jamaica, Guatemala and Colombia have broken new ground, revealing wide differences between beliefs of policymakers about forms of violence and the realities experienced by ordinary people (Moser and McIlwaine, 2004). In Peru, participatory timelines, matrices and maps were used in Ayacucho as part of the Colectivo Yuyarisu ('We remember') process of the Truth Commission (Comision de la Verdad y Justicia): using these methods, over 100 groups recollected and reconstructed human rights violations which had taken place in the era of political violence 1980–94 (Francke, *pers comm.*). In many contexts, domestic abuse and violence against women has been brought out into the open. An early example was an all-women's PRA activity in Tamil Nadu in 1990 (Sheelu Francis and John Devavaram, *pers comm.*) in which women mapped households and marked with a yellow circle those where the husband was a drunkard. The Voices of the Poor study included perceived prevalence and trends of domestic violence against women. Another illustration is the Internal Learning System introduced into parts of India.[2] Women individually and in groups have kept visual diaries which they update every six months. In these they score from 1 to 5 for aspects of quality of life such as husbands drinking, domestic violence, Dalits having to drink out of separate glasses, Dalits being made to carry dead bodies or dead animals, and whether a girl can select her life partner.

6. *Open defecation.* A final example is *open defecation*, widespread in South and Southeast Asia and a major source of sickness, mortality and ill-being for all, especially women who lack access to the privacy of a latrine. Women in South Asia are subject to gross gender discrimination, being compelled by custom, unlike men, to defecate and urinate unseen. Without access to latrines this means only before dawn or after nightfall. The participatory approach of Community-Led Total Sanitation[3] enables communities to confront and

---

1. For example, a group of seven school girls in M'tendere Compound, Lusaka, matrix scored a typology of sex partners and preferences, with 16 categories of male partners scored against 5 criteria (Shah et al., 1999: 52).

2. For the Internal Learning System see Nagasundari (2007), Narendranath (2007) and Noponen (2007).

3. www.communityledtotalsanitation.org is a regularly updated source. For others sources, also downloadable from the website, see Kar (2003), Kar and Pasteur (2005), Kar and Bongartz (2006), Kar with Chambers (2008), Bongartz and Chambers (2009). See also Mehta and Movik (eds) (2011) *Shit Matters.*

face these realities, often spurring them into action. A facilitator initiates the process. Community members make maps on the ground to show their communities and the areas where they defecate. They then walk and stand in those areas, face, smell and discuss the reality. They calculate the cartloads of shit (the crude local word is used) produced. They identify pathways from faeces to food and mouths and come to realize that they are 'eating one another's shit'.[1] This frequently triggers self-help action to dig pits and adopt hygienic behaviour. Many thousands of communities in South and Southeast Asia and Africa have proudly declared themselves open defecation free now. The gain in well-being for women is suggested by an inscription on a wall in a totally sanitized village in Maharashtra: 'Daughters from our village are not married to villages where open defecation is practised'. In rural South Asia alone the scale of potential gains in health, expenses saved, reduced mortality, improved nutrition, and well-being for millions of women, children and men are so vast that they are difficult to grasp.

India, for instance, has been reported to have 58 per cent of the open defecation in the world (WHO/UNICEF, 2010: 22), over one third of the people living on less than $1.25 a day, and one third of the undernourished children. This amounts to some 46 per cent of the children in India. There are many faecal infection-related causal links from open defecation and lack

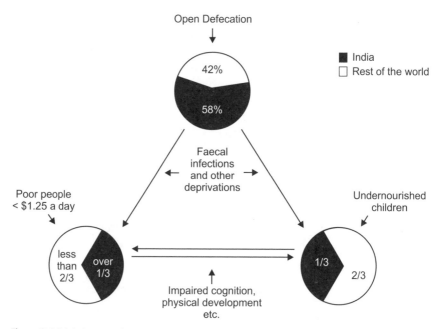

Figure 2.1 Global proportions

---

1.   For a glossary of over 200 words for shit, visit www.communityledtotalsanitation.org

of hygiene to undernutrition (see e.g. Prüss-Üstün and Corvalán, 2006; World Bank, 2008). Open defecation and lack of hygienic practices appear deeply implicated in the undernourishment of so many Indian children.

Concluding

The importance of opening up these six subjects can scarcely be exaggerated. When they are not surfaced, analysed and confronted, much avoidable ill-being persists. Conversely, the potential for enhanced well-being from improving the places of the poor, reducing poverty of time and energy, recognizing the body as an asset and providing good affordable and accessible medical treatment, improving sexual and gender relations, tackling and reducing or eliminating violence in its many forms, and ending open defecation with gains in health and for the well-being of women, children and men – each of these can only be described as phenomenal. Participatory approaches and methods, well facilitated, cannot fully solve these alone; but there is enough evidence now to realize that they can take us a long way by establishing bridgeheads and becoming transformations and movements.

Poverty in diagrams

Again and again the interlocking nature of deprivations, and of dimensions of well-being, is revealed by the lives and livelihoods of people living in poverty. Linear sentences cannot express these linkages. They are best shown in diagrams. The same is true of the season blindness of professionals (see page 72). So here are some modest attempts. The challenge throughout is to find ways of weakening and eliminating the negatives of ill-being, enabling people to move towards the positives of well-being.

I hope this provokes you into drawing your own diagrams, including more with positive linkages. And facilitating those who suffer to draw their own so that we can learn from them.

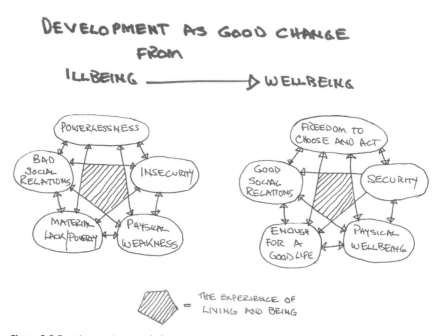

Figure 2.2 Development as good change

All five dimensions of ill-being are points of entry. Which are most important and most feasible, in which contexts, for whom? And what are the linkages? Can you list examples of how all the 20 linkages can play out? Negatively and positively?

Take, for example, physical ill-being. Who is most vulnerable to it? What are the most feasible and effective points of entry for enabling them to shift from physical ill-being to physical well-being, in which contexts? Sustainably. What are the implications for policy and practice? A provocation: the most common proximate cause of people falling into poverty is sickness and accidents. There is a strong argument that it is cheaper to prevent people falling into poverty in these ways than it is to enable poor people to become less poor.[1] If this is true, who should do what about it?

Figure 2.3 is another web of linked dimensions for review and reflection. Notably it includes, Behaviours: disregard and abuse by the more powerful.

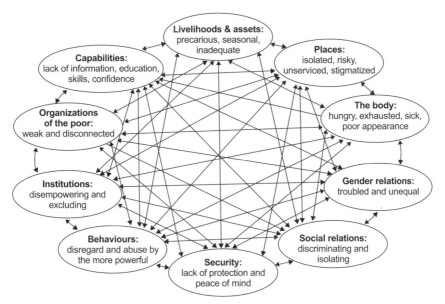

Figure 2.3 Dimensions of powerlessness and ill-being
Source: Narayan et al., 2000b: 249

You may wish to draw your own diagram from scratch, with fewer or more circles, with different categories, and not necessarily all connected. Or you may wish to study the examples that follow overleaf of illustrating these categories for a particular group of people, as Susie Jolly has done with examples related to sexuality. There is a blank template for this with the same categories in the circles on page 64.

Finally, on a positive note, we now know through hard won experience many ways of enabling 'the world's extreme poor' to gain better lives. As never before, these are presented and analysed authoritatively in a book published in 2010. This is David Lawson, David Hulme, Imran Matin and Karen Moore (eds) *What Works for the Poorest? Poverty reduction programmes for the world's extreme poor* (Practical Action Publishing). I endorsed the book:

---

1.   This has been cogently argued by Anirudh Krishna on the basis of widespread research in different countries and continents. See for example Krishna (2010).

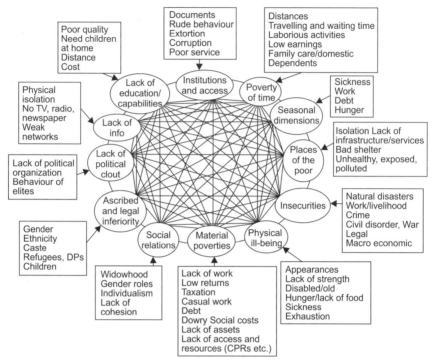

Figure 2.4 Web of Poverty's disadvantages
Source: Narayan et al., 2000b: 249

For too long development practice has focused on the moderate poor and left out those who suffer from extreme and chronic deprivation. Now at last, by gathering and presenting current ideas and experience on assisting the poorest and helping them to help themselves, this book does an outstanding service. If all development professionals were to go into retreat for three days and read, reflect and debate this book, and then apply it in their work, it could touch and transform the lives and livelihoods of many tends or even hundreds of millions of those who are most deprived and excluded. *What works for the poorest* is one of the most important development books of the decade – a treasury of ideas and experience.

Was I over the top? Get the book and make your own judgement.

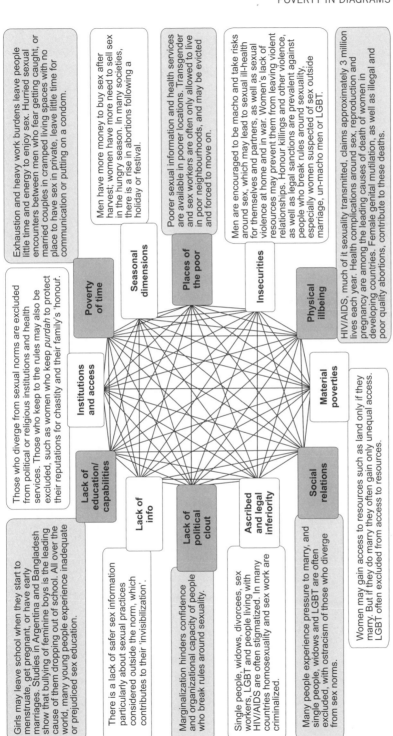

Figure 2.5 Web of Poverty's disadvantages – with examples related to sexuality
Source: Jolly, 2006

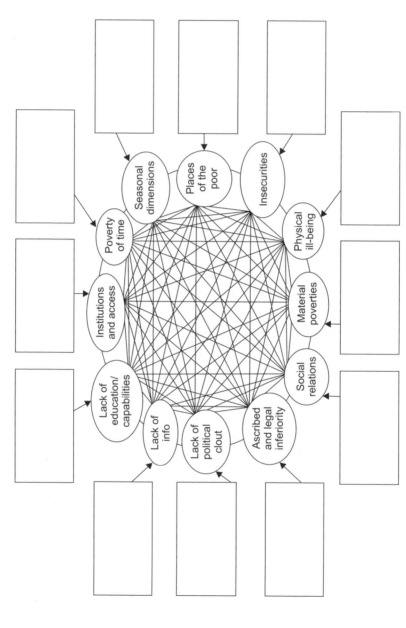

Figure 2.6 Web of Poverty's disadvantages – with blanks to fill in, if you wish, for people who are poor, powerless, vulnerable, marginalized, excluded, or stigmatized. This can be for a particular individual, household, group, gender, age group, occupation, ethnicity, religion or other category of people.

Integrated: seasonal poverty, season blindness

About 1976, in a seminar in the Institute of Development Studies, someone reported that in their fieldwork in Bangladesh they had found a peak of births during the monsoon. Richard Longhurst, who had just returned from his fieldwork in Northern Nigeria, said he had found the same. An ahha! moment. Was this a coincidence or a feature of tropical seasons? So Richard and I got together with David Bradley and Richard Feachem of the London School of Hygiene and Tropical Medicine, and convened a conference in 1978. And then 31 years later, finding that nothing much had changed in professional awareness of seasonality, Stephen Devereux, Rachel Sabates-Wheeler, Richard and I were involved in convening another. For this I wrote the following.

Integrated Seasonal Poverty

Of all the dimensions of rural deprivation, the most neglected is seasonality. Vulnerability, sickness, powerlessness, exploitation, material poverty, under-nutrition and malnutrition, wages, prices, incomes ... these are recognized, researched and written about. But among them again and again seasonality is overlooked and left out.

Yet seasonality manifests in all these other dimensions and in how they interlock. This is almost universal for poor people, but especially in the rural tropics. There, during the rains, poor people are repeatedly oppressed and screwed down by cruel combinations of adverse factors: lack of food, lack of money and high food prices reflecting scarcities before harvest; physical hardship from wet and cold, and collapsing and leaking shelter; hard work, vital for earning wages or for family farm cultivation, especially weeding, usually the work of women and critical for the final crop; and debilitating sicknesses like diarrhoeas, malaria, Dengue fever, Guinea worm disease, and skin infections, accidents slipping and falling,[1] and snakebite too when snakes are flooded from their holes.

Then there is isolation and lack of access to services, some areas being cut off for weeks or months. It is then during the rains that poor people are materially most poor, most short of money, most vulnerable, most powerless, most exploited, most isolated, and most short of food. It is then that these dimensions most tightly interlock and reinforce each other. It is then that the opportunity cost of not being able to work can be at its highest. As a Gambian

---

1. The SDC Views of the Poor study in Tanzania reported for one community that for fetching water 'The biggest problem is the terrain which is steep and slippery during the rainy season ... people in the villages have had accidents carrying water' (Jupp, 2003: 36).

woman said to Margaret Haswell (1975: 44) 'Sometimes you are overcome by weeds through illness or accidents'. Distress migration too is often seasonal. For many reasons it is during the rains then that poor people suffer most and are most vulnerable to becoming poorer.[1]

Seasonal undernutrition, malnutrition, sickness and poor hygiene interact. Hygiene is harder to maintain. Food is more likely to be infected: busy and exhausted mothers are more likely to leave cooked food for eating later, and in hot humid conditions, bacterial overgrowth is faster (Schofield, 1974). In triggering Community-Led Total Sanitation (Kar with Chambers, 2008: 27–31) participatory mapping includes villagers putting yellow powder (or sawdust) on their social map to show where they defecate. Typically, this is around the edges of their settlement. But people with urgent and painful acute diarrhoea may not be able to go far. When asked where they go at night during the rains, embarrassment and laughter are common as the powder is put close to dwellings. Liquid stools mixed with the rainwater may be trampled back inside. This scenario is the more likely because pit latrines tend to be less used during the rains. In Bangladesh, unlined pit latrines quite commonly collapse and become unusable during floods. In Cambodia, a sharp drop in latrine use is reported during the rainy season. On top of all this, diarrhoeas and other intestinal infections reduce absorption. And with tropical enteropathy, the energy needed to make the antibodies to fight infections from faecal-oral contamination that gets into the blood-stream, together with reduced food absorption, may contribute more to undernutrition than diarrhoeas themselves (Humphrey, 2009).

The rains are also a time of social and economic differentiation: some can gain. A poor farm family may in desperation have to work for others first for food or cash before they cultivate their own small land in a less timely fashion and so get less at harvest. Those in communities who have food surpluses can sell them for high prices or as loans with high interest rates; relationships of dependence are reinforced; and those who need agricultural labour can get it cheap. In an Indian village a group of women told me the rains were their best time of year: there was lots to do, a sense of urgency and purpose, and they enjoyed that. But then these were well-built, healthy, strong women with good stone houses and by no means poor. Mindful that south of the equator Christmas comes at the worst time, in the middle of the rains, I was startled when a student from Malawi told me that before Christmas was a very good time in his village. Labourers would do a standard amount of agricultural work for his family for only one kwacha. But after Christmas for the same work you had to pay four. The rains are indeed a good time for some.

Bargaining power is affected. The normal view is that wages rise with demand and so should rise during labour peaks such as weeding and harvest.

---

1. There is a considerable literature on tropical seasonality and poverty. See Chambers et al., 1981; Longhurst, 1986; Sahn, 1989; Gill, 1991; Devereux et al., 2008; Hadley, 2010; Devereux et al. (eds) forthcoming, in which this section is a chapter.

This may well be the general tendency, depending on contextual conditions, but in most analysis bargaining power is omitted. Bargaining power is gendered to the disadvantage of women (Jackson and Palmer-Jones, 1999: 563–4). Weak bargaining power, whether because supply exceeds demand, or because labourers are women or weak, hungry and desperate, can depress wages, as in this lament from Malawi:

> the problem is that these boat owners know that we are starving, as such we would accept any little wages they would offer to us because they know we are very desperate...we want to save our children from dying. (Khaila et al., 1999: 66)

The seasonal significance and vulnerability of shelter is another dimension easy to overlook.[1] But a participatory appraisal with very poor families in Tanzania (Jupp, 2003) found that shelter was a higher priority for them than outsiders had supposed:

> Most of the rural study households had houses with grass thatch roofs in poor condition and leaking roofs were nearly always mentioned as one of the worst aspects of their lives...The urban households either had very old corrugated iron roofs which leaked badly or a crude 'thatch' of plastic bags and cardboard.

Disasters and contingencies are common. Theft of food or livestock can be serious. In Malawi, rural people used to store food in structures outside their dwellings; now for fear of theft they store it inside. In Ethiopia, farmers have abandoned growing faba beans, good for nutrition, because theft has got out of hand (Boudreau, 2009). Problems of leaking and collapsing roofs, flooding, water and dampness within shelters and wet sleepless nights can compound other stresses. The Malawi Voices of the Poor reported that the problem of collapsing houses had come about because of heavy rains: houses were made of mud and thatched with grass and could not withstand the heavy rains (Khaila et al., 1999: 82); and having a house that did not leak was an indicator of well-being. A woman said that houses should not make people wake up and stand when it is raining like in a court when the judge is arriving and people say '*khoti liime*' – Court stand! (ibid.: 32). In Bangladesh many, perhaps most, of those in the slums of Dhaka originally went there because they lost their land and/or houses to riverbank erosion with seasonal floods in the big rivers. Then there are funerals with the big demands they make on time and resources.

Climate-related disasters and stresses are becoming more common. Meteorological data and farmers' accounts in a range of countries in East Asia, South Asia, Southern and East Africa and Latin America are consistent in indicating that the start and end of rains has become less predictable,

---

1.   Shelter is not a topic in the book of the 1978 Conference on seasonality (Chambers, Longhurst and Pacey, 1981). It was simply not on our mental map.

and rainfall has become more intense and more widely spaced, with serious consequences for agriculture and food production (Jennings and McGrath, 2009; also Patt, 2005). Storms and hurricanes are widely believed and predicted to be becoming more frequent and intense and have their own seasonalities. And most famines in which climate is the cause or main cause, originate in the failure of seasonal rainfall: seasonal hunger is the father of famine (Devereux et al., 2008).

The rains are a bad time for children. Many factors – shelter, cold, wet, poor quality food, sickness and undernutrition apply. Reflecting a peak of conceptions in the cool dry season, late pregnancy and births peak, and babies are small. Mothers sometimes stop breast feeding shortly before the rains, anticipating hard work away from the home. On top of this adults have less time for child care. Seasonal migration besides other stresses and disruptions affects and may prevent children's education (Smita, 2008; Hadley, 2010).

Reflecting on all this, let me invite you to a puzzle. Here is a scenario and question:

> In the middle of the rains, parents in a poor rural family decide not to take their very sick child to the clinic 8 km (5 miles) away when, had it been the dry season they would have taken the child.

What are possible reasons?
If you wish, reflect and make your own list before turning to page 71.

Box 2.1 My reflections on the scenario: possible reasons for not taking the child to the clinic

•

•

•

•

•

•

•

•

•

•

Integrated Season Blindness

'Come let us mock at the wise;
With all those calendars whereon
They fixed old aching eyes.
They never saw how seasons run,
And now but gape at the sun'

W.B. Yeats

Development professionals are season-proofed and season-blind. We are season-proofed – insulated and protected by our housing, air-conditioning, fans and heaters, clothing, urban facilities, incomes, food supplies, protection from infection and access to health services. We are season blind – we travel least during the bad times of the rains and before the harvest, and when we do, stick more than ever to tarmac and places close to town. Except in full-blown famines, we rarely encounter or perceive the regular seasonal hardship, hunger and starvation of remoter poor people. Cyclical seasonal hunger is quiet and hidden. When the rains are over, the harvest is in, and people are through the worst, then it is that urban-based professionals travel again and venture further afield. That is when there are health campaigns. Sometimes that is even when nutrition surveys are carried out. And this is compounded for international visitors from the North who have their own reasons to want to travel to the South in January, February and March. Indeed, in Bangladesh, these visitors are known as *sheether pakhi* – winter birds, who come in January to March. When in 1978 the Select Committee on Overseas Aid of the British House of Commons wanted to visit India in the first quarter of the year, the Indian authorities requested postponement as it was near the end of their financial year in March; but the convenience of the MPs prevailed and they went at what for many poor people in India was their best time of year – cool, relatively dry, healthy and after harvest. So impressions come from the best times, missing the worst. We are systemically misled.

When we professionals do perceive seasonality it tends to be in our own discipline or specialization. The interlocking connections with other domains as they affect poor people are unlikely to be seen. Those concerned with hunger and nutrition overlook sickness. Those concerned with health overlook hard work and the poverty of time. Statistics too, as suggested in Box 2.2, may have built-in biases, underestimating the deprivations of the rains. Or data may be recorded without including seasonality. We may see seasonality to a degree but our sight is impaired.

This blindness is shockingly reflected in publications – books and reports – to an extent that almost beggars belief. Indexers are in part to blame. I first go to the index, and if seasonality is not there, search the text with mounting morbid glee. It is not in the index of Michael Lipton's classic *Why Poor People Stay Poor* (1977) but Lipton had spent most of a year living in an Indian village. And indeed, as expected, seasonality and some of its interlinkages are there in the book (pages 243–4). And he has written elsewhere about seasonality and ultra-poverty (1986).

Books in which seasonal dimensions and their significance appear to be missing include:

Peter Townsend *The International Analysis of Poverty* (1993)
Jeffrey Sachs *The End of Poverty* (2005)

More surprising is to find it missing in otherwise excellent recent works:

Paul Spicker et al. *Poverty: an International Glossary* (2007) despite 27 other entries under the letter under S
Paul Spicker *The Idea of Poverty* (2007)
Potter et al. *Geographies of Development* (2008)

To season blindness there are remedies:

- Include seasonality in terms of reference for consultants
- Interrogate research proposals to find if it is there
- Read texts to assess whether it is included and adequately treated
- Instruct indexers to include it
- Raise it in committees and discussions
- Travel and immerse in the rains

And one might add, enjoy seasonality as a focus and concern, because it is not only so important and neglected, but also intriguing and fascinating, both intellectually, and in terms of puzzling through the practical implications and identifying the opportunities it opens up for making a difference.

Box 2.2 Workshop participants' reflections on the scenario

- One or both of the parents are themselves sick
- The parents are exhausted, weak and short of food and energy
- The mother is in late pregnancy or has just given birth [births tend to peak in the rains]
- Another of their children is sick
- With rain and cold the child would suffer on the journey
- They have no umbrella, big banana leaf or waterproofs
- Carrying a child in wet and slippery conditions would be difficult, exhausting, even dangerous
- Transport (bicycle rickshaw, minibus, bus) during the rains is less reliable, costlier or non-existent
- The opportunity cost of not working (especially weeding) is high
- It is difficult to ask neighbours to look after their other children because neighbours are in the same state, and the opportunity cost of their time is also high
- They fear theft of food stocks, livestock, tools or other possessions in their absence
- They are short of or out of cash, loans are harder to get and carry higher interest rates, and they fear indebtedness
- The clinic staff may be charging more for drugs because demand exceeds supply in the rains
- The clinic may be out of drugs because of high demand or failures of supply
- The clinic may not be open and they cannot know because people are not travelling bringing news [less likely now with mobile phones]
- There is a risk of getting to the clinic and not being able to get back again (flash flood, landslide etc)
- Their shelter is damaged or has collapsed and needs repair
- Herbal remedies are more available in the rains

It may need only a few of these interlocking, or sometimes only one on its own, to deter the parents. When several combine, they are more than ever likely to mean that the child is not taken.

So, if these deterrents, and their opposites during the dry season, are widespread, and many of them can affect adults as well, what effects can be expected on clinic attendance figures and on professional perceptions of the incidence of diseases? Will these be undercounted during the rains, and relatively over represented after them when people can and do go for treatment?

Two syndromes of seasonality

Figure 2.7 Integrated season blindness

Figure 2.8 Integrated seasonal poverty
(especially in tropical wet seasons)

Warning: There are many local variations, nuances, paradoxes and exceptions. The inner circle is really an interconnected web. These are factors which are mostly regular, continuous, predictable and expected – *screws* which combine to press people down into poverty and deprivation. The outer events are vulnerabilities. These are mostly sudden, unpredictable and unexpected – *shocks* with ratchet effects, which abruptly deepen poverty and deprivation. The screws aggravate the impacts of the shocks, making them harder and more costly to handle and more likely to have irreversible ratchet effects.

For professionals, a time to provoke

To everything there is a season, and a time to every purpose under the heaven... A time to weep, and a time to laugh...
The Bible, Ecclesiastes chapter 3.

Normal and new

Normal professionals face the core
And turn their backs upon the poor
New ones by standing on their head
Face the periphery instead

If you're inspired by wild ideas
Do not pander to your peers
Don't go to a Dean's confessional
Come out as a new professional

Whatever next you will propose
If upside down we know it goes
Stand on your head, reverse your role
And kick the ball in your own goal

Whose back to whose, or face to face?
If you're confused it's no disgrace.
Fear not. Have faith. Together pray:
'Dear Edge of Chaos save the day'

So let us hope this little verse'll
Help you make a full reversal
March up and down, banner unfurled
New professionals change the world

In vino

Normal professionals, dull and dry
View things downwards from on high
Only when higher in their cups
can they reverse with bottom-ups

Economists

Economists have come to feel
What can't be measured isn't real
The truth is always an amount
Count numbers, only numbers count

Number stew

With huge numbers you thought that you knew
When in fact what you had was a stew
All the same you were able
To put crap in a table
When it should have been flushed down the loo

Seed breeders

To be a top seed-breeder
Professionally a leader
Stay simple. Measure in the field
By only one criterion – yield[1]

Corruption

Where markets rule, the mantra says
The client's right, politeness pays
But in the bureaucratic way
Clients are wrong until they pay

Justice (India, c. 1983)

They clap in gaol, they are so cruel
Poor folk who pick dead wood for fuel
But let rich loggers go scot free
Who fell and steal the living tree

---

1. This was more justified when it was written than it is now. Following the Green Revolution in India in the late 1960s, breeders did indeed indulge in this sort of reductionist competition. But in 2011 many other criteria are brought to bear, and participatory seed breeding has shown extraordinary success.

Professionals on Canal Irrigation

This dates back to work on canal irrigation in India in the early 1980s. I know I should not include it, but naughtiness has got the better of judgement. There is a personal dimension under the (water) surface in that for reasons we need not go into, since early childhood I have been fascinated by controlling and diverting water flows and still lose myself happily playing with streams on the beach, explaining myself to passers-by as being in my second childhood, though in this respect I never left my first.

Topenders revel in the flood
Perpetual water, soaking mud
Let sluices flow and fields get wetter
Water is good and more is better

Tailenders shrivel in a drought
They cannot bathe; they do without
Their water flows are few and fickle
At worst no drop; at best a trickle

To solve this water problematic
Shrinks can make us systematic
Psychologists can take a hand in
Water-passing understanding

Permissive managers we know
Do not care where waters go
As adults, lax, they in some sense
Relive the child's incontinence

Not so disciplinarians
Who penalise all forms of variance
Their kicks as any Freudian knows
Are childhood joys controlling flows*

In things designers plan to do
Dreams and fantasies come true
Surrogate spouts and flumes of beauty
Help them do their water duty

In water doctors' jaundiced view
Sees hepatitis, schisto too
When vectors breed the sick lie prone
On water doctors stand alone

Deprived of water crops may wilt
But engineers will feel no guilt
Their conscience never suffers harm as
They can always blame the farmers

Economists have other vices
Shady loves for shadow prices
If water's trickling or in spate
They'll solve it with a water rate

Last, politicians' irrigation
Calls for speedy consummation
They demand a quick erection
– dams before the next election

[*another school thinks they are happy
 peeing freely in the nappy]

On Value for Money in Research

Towers were ivory once, now they're steel
Built by business that strikes a hard deal
        What you'll find they will say
        Good researchers obey
Dogs on salaried leads brought to heel

Money talks and will tell what to find
To all contrary data be blind
        To assure the fat cheques
        Always find good effects
Put discrepancies out of your mind

        For the pharmas who fund we declare
        That their patents and prices are fair
        Doubly blind our research shows their pills
        Though placebos, will cure any ills

        For the brewers who pay us we find
        Alcoholic intake helps the mind
        Those who drink become better and stronger
        And live their lives fuller and longer

        When the donors of aid fund our work
        We have duties we never should shirk
        With detached objectivity we
        Find their projects reduce poverty

How to fiddle your findings is fun
And exploring that frontier's begun
        One good ploy, most agree
        Is to hide what you see
        Be opaque and the battle's half won

Use equations and jargon galore
Complicate, obfuscate more and more
    But cap the confusion
    With one clear conclusion
Such as 'This has been good for the poor'

Indeterminacy sets us free
What our sponsors want's then what we see
    We select every sign
    That their products are fine
And unblemished their morality

So like dogs, as old Pavlov explained
Let's have reflexes carefully trained
    While real dogs salivate
    We instead fabricate
And our livelihoods thus are sustained

Professionals and Seasons

Ode to the Seasons Conference (July 1978)

Assembled here in sunny Brighton
We hope our meeting will shed light on
Seasons. Is this good or bad?
Another conference? One *more* fad?

The answer is we're in a trap
We don't have seasons on our map
Our disciplines aren't trained to see
The range of seasonality

First, anthropologists I swear
To seasons have been far too near
Immersed in culture, rain or dry
They have not seen the clouds pass by

And sociologists, even worse
With questionnaires and questions terse
Snatch instant truth, one-off. It's rare
To find them survey all the year

Nutritionists with careful plan
Conduct their surveys when they can
Be sure the weather's fine and dry
The harvest's in, food intake high

Malariologists can claim
Their pattern is not quite the same
Superior in virtue they
Migrate to *face* the rainy day

Economists, that super breed
Show seasonal supplies exceed
Demand: result – the landless poor
For less and less work more and more

And statisticians too declare
They have a seasonal nightmare
An average is but a dream
With seasons means aren't what they seem

Geographers – complacent crew
Will say – of course they always knew
What others now just come to know
That seasons come and seasons go

Contrariwise plant breeders say
Not seasons but the length of day
Is critical. The key they've seen
's a photoperiodic gene

Demographers now wonder why
We do it when it's cool and dry
Conversely when it's wet and hot
It seems we tend to do it not

Now epidemiologists
Will say the worst is when it's [poured][1]
With rain for that's when vectors vect
And swarms of small insects infect

Then students seeking PhDs
Believe that everyone agrees
That rains don't do for rural study
Suits get wet and shoes get muddy

And bureaucrats, that urban type,
Wait prudently till crops are ripe
Before they venture to the field
To ask their question: what's the yield?

---

1.   It is a reflection on changing mores that in 1978 I held back from writing pissed. In 2010
     I would not hesitate.

The international experts' flights
Have other seasons winter nights
In New York, Paris, Brussels, Rome
Are what drive them in flocks from home

And Northern academics too
Are seasonal in their global view
For they are seen in Third World nations
mainly during long vacations

The rural people – I forgot
Know what some others still know not
Long life and leisure, food and health
Belong to those who have the wealth

They do not need research to show
The troubles they already know
Oppressed by hunger, sickness, debt
They know the worst is when it's wet

But wealthy ones dislike life dry
The poor may thirst but we'll get by
Eating and drinking, within reason
Steadily through the conference season.

And its more staid sequel:

Sonnet for the Seasonality Revisited Conference (8–10 July 2009)

And now we sup here after thirty years
And wonder what has happened in between
And blame ourselves for all the needless tears
That fell because the seasons stayed unseen.
Though much has altered much remains the same
Those screws and ratchets still keep down the poor
But global warming's changed the farmers' game
With loaded dice that make the risks hurt more.
Our eyes are opened. No more season-blind
Our vision can be positive and green –
A world that's season-proofed for humankind
In thirty more years let's transform the scene

Let's go for change. By then may all have found
Not pain but pleasure in the seasons' round

Banks, shares and beyond the dreams of avarice[1]

Financial pundits search for reasons
Why money matters have their seasons
In July take out your savings
August's the month of big bank cave ins[2]

Prudent investors, too, remember
Sell your shares off in September
Safer to have it all in cash
October's when the markets crash[3]

But wait! Mean monthly values tell
Another tale of when to sell
November is the month to buy
And hold till April hits its high

Sell then, sit pretty through the crashes
Then buy up October's ashes
Your wealth should grow, through this advice
Beyond the dreams of avarice

---

1. For alerting me to these seasonalities and to sources of information about them I am grateful to Tom Lines. Responsibility for the content of these verses is, however, mine, but not in any respect including any losses occurring as a result of taking the advice. If, on the other hand, you make a killing, I will not refuse a modest commission. See http://ftalphaville.ft.com/blog/2009/07/13/61596/beware-the-out-of-office-indicator/ which suggests possible explanations including illiquidity during July and August summer holidays in the Northern hemisphere. Analysis of 30 years of monthly changes in stock market values in Europe and the UK show the biggest average drops in September and the biggest average rises in December and April http://ftalphaville. ft.com/blog/2010/12/13/435021/ding-dong-merrily-on-high/
2. For example Mexico 1982 and Russia 1998. The period can start in July, as in the Asian crisis of 1997. (P.S. This was written before the crises of the euro and the United States debt in late July and August 2011. By the time this is read, it will be evident whether November 2011 was a good time to invest.)
3. For example Wall street and other markets in October 1929, 1987 and 1997. Of the ten largest one day falls on Wall Street up to 2003, five were in October http://news.bbc. co.uk/1/hi/business/2131739.stm [accessed 29 December 2010].

Participation: tyrannical or transformative?

The 1990s were the heyday and a heroic age for some participatory methodologies. PRA (Participatory Rural Appraisal) was one of the best known and widespread of these. It had its passionate champions. It also had its opportunistic adopters who used the label without the substance of changes in behaviour and attitudes. Donors demanded PRA and consultants said they would supply it. There was much abuse. Some academics even tried what they called PRA and then criticized PRA for their own bad practices, for example holding large community meetings. A backlash was inevitable. It came in 2001 with a book edited by Bill Cooke and Uma Kothari, Participation: The New Tyranny? *This took a critical but not always well informed stance. The title of the book was arresting and it has been much cited. The question mark was often forgotten. Its orientation appeals to negative academics. And in its turn, it provoked a response:* Participation: From Tyranny to Transformation? Exploring New Approaches to Participation in Development, *edited by Samuel Hickey and Giles Mohan, Zed Books, London and New York, 2004.*

This review was published in Development in Practice *vol 15 no 5, August 2005, and reflects my own experiences and biases.*

From Tyranny to Transformation? has appeared none too soon. Its predecessor, *Participation: the new tyranny?*, edited by Bill Cooke and Uma Kothari, and published in 2001 also by Zed Books, was more in the tradition of the negative academic who relishes finding things to criticize. These were the many actual and potential defects of practices labelled as participatory. Its question mark was overshadowed by the clever paradox of the rest of the title, which must have ensured a wide readership. Unfortunately, the style and orientation of that book were more prone to breed cynicism than to encourage action and trying to do better. It is, of course, vital to recognize and learn from the widespread bad practices perpetrated in the name of participation. But any balanced view must also include the gains that have been made, some of them extraordinary. *From Tyranny to Transformation?* takes us in that direction. It has the sharp critical edge we will always need. At the same time it is better informed and more perceptive and judicious than its predecessor. While its title retains the question mark, as it should, the word 'transformation' points us forwards.

No short review can do justice to the wealth of comment and insight presented in the book's 18 chapters. One strength is the presentation and analysis of examples to give an empirical grounding. Quite extensive case material is drawn from Bolivia, Brazil, Cameroon, Ethiopia, Ghana, India, Nepal, Peru, Sierra Leone, Zimbabwe and elsewhere.

There are some useful concepts, examples of participation, and reminders of its dimensions that give pause for reflection. Among others, John Gaventa describes new forms of citizen-state engagement. Andrea Cornwall explores spaces as metaphor and reality, using the distinction between those which are 'invited' and those which are 'popular' or 'autonomous'. Ute Kelly gives us 'the tyranny of safety', suggesting that making spaces 'safe' for people to express and change their views can discourage precisely the open, honest discussion that is sought. Glyn Williams finds participation 'a highly malleable discourse in political terms' and argues that it should be re-politicized. Mark Waddington and Giles Mohan refer to 'deep political literacy' linked to REFLECT (originally Regenerated Freirian Literacy through Empowering Community Techniques, now more usually simply Reflect).

Codes of practice and ethical considerations are central to only one chapter. In this Bill Cooke lists his rules of thumb for participatory change agents. Individually, these are salutary shocks not least to those who gain their livelihoods in consultancy and research. But they could tyrannize more than transform: don't work for the World Bank; data belong to those from whom they were taken; work only in languages you understand as well as your first; always work for local rates, or for free – each of these invites a 'Yes, but...'. Life and ethics are not so simple. Development professionals who practise responsibly are faced with dilemmas: and these are interwoven with personal and professional tensions and contradictions, demanding trade-offs and compromises which are sometimes stark and sometimes subtle, if they are to engage actively rather than carp and prescribe from the sidelines. This applies not least to decisions and actions when engaging with process, when dealing with difference and conflict, when seeking to make spaces safe but not too safe or safe in the wrong way, and when facilitating exchanges, negotiation, and mutual understanding. Not to engage, and so to avoid having to make choices with trade-offs, is itself an ethical decision. Questions of responsibility apply to what is not done as well as to what is.

Power and agency are pervasive themes in this collection. Gaventa writes on the significance of power relations in participatory spaces, Cornwall on spaces for transformation, Kelly on how shifts in power can be difficult and painful for all who are involved, and Williams on calling power to account. And other chapters pick up on these themes. While it is good and overdue that power and agency have become more central concerns and more discussed in development, there is a danger that they become top-down priorities, a point made by Frances Cleaver: in analysing the social embeddedness of agency and decision making, she adds the salutary caution that in terms of poor people's priorities, empowerment and transformation are not just matters of spaces and voices, but entail more prosaic forms of material and social transformation of everyday life.

The frontiers of participatory practices move fast; and given the delays of authors, editors, and publishers, books on participation are vulnerable to being overtaken by events by the time they are published. It is also easy for them to overlook some of the myriad innovations and applications that manifest almost every month. So it is not surprising that some strikingly original and transformative developments are not in this book, for example applications of participatory approaches and methods to violence, to guns and disarming, to sexual and reproductive health, to community sanitation, to boundary disputes and conflict resolution, and to tertiary education. As Tony Bebbington remarks 'the frontier of what can be done around participatory development and social change has expanded enormously'. It continues to do so. *From Tyranny to Transformation?* does not explore the full span of potentials and applications on that frontier, but does a service in summarizing much recent experience, and doing this in a manner which is variously provocative, critical and balanced. It deserves to be widely read and reflected on by those who are engaged in and concerned with participation.

Negotiated learning: collaborative monitoring in resource management

Every few years there is a book which shakes unquestioned assumptions. Monitoring and evaluation was prefixed with Participatory to become PM and E in the 1990s. Participatory meant either that indicators were identified in a participatory manner, or that local people took part in assessing and reporting them, or both of these. They might learn in the process, but the prime beneficiaries were the organizations that initiated the process. The rationale was not learning by local people, though they might learn coincidentally, but learning by us: it was basically a way of improving the upwards flow of information and accountability. As this foreword to Negotiated Learning *affirms, and as its title indicates, a further step was taken in which how outsiders and local people could learn together was itself negotiated and evolved jointly in a participatory process. If the foreword intrigues you, or irritates you with its unexplained allusions, I shall be delighted if this provokes you into borrowing or buying, and reading the book. It will then have served my purpose. The book is: Irene Guijt (ed.)* Negotiated Learning: Collaborative Monitoring in Resource Management, Resources for the Future, *Washington DC, 2007.*

This important book breaks new ground. Monitoring has often been associated with upwards accountability; the measurement of centrally determined indicators; regular, repetitive and routine reporting; and, quite often, accumulated sediments of information that are unread and unused. In English, the word 'monitoring' has unfortunate undertones of surveillance. As noted by contributors to this book, it can also translate into other languages as words that imply control and even policing.

For CIFOR (the Centre for International Forestry Research), which supported the research initiatives discussed in this book, monitoring was structured around a hierarchy of four concepts: principles, criteria, indicators and verifiers. Attempts were made to apply these by teams of facilitators in a participatory action research mode in Bolivia, Brazil, Cameroon, Ghana, Indonesia, Malawi, Nepal, the Philippines and Zimbabwe. Their experiences have generated rich, reflective and insightful accounts of learning and change that show us new potential.

Though the case study experiences naturally differ, their commonalities are significant. First, teams found that detailed use of indicators, while logical from a research and information perspective and prevalent in the world of monitoring and evaluation, impeded learning and contributed little to resource management. Of the four concepts, that shape CIFOR's indicator framework, it was only 'verifiers', close to the realities of local participants, that made some sense. Second, the teams' participatory approaches had to evolve to be relevant in complex, diverse and dynamic local conditions. Often there were many actors with different and at times conflicting views and interests. Preset methodologies, so prevalent in the world of monitoring and evaluation, were of little use. The teams had to become not just facilitators but negotiators, and innovators of methods. Third, the teams found themselves co-learners. They entered and explored a world of 'collective sense-making through critical analysis of information', of 'facilitated reflections', and of 'co-creating meanings through joint reflection'. And much of what is new and important in all this is captured and expressed in the phrase 'socially negotiated learning'. This in turn leads to adaptation and action, feeding into the cycle of action, observation, reflection, planning and then action again.

Paradigmatically, this is a new world for monitoring. It goes beyond the prevalent monitoring of participatory monitoring and evaluation, in which local people participate within frames that are externally determined, observing and measuring indicators that are passed down to them, and then passing the findings back up. Instead, monitoring as socially negotiated learning requires information seeking, critical analysis, and process facilitation in equal measure. Monitoring focuses on co-learning and adaptive management by local actors. Local actors include not just those who use the resources, but others like forest rangers and government officials who influence resource decisions and implement resource use legislation.

Monitoring in this mode fits, flows from and functions in the world of local complexity, diversity and dynamism. Unpredictability is inherent; surprise is expected and sought. Imposed top-down categories, lists and indicators are then destructive. There is no blueprint. Rigour is not in rigidity but in relevance of learning. This in turn derives from the quality of process, interactions and relationships. The calibre, orientation, behaviour and attitudes of facilitators, and the organizational understanding and support they receive, are crucial.

Negotiated Learning: Collaborative Monitoring in Resource Management is about much more than participatory *forest* management. Its lessons apply to all participatory *natural resource* management. Beyond that, both deeper and broader, it has messages for all development professionals about how 'we' think of and go about development. The experiences it reports challenge central mindsets, the paradigm of preset research, and the rationality of bureaucratic accountabilities. Those currently frustrated by ineffective ways of working may now see collaborative monitoring and negotiated learning as personal, professional, and institutional paths to innovation with procedures, accountabilities and priorities.

Let me hope that this volume will be widely available and reflected on. It should be read by teachers and should enter the curricula in universities, institutes of forest management, and organizations that educate and train for the management of other natural resources. It should lead to decisive and imaginative action not only in adaptive collaborative management but also in development more generally. For it opens up and illuminates the world of potential through facilitation, process, relationships and social learning. This is a wave of the future for many professional fields. May it inspire many others to follow where it leads.

Measuring empowerment? Ask them?
A win–win in Bangladesh

Uppers – those who are dominant, senior, powerful in a context – tend to underestimate what lowers – those who are subordinate, junior, weaker in that context – know and can do. This seems to be so widespread as to be almost universal. Adults and children, teachers and pupils, doctors and patients... long lists can be drawn up, and readers may wish to have some fun by making their own. This can apply to professionals and members of the public, to donors and recipients, to consultants and their clients... When the PRA principle of 'They can do it' – assuming that lowers and local people can do something until it is robustly proved otherwise – is internalized in upper-lower relationships and reflected in behaviour and attitudes, it is often astonishing what children and other 'lowers' show they can do (for children see Johnson et al., 1998 Stepping Forward *pp. 204–206).*

One way into this is another PRA principle 'Ask them'. Here is a remarkable case where that was applied in Bangladesh. It defied conventional professional wisdom, proved popular and empowering, and enabled groups of poor people to define and co-evolve their ideas of the social changes they wished to achieve.

The story is this. Sida as a funding agency wanted an evaluation of empowerment in a large social movement it supported in Bangladesh. For this donors tried to impose logical frameworks and standard monitoring and evaluation approaches but the movement resisted. When outside design consultants were asked to suggest indicators for empowerment they came up with membership characteristics, leadership and group cohesion, collective action and wider networking, autonomy and maturity, and key benefits achieved. Then a team led by a consultant used an array of PRA tools, a listening study, and drama to generate value statements from members of the movement. The over 8,000 resulting key statements from groups and committees were 'peppered with perspectives which had never occurred to staff'. When grouped, the statements emerged and cohered as 132 indicators clustered under four headings: awareness; confidence and capability; effectiveness; and self-sustaining. A system of reflection sessions was then introduced in which groups assessed themselves against the criteria with either a happy or unhappy face, according to their satisfaction.

However, an outside review later said that 'in order to be a realistic monitoring tool it needs to be streamlined to reduce the number of indicators and the time taken to complete'. Participants in a donor consortium observed the group reflection process in action and dismissed the approach:

'How can poor people engage in a process which takes three hours or more... they have mouths to feed. This is an imposition on their time. Either that or this is not the target group we thought we were supporting'

When these observations were taken back to several member groups 'they were flabbergasted':

> *'We do this because it is important to us. Yes, it takes a long time but it is time well spent. How could we review everything we do with only a few statements to describe it? These people do not understand – we never talked about these things properly before – it has opened our eyes'*

The outsiders' concerns about time were based on sensitivity to the widespread experience with the extractive M and E of focus groups and questionnaire surveys. But this situation was different. The meetings mattered to the participants and were found valuable by them. They were even facilitated by members of the movement. There were other paradigmatic differences – for example the way empowerment was a moving target, as groups changed the indicators, seeking to achieve more: goals themselves can change in participatory processes; indeed, one indicator of a good participatory M and E process is that the indicators do indeed change. If they do not, something may be wrong.

Here is the foreword, written in 2008 to Dee Jupp and Sohel Ibn Ali with contributions from Carlos Barahona (2010) Measuring Empowerment? Ask Them: quantifying qualitative outcomes from people's own analysis – insights for results-based management from the experience of a social movement in Bangladesh, *Sida, Stockholm.*

We, development professionals, are lucky to be living and working at this time. For there is an explosion of participatory methodologies, and a constant opening up of possibilities. Tragically, though, many innovations are one-off, never written up, and never shared. The innovators may not see their significance. Managers in organizations and sponsors in donor agencies have other priorities. And methodologies with potential to transform the quality of what is done in the name of development are all too often one-off and never spread.

Here, though, we have an outstanding exception: a methodological breakthrough made accessible to the development community at large.

Consider the context. For over a decade empowerment has been prominent in the rhetoric of development. Attempts to monitor and measure it have typically relied on indicators decided by outsiders for their own information and use. Professionals have believed that people's own assessments could only be simple and qualitative and could not be aggregated; that little of local people's time should be demanded; and that local-level staff had to facilitate analysis.

Now we have an approach and methods evolved with and for a social movement in Bangladesh which turns these on their heads. Groups assess themselves using indicators generated earlier through a participatory process; the indicators are many – 132; an elegant method quantifies and aggregates them to show distributions, trends and surprises; local people themselves facilitate group analysis, releasing staff time and avoiding deferential responses; and people enthusiastically give time to assessments because they are important for their own learning, planning and progress.

Such radical reversals were not easy. Salaried field staff felt threatened by some findings. Donors were sceptical until they had direct experience of the group reflections; and when new donors and their consultants arrived, it was back to square one again. This should never happen again. Let sceptics read the balanced evaluation by Carlos Barahona, made with the authority of a critical professional statistician. *Measuring Empowerment?* shows how participatory assessments can empower and transform relationships, and at the same time generate reliable and valid statistics for what were thought to be only qualitative dimensions.

A big lesson has been that to invent, evolve and establish such a participatory methodology demands creativity, tenacity, continuity and champions. It shows that the gains can be all round. Reports were more credible and insightful. The movement's salaried staff learnt with surprise about the range of activities and diversity of benefits perceived by members. The process of assessing empowerment was itself empowering for local groups, whose members are the primary users. This is a methodological breakthrough, a remarkable win–win for all concerned.

This is a 'must-read' for all who are committed to empowerment, rights-based approaches and good governance. It shows the power of privileging the realities and priorities of those who are marginalized and living in poverty. I defy any committed and open-minded professional to read this without feeling excited. May what is written here be internalized and acted on by all concerned in lender or donor agencies, governments, NGOs, social movements, research institutes and universities. May they be encouraged by its approach and example to invent, spread and share other participatory methodologies. Well facilitated and taken to scale, approaches like this have huge potential to transform our world.

Congratulations to the pioneers of this approach for their creativity and persistence, to the Movement, its members and staff, for showing what it could do, and to Sida for sponsoring it and having it written up. May other donors follow suit whenever there is need and opportunity. May this publication be seen and read by many. And may others be inspired by its example to do likewise.

Participatory numbers and statistics

Why are we so blind, so conservative, so slow to recognize and exploit this win–win waiting in the wings?

I will not beat about the bush. I am angry and frustrated. There is an abundant accumulation of evidence that well-facilitated participatory approaches and methods can generate good numbers and statistics. Let us call them Participatory Methods and Methodologies that Quantify (PMQs). They have much to recommend them. Yet they have not entered any mainstream. They can probe and throw light on dimensions inaccessible to questionnaires. Repeatedly and in many respects they have demonstrated advantages over conventional questionnaires of any length.[1] Yet the reflex, again and again and again, is so predictable. You want numbers and statistics? How? Long and over inclusive questionnaires.

As with *Measuring Empowerment? Ask Them* PMQs can be a win–win. In many circumstances local people learn and are empowered through their own appraisal and analysis, and outsider professionals are informed and kept in touch and up-to-date. For local analysts PMQs can generate credible numbers for use in advocacy.

So what do we know about PMQs?

Participatory numbers can be analysed like other statistics. The classic works on this are by statisticians at the Centre for Statistical Services, Reading University, who have facilitated participatory numbers from various methods, and have devised ad hoc sequences for specific purposes (Burn, 2000; Barahona and Levy, 2003, 2007; Levy, 2003, 2005, 2007). Andy Catley and his colleagues have extensively used PMQs in East Africa (see e.g. Abebe et al., 2009) and have compiled an excellent guide for practitioners on *Participatory Impact Assessment* (Catley et al., 2008) with examples of ranking, scoring, estimating, matrix scoring and causal attribution, and a diagram (p. 58) which illustrates triangulation. For analysing the outputs they have applied standard statistical methods.[2]

PMQs can quantify the qualitative. PMQs can quantify almost any qualitative dimension open to human judgement, for example aspects of well-being (White and Pettit, 2004). As we have seen above in *Measuring Empowerment?* aggregation from focus groups can quantify dimensions of social change.

---

1. For evidence see Chambers, 1997: 122ff; Barahona and Levy, 2003; Chambers, 2008: chapter 6; Catley et al., 2008.
2. For example SPSS, the Kendall coefficient of concordance, and the Wilcoxon Signed Ranks test.

PMQ numbers are often better than those generated in other ways.[1] The word 'alternative' as in 'alternative statistics' (Archer and Newman, 2003) applied to such numbers should not give the impression that they are soft or second best. To the contrary they are usually more accurate and relevant than those from questionnaires and censuses, sometimes spectacularly so. Ad hoc inventive design can lead to tables with a credible rigour and accuracy inaccessible by other means (see e.g. Levy, 2003, 2005). The rigour of trustworthiness and relevance manifests through design, critical participatory facilitation, and observation of group-visual synergy – participants committed to 'getting it right' and triangulation with visual cross-checking and progressive interactive approximation (Chambers, 1997: 154–61; Catley et al., 2008: 58). Evidence of the accuracy and power of participatory numbers has been accumulating over the past two decades. Summaries, overviews and critical analyses (e.g. Abeyasekera, 2001; Burn, 2000; Barahona and Levy, 2003, 2007; Chambers, 2008: chapter 6; Mayoux and Chambers, 2005) present evidence from many domains. A remarkable case was the credible identification of a census undercount of the order of 36 per cent found in the rural population of Malawi through participatory census mapping triangulated with a one-page questionnaire (Barahona and Levy, 2003).

PMQs can be cost-effective and give numbers and otherwise inaccessible insights. Unanticipated aspects and consequences can come to light. We are now, in 2011, in a new space where combinations with mobile phones, ICTs and Web2.0 have opened up an explosion of new opportunities with an epicentre in Kenya.

So why is it that PMQs have not yet become the norm?

Here are some likely reasons:

Ignorance – Those who commission work do not know the potentials.

Risk aversion – Fear the unknown. Lack of guts.

Lack of creative and inventive innovators who can develop, pilot test, and evolve methodologies fit for purpose and context.

Few facilitators – there are armies of enumerators who have been trained to administer questionnaires, and fewer who are competent facilitators. Facilitators may have to be trained.

PMQs often take time to develop and test, though once developed they generate data very fast.

---

1.   This assumes similar quality of facilitation and implementation in the approaches being compared. There is a wealth of evidence to support this rather modest assertion. See for example Chambers, 1997: chapter 7, and 2008: chapter 6, and Barahona and Levy, 2003 and 2007. The rigour of triangulation, successive approximation and emergence in observed group-visual synergy (Chambers, 1997: 158–61) is still almost entirely unrecognized in the mainstreams of orthodox professionalism. The issue is paradigmatic, between dominant neo-Newtonian practices and participatory and adaptive pluralism, which accommodates and expresses complexity and emergence (see pp. 194–6 and Chambers, 2010).

Let us unpack this last point. To evolve fitting participatory methodologies requires participatory attitudes and behaviour. Participatory methods, like mapping or matrix scoring, are versatile and fairly straightforward; they do not require extensive trials. In contrast, to evolve a methodology that combines methods and approaches to fit a context and purpose can take time, skill, inventiveness, patience and progressive piloting. To develop the methodology used in Malawi for impact assessment of the 'starter pack' with farmers' indicators of sustainability (of which there came to be 15) (Cromwell et al., 2001) took a team three weeks of continuous and intensive participatory fieldwork and trials (Fiona Chambers, *pers. comm.*). The impact assessment methods and processes used with pastoralists in East Africa to generate relevant statistics and insights were developed over a matter of years (Catley, 2009; Catley et al., 2008).

So we can understand some of the obstacles although what is on offer is win–wins, which may often be the best of all worlds – qualitative, quantitative, participatory, empowering and generating statistics.

I want to provoke you now. Have you used these approaches? If not, why not? Will you be a pioneer? Will you help to mainstream these win–win ways of generating statistics, of gaining better data, of learning at the same time as empowering? Will you ally with others and support them in doing likewise? Will you write up and share the experience, or sponsor others to do so?

Will you dare? Have you got the guts and imagination? Or do you prefer to hibernate, snug and safe, in your old warm comfort zone? Come on. Wake up. Spring is here.

PRA: start, stumble, self-correct, share

This dates back to 1992 and the early days of PRA. It urges us to engage, to make mistakes, to fail forwards, to learn, to correct and to share the experience. I say 'us' to include myself because I persistently want to withdraw to the security of known comfort zones and will never dare enough. In being bold, we must take care not to hurt others, especially others weaker than ourselves: do no harm is a good injunction. But we have to learn and change. Can we act responsibly without taking risks? Does this mean being alert, aware, nimble, improvising and adapting. If so, does what follows still apply?

Participatory Rural Appraisal is a label. More and more people are adopting it, and calling what they do PRA. More and more influential organizations are requesting or requiring that PRA be carried out.

This brings dangers and opportunities.

The dangers are that the label will be used or claimed for activities where behaviour and attitudes are not participatory; that these activities will do badly; and that good PRA will be discredited. There is a danger too that the demand for training in PRA will so outstrip good supply that some will claim to be PRA trainers when they have no direct personal experience of good PRA. This has already happened.

The opportunities are hard to assess but look big. Time, though, will show. Perhaps we have in good PRA one among a family of approaches for reversing centralization, standardization, and top-down development; and for enabling and empowering rural communities and the poor to do more of their own analysis, to take command more of their lives and resources, and to improve their well-being as they define it.

So what is the core of good PRA?

We should all have different answers. It is more important to ask the question, and to puzzle and puzzle about good answers, than to have one right answer. It is more important for each person and each group to invent and adapt their own approach, methods, sequences and combinations than to adopt a ready-made manual or model. Let a thousand flowers bloom (and why only a thousand?), and let them be flowers which bloom better and better, and spread their seeds.

Here is one personal set of answers. If you read them, criticize them. Reject them. Think out your own, from your own ideas and experience.

In the words of the one-sentence manual
'Use your own best judgement at all times'

The core of good PRA is in us. It is our behaviour and attitudes. It involves:

Being self-aware and self-critical
Embracing error
Handing over the stick
Sitting, listening and learning
Improvising, inventing, adapting
Using our own best judgement at all times

So we can ask:

Who lectures? Who holds the stick? Whose finger wags?
Whose knowledge, analysis and priorities count?
Ours? Theirs, as we assume them to be? Or theirs as they freely express them?
Good PRA is empowering, not extractive.
Good PRA makes mistakes, learns from them, and so is self-improving.
Good PRA spreads and improves on its own.
So START. Do not wait. Get on with it. Relax. Try things. Learn by doing. Fail forwards. Experiment. Ask – what went well? What went badly? What can we learn? How can we do better? How can we help others to do better?

Remember the three pillars

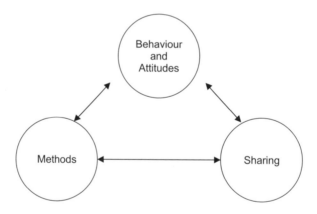

Done well, PRA becomes self-improving and self-spreading: self-improving through critical awareness, embracing error, failing forwards, and learning what works; and self-spreading through sharing.

Start with behaviour and attitudes. Ours. And use the methods at once to help.

Or start with a method, and observe and reflect on your behaviour and attitudes as you use it. Relax. Listen. Keep quiet. Allow fun. Learn. And learn how to do better.

PRA is what we make of it. If you do not like it, leave it. No one will mind. It is not everyone's cup of tea. But if you like it, and use it, share it and help others to share.

PRA is not a panacea. It is a potential. For us. And through changes in us, for them.

Do you want to realize it?

Then later this led to an invitation in 2002 to be adventurous – easy to write, so much harder to live. What follows now was the first of 21 entries each with 21 points or activities in a book of serious fun on Participatory Workshops *and facilitation.*

PRA behaviours: 21 do's

If you are repeating what you did two years ago, is something wrong?

When in doubt,

- Do something new
- Be of good heart
- Fail forwards
- Bounce back
- Celebrate learning

and

- experiment
- innovate
- invent
- improvise
- dare
- risk
- seek
- explore
- discover
- collect

- adapt
- combine
- vary
- sequence
- reflect
- self-critique
- change
- share
- spread
- enjoy

and

- make your own list

These were listed for facilitators of participatory workshops not for the rest of living. But is there an overlap? How would you rank these for importance? For yourself? For others? And what would your own 21 be? Does this provoke you into making your own list?

From a little book on *Participatory Workshops* (Chambers, 2002: 3).

PART III
Aid

Provoking aid

Over the years I have engaged with aid from inside and outside: inside with UNHCR working as evaluation officer concerned mainly with rural refugees in Africa; half in half out as a consultant of dubious competence for a number of agencies; and outside as beneficiary of grants, observer and critical friend. I will not hide the fact that this has been immensely enjoyable. Much of the time it has meant access without responsibility. For this I owe much to those in aid organizations – multi- and bi-lateral official agencies, and INGOs, who have opened doors and shared ideas, and trusted me with insights and information.

I tend to meet and mix with the like-minded and so am vulnerable to imagining that others in aid agencies are like them; I may consequently underestimate the obstacles to good change. Some who may know better think that aid is so bad that it should be wound up. I am not one of those. Rather I believe in engagement and struggle. In aid, relationships should change, realizing and recognizing reciprocities of mutual learning and co-evolution. Institutional and personal learning and change are permanent priorities. In my view, 'rational' procedures – the logframe, results-based management, upward accountability – should be transformed to minimize bad effects and maximize good. And so it goes on…should…should…should. It is so easy to be a negative academic, carping from the sidelines without practicable solutions. But in 2011 aid has become pathologically controllaholic: more controls make for worse performance. So let me salute those who struggle to protect responsible autonomy against the linear magnetism of top-down demands and controls. Let me hope that they will be rewarded with the liberations they deserve. And that this will mean many gains for the hundreds of millions of those living in poverty whom they and aid programmes are meant to serve.

These papers have been selected from the past for their contemporary relevance, concluding with 2011.

How do you change self-awareness and behaviour in an international organization? One way is to bring people from different organizations, or different types of organization, together, and ask them how they see themselves, how they see the others, and how they think the others see them, as in **How development organizations see each other and relate**. Another is retreats and workshops in which people live, work, sleep, relax and, if so inclined, drink together, as was the background to the **Rugby International: UNHCR vs NGOs**.

As the first evaluation officer in UNHCR in the mid 1970s, I found that many of my colleagues were experienced lawyers from Europe who were having to deal with massive problems of hundreds of thousands of rural refugees in Africa. All were subject to pressures of time that trapped them in headquarters and in capital cities. So I tried at least to tackle that and wrote tips for field visits. Though I thought badly needed they were resented as patronizing, and ignored. So I tried another tack and composed **My visit to a rural settlement**. It did not work either but it was fun to write.

People uprooted by conflict and persecution, both refugees who flee to another country, and internally displaced people, are a disgraceful blot on our human record. In 2010 there were over 43 million people forcibly displaced from their homes, the most there had ever been. More than any other, Barbara Harrell-Bond's 1986 book *Imposing Aid: Emergency Assistance to Refugees* revealed the realities of such people and of the organizations that set out to help them. I was invited to write a *Foreword*. The book is a classic and as relevant and disturbing today as ever.

Procedures have a strong influence on performance and relationships. In 1996 tentative feelers were put out for a marriage between ZOPP (Zielorientierte Projekt Planung) (the aspiring bridegroom), and PRA (Participatory Rural Appraisal) (the would-be bride). ZOPP is a sibling, if not twin, of the Logical Framework aka Logframe. Social anthropologists in GTZ (Deutsche Gesellschaft für Technische Zusammenarbeit) convened a stimulating and enjoyable two-day workshop. Inputs and outputs there were, and much interaction, but neither betrothal nor any premarital consummation. In 2011 the tensions and contradictions are even more relevant than they were in 1996. **ZOPP marries PRA: whose reality, needs and priorities count?** was an input to the workshop. And **Reversals, realities and rewards** were designed to provoke reflection and action. Who agrees with them? And if you agree, so what? In the meantime, GTZ was and remains a leader in procedural innovation, a space for would-be reformers to watch. As for PRA, it was often undermined and abused by demands to go rapidly to scale.

The 1970s and 1980s were the heyday of heavy lending. Banks of the world were flush with petrodollars, and the World Bank led the way with large loans to developing countries, encouraging private sector banks also to invest. The disastrous results are notorious: structural adjustment, declining health and education, deteriorating infrastructure, and terrible avoidable suffering. How does one express anger and outrage? Verse is one way. Fury can be dressed as fun. So it came out as **On lenders, donors, debt and development**.

In the 1990s it was the turn of participation to have its heyday in the World Bank. SIDA provided a Trust Fund for a Participatory Learning Process. The Participatory Development Learning Group had 60 members. Aubrey Williams and Bhuvan Bhatnagar were committed and tenacious in leading and pushing the process. As the responsible person in SIDA, Gunilla Olsson, in alliance with Sven Sandstrom, one of the four Managing Directors of the Bank, gave crucial support. Big workshops were held in Washington in 1992 and 1994. *The World Bank and Participation* (World Bank, 1994) and *The World Bank Participation Sourcebook* (World Bank, 1996) marked a peak of enthusiasm and commitment. As a participant observer in the workshops I was given time to make some remarks, extracts of which are here as **The World Bank: what next?** Some shifts did take place in the Bank, and were followed through in James Wolfensohn's time as President. Rhetoric changed. *Participation* and *participatory* peppered project proposals and official papers. More and more projects labelled themselves as participatory. But the unparticipatory logic of speed and scale scarcely changed. **Participation and PRA for donors** was an exhortation to donors to be sensitive in how they supported PRA, and continues to apply with participatory approaches, not least Community-Led Total Sanitation.

'Participation' became a widespread aspiration. CBD (Community-Based Development) and CDD (Community-Driven Development) became all the rage in the World Bank. More and more projects were given these labels. Then the Bank's Operations Evaluation Department conducted an evaluation of CBD and CDD. Near the end of the process an invitation came to be a member of a panel to review the evaluation. In IDS Andrea Cornwall and I enjoyed puzzling and debating whether it would be right to accept and if so who should go. In the end I went. After the review, members of the panel wrote comments. Mine were critical. There was a long delay before Management in the Bank approved the report. To the great credit of the Bank, my reflections were posted on the World Bank website as part of advisory committee comments (presented here in **The effectiveness of the World Bank support for community-based and -driven development**). Do the points about this sort of large-scale evaluation apply more widely? And was I right or wrong to go beyond my brief and offer gratuitous advice? Well, it upset some in the Bank who believed themselves to be working for good on the side of the angels. Unsurprisingly, the advice to declare a moratorium on such projects was not taken.

After the World Bank, DFID is one of the most influential donors. To a degree it is a trendsetter. Tragically, the British Treasury set it on a course of having to reduce its staff even while its budget doubled. I favour increasing the aid budget, and at the time of writing in early 2011 all major political parties in the UK remain committed to this, quite remarkably given draconian cuts in other departmental budgets. But I favour the British taxpayers' money being spent as effectively as possible. This needs more, not fewer, staff in DFID. So in 2007 when some of us in IDS were asked **What DFID should do** – 'We hope for balanced entries that are challenging but constructive', here is what I wrote. Was I right? Did I overstate it? Understate it? And now in 2011 does what I said apply with even more force? And does it apply to other aid organizations as well?

Tragically, the losers from reducing staff while raising the budget were and would continue to be the people whom the money is meant to help, the hundreds of millions who live in poverty, the poor, the vulnerable, the marginalized – children, women, men. They have not been gaining what they could and should gain. There is some hope though. More staff in-country will now in 2011 be recruited on programme budgets, though whether this will go far enough remains to be seen.

Then there is the recognition that where the poor are has changed dramatically. In 1990 some 93 per cent lived in Low Income Countries. In 2010 three-quarters, almost a billion 'The New Bottom Billion' lived in Middle

Income Countries. This demands a radical rethink of aid, the question raised in **Aid and the new bottom billion**.

And finally, The big push back, and the big push forward draws on a well attended workshop convened by Rosalind Eyben in IDS, reflecting on increasing donor demands for measurement and the damage that these do. Which points us forwards to how we make a better future.

How development organizations see each other and relate

Anyone who has worked in a UN agency, a multilateral lender or a bilateral donor, and many of those who have worked in INGOs, will be well aware of differences of cultures, policies and practices between them. It is fascinating, and revealing, to bring together representatives of these groups. An exercise I warmly recommend has been called Images. For this, go to pains to take time to create a friendly and undefensive environment. Here is a description from Participatory Workshops *(Chambers, 2002: 112–13).*

An absorbing, even riveting, source of awareness of how different groups see one another. Divide into groups according to type, often type of organization (e.g. government, INGOs, NGOs, donors). It is easier with only two types, but three is possible. The description that follows is for two groups.

Each group takes a flip chart sheet (or two or more taped together), draws three columns and brainstorms adjectives that describe:

1. How they see themselves (column one), and then
2. How they see the other group (column two), and then
3. How they think the other group sees them (column three).

Display and compare the sheets. Invite reflection and comment. Considerable discussion can ensue. Allow plenty of time for this, with groups separate or all together depending on dynamics and purpose.

Tips

*   Loosen up with an energizer before this. It is better in, say the second half of a one-day workshop, when participants have met on a friendly basis and relaxed a bit.
*   Ask groups to use adjectives not descriptions
*   Allow anything from 30 to 90 minutes, or even more for follow-up discussions
*   Keep a record and later send a consolidated copy, showing the comparisons, to all participants

This was done in Kathmandu with three groups – donor and lender organizations, International NGOs, and national NGOs. The perceptions were often humorously self-critical and quite strikingly similar. The fit was close between how they were seen by others and how they thought others saw them. The biggest discrepancy was that the national NGOs thought they were seen more favourably than they were.

Rugby International: UNHCR vs NGOs

*In 1985 a need was felt for UNHCR and NGOs to work more closely together.
So we had an amiably combative meeting in Switzerland, with about fifteen
from each side. This provoked (with apologies to non-Rugby enthusiasts):*

Two teams – the UNHCR
And NGOs arrived by car
To play a game of rugby, far
Away in Vaud, at Cret Berard

Both teams, though amateur (dare I say?)
Assessed their needs without delay
Co-chairs argued on rules of play
To cook the books each others' way

The game was not a normal thing
The NGOs all played left wing
While HCR repulsed attack
With 15 players at full back [*]

The NGOs showed deep revulsion
For any nuance of compulsion
Their contracts, please should always state
Refugees *must* participate

Poor HCR so tight contained
They lost an inch for each inch gained
For each solution there's a problem
Political factors always hobble'em

Money is short but there's a feeling
Helping the poor should have no ceiling
Give us this day our daily bread
To meet EAA's overhead

And so they found a common goal
To hold the same big begging bowl
Thus sharing, one could not detect
The slightest mutual disrespect

The game's well played. Both sides have won
The scoring was non-zero sum
The aim for all each player agrees
's a better life for refugees

---

[*]   My own ambition was to enter
      the NGOs' team as extreme centre
      but in the scrum I found instead
      that I was playing as loose head

My visit to a rural settlement

Written for UNHCR staff in 1976 after Tips for Field Visits had been a lead balloon.

I planned to visit Nitashindwa settlement leaving the capital early on the morning of August 2nd, arriving there on the same evening, spending 3rd and 4th there, and returning on the 5th. In this way I thought I would get two clear days at Nitashindwa, allowing plenty of time to check up on progress in building the two schools and the health centre, see how the seed distribution programme was getting along, meet some of the secondary schoolboys who wanted to continue their education, have a thorough discussion with the Commandant and broach with him some of rather delicate protection questions, see if the food issues were adequate and why the reporting system seems to have broken down, check what wages are being paid and of course have plenty of time to meet and listen to the refugees.

Unfortunately, on the evening of 1 August:

- The Minister of Home Affairs sent a message asking to see me the following morning,
- The Landrover broke down,
- I received a cable from Geneva asking me to meet a journalist on the afternoon of 2nd,
- My child was sick,
- I developed psychosomatic dysentery (I detest field visits),
- I realized that 4th was a national public holiday.

But I am made of stern stuff. I did not give up. I

- Saw the Minister,
- Borrowed a Landrover from UNDP and sent the UNHCR one for repair,
- Saw the journalist,
- Took my child to hospital and comforted my wife,
- Dosed myself with Mexaform,
- (of course) put duty before holidays,

and just managed to leave with the office driver after supper on the evening of 2nd. We drove through the night, stopped at midnight at a small hotel, and continued the next morning, arriving at 14.00 on 3rd. It was hot and I was tired. The Commandant was nowhere to be found, but his clerk said that as I had not arrived the night before he had cancelled the programme for my visit. I was to have seen the schoolboys that morning.

The clerk said that the Commandant had gone to the far end of the settlement, so I set out to look for him. When we returned to the headquarters it was already 17.00. I was reluctant to do anything before I had seen the Commandant, but I decided to see the Agricultural Officer. Unfortunately, he had just left for his home some 40 miles away in order to spend the public holiday there. By now my stomach was giving trouble again, so I went to the Guest House and tried to recuperate. Just as it was getting dark the Commandant turned up. He did not seem very pleased. He said that it would be impossible to reassemble the secondary schoolboys. He himself had to go the next morning to the regional headquarters for the celebration of the national holiday, and the food distribution staff would be all off work. He did not seem in a very good mood. I offered him a drink. He said he had been a teetotaler for twenty years. It did not seem opportune to broach the delicate protection questions.

In the night it rained. The next morning I felt a bit weak and depressed but after a breakfast of buttered Lomotil, as used by the astronauts, (the Mexaform had not been strong enough), I set out for my remaining day on the settlement. Unfortunately neither my driver nor I spoke the refugees' language. I decided that the best thing to do was to look at the two schools which were under construction and also the health centre buildings. Then at least I would have something to report when I got back. Unfortunately, when we were about five miles from the Headquarters the Landrover got stuck. It began to rain again. Some refugees pushed us out. We got stuck twice more before reaching the school at midday. Unfortunately, the teachers and contractors were all away, but I could see that much more work remained to be done than had been reported. I took detailed notes. I was worried whether we would be able to get back to the Headquarters, so we abandoned the proposal to visit the second school and Health Centre and set off back. On the way we got stuck again. A gust of wind blew my notes out of the Landrover. They fell with writing side downwards on wet mud. Some refugees pushed us out. One of them was a secondary schoolboy who spoke a very little English. He seemed to be saying that the refugees had no food, but I could not make much sense out of it all. We got back to Headquarters as night was falling.

The next day we drove back to the capital. My child had recovered, the Landrover had been repaired but I remembered that I should have obtained authorization from Geneva before having the work done. I wrote a report from memory about the unfinished school.

I do not think I shall be able to get away to the rural areas again for some time. There is much to do here in the city. You have only to look at the queue of refugees outside my door to see what I mean.

Imposing aid

In 1986 Barbara Harrell-Bond published Imposing Aid: Emergency
Assistance to Refugees. *At that time she was founding the Refugee Studies
Programme at Queen Elizabeth House in Oxford. Thanks to the generosity and
vision of a private benefactor, Hugh Pilkington, the print run of the book was
multiplied several fold: Oxford University Press printed 10,000 paperback copies
and put them on the market for £2.50 when they would otherwise have printed
only 2,500 with a retail price of £10. Some of the new professionalism which
refugees deserved in the mid 1980s has been achieved. But the challenges will
always be formidable, and the book is as disturbing, challenging and relevant
as ever. It should remain on the reading list for all who work in relief.*

Foreword

The intractable problem of millions of refugees, displaced persons, and victims
of famine in rural Africa will not go away. The famines of Ethiopia, Sudan,
Chad, and other countries in 1984 and 1985 have attracted attention as sudden
emergencies, but underlying them are long-term trends. Even on an optimistic
view, the future prospects in sub-Saharan Africa are appalling. Over the past
two decades, the numbers of political refugees have grown from hundreds of
thousands to millions. To these are now added millions who move *en masse* in
distress because of loss of livelihood and starvation. Population in sub-Saharan
Africa is projected to grow by 3 per cent per annum for the next two decades,
with a doubling time of some 24 years. The rural population, after allowing
for large-scale rural to urban migration, may rise by at least 50 per cent during
the same period. On top of this, environmental degradation is widespread,
with soil erosion, deforestation, and desertification. For tens of millions of
rural people, economic decline, political instability, and ethnic tensions
promise a worse future. Even if the rainfall failures of the early 1980s prove
exceptional, the next two decades will probably see more, not fewer, crises,
involving more, not fewer, people in the terrible decision to leave their homes
and flee, destitute and desperate, from fighting, persecution, and famine, in
search of safety, shelter, and food. At the same time, deeper indebtedness and
the poverty of African Governments, less land for agricultural settlement, and
fewer work opportunities in downwardly spiraling economies, will make it
harder to host and help refugees, and harder for refugees to help themselves.

Despite the scale and awfulness of these forced mass migrations, there has
been little systematic study of rural refugees and rural refugee work in Africa or
indeed elsewhere. Until recently, refugee studies itself has not been recognized
as a subject. Most books and papers on refugees and refugee programmes have
had urban and elite biases to the neglect of those – in Africa the vast majority
– who are rural, less well-educated, and poorer. Until recently, rural refugees
have rarely been the starting point or central concern of research; they have

usually been noticed and mentioned only in passing and not as the primary focus. In consequence, debates on policy questions like the relative merits of organized agricultural settlements and self-settlement have not been well-informed. It has been easy to think of rural refugees as an undifferentiated, uneducated mass. The points of view of refugees themselves have not been well represented. Nor have the attitudes, behaviour and problems of those who work in humanitarian and government agencies been examined. On the positive side, able efforts have been made to consolidate and communicate professional knowledge, for example in the journal *Disasters* and in the excellent UNHCR *Handbook for emergencies*. But the fact remains that at a time when unprecedented numbers of desperate people have been migrating, struggling to survive in or out of camps, and dying, we who are not desperate or dying have still been negligently ignorant of what is really going on.

Just how ignorant we have been is exposed in this book. To my knowledge there has been no previous study like it. Conrad Reining, also in the south Sudan, was the first social anthropologist to see colonial officials as part of his field and write them up in his classic, *The Zande Scheme* (Reining, 1966). With *Imposing Aid,* Barbara Harrell-Bond has given us a successor from the same region but with differences. The period is post-colonial, the occasion the crisis of massive influxes of refugees from Uganda. The people in this field are the refugees, their Sudanese hosts, and the staff of voluntary, humanitarian, and Government agencies. The book is timely and immediately relevant. In a more leisurely tradition, Reining took ten years from fieldwork to publication; but in keeping with the scale, importance, and urgency of the issues, Harrell-Bond with assistance from the Oxford University Press, has taken a matter of months. The main fieldwork, as researcher and participant-observer helping in the administration of official programmes, was conducted in 1982–3; and several chapters also draw in the experiences and findings of a team of committed researchers from Oxford who spent two months in the area in 1984.

There is much here that will be seen as new. Many readers will, like me, be surprised and shocked at how much we have been wrong and how much we have to learn. Those concerned with food supplies, nutrition, health, planning and implementation in emergencies, and management and administration of refugee and other relief programmes, will find much to ponder. Perhaps more important, though, are the changes of perception which are opened up. Refugees speak and show the vivid awfulness of their experience, the brutality, terror, and desolation. Stereotypes dissolve under the impact of examples. Rural refugees in Africa, so easily thought of as statistics, are revealed as intelligent, articulate, and different individuals. Like other human beings, only more so than most others, they suffer, struggle to survive, need their self-respect, and have to mourn their dead. Convenient myths that somehow rural Africans are different – less sensitive, less individual, less vulnerable to trauma than others – cannot survive this book.

No one will feel comfortable with this book. Much of it disquiets, not least the difficulties, conflicts, and shortcomings of voluntary, national, and international agencies. Evenhandedly, Dr Harrell-Bond spares neither herself nor others in recounting what happened, what was said, what was done and what was not done. In a fine tradition of social anthropology, she has not only observed others, but also herself, and reported on her own fallible human reactions and behaviour as well as those of others. In doing this, she sets a standard of introspection and honesty for others to follow, and shows us at first hand, from within, some of the personal stresses and dilemmas of those who work in mass refugee situations, and the courage and commitment needed to deal with them. She takes us intimately into the relations of refugees, hosts, and voluntary and official organizations, laying bare realities which have to be faced in order to learn how to do better.

The danger is, though, that strong reactions will distract readers from learning and from pondering and acting on the many positive lessons of the book. One such reaction could be to blame organizations or individuals. An antidote is to ask how one would have behaved oneself in similar conditions, under similar stress. Another reaction is defensive. Some who work in voluntary, humanitarian, or government organizations may feel threatened by the critical self-examination which the book invites. Some may even be tempted to search the text for error to justify rejecting the larger lessons; but if they do so, they, and future refugees, will be the losers. And yet another reaction could be the most damaging: to condemn aid and urge its termination. Negative academics will find here plenty of grist to their mills. They will not lack bad incidents to feed destructive cynicism. They will find plenty to quote selectively to argue that it would be better to do nothing. But before reaching such conclusions, they should reflect: on the terrible suffering of so many; on how difficult it is for those who try to mitigate that suffering: and on how much worse things would be if nothing were done. Moreover, Dr Harrell-Bond is clear on this point. The sane and humane thing to do is not to stop aid, but to augment and improve it. Honest examination of reality, however unpalatable, is a necessary painful means to that end. The challenge of this book is to recognize, embrace, and correct error. The message is not to do less, but to do better.

Let me commend this book to all concerned. They are many: refugees, who speak through these pages with such eloquence and who may come to understand more about humanitarian agencies; academics, activists and journalists concerned with mass deprivation and migration; and especially those involved in humanitarian work, whether in headquarters or the field, and whether in foreign or national voluntary agencies, host Government departments, bilateral aid agencies, or international organizations like UNHCR, UNICEF, WFP, FAO, or WHO. They in their turn may come to understand better both refugees and themselves, and to see themselves the other way round, in the refugees' eye view.

Imposing aid applies most directly to refugees and rural Africa but its value and relevance is wider, touching the behaviour and attitudes of the development and social welfare professions and their clients generally, on the organization of relief, and on the survival strategies of those who endure extreme deprivation. For all those concerned with refugees and others who migrate in distress, this is more than essential reading; it is essential learning. To the new professionalism which refugees deserve from those, not themselves refugees, who work with and for them, this book is a major contribution.

ZOPP marries PRA: whose realities, needs and priorities count?

In the mid-1990s ZOPP[1] (a relative if not ancestor of the Logical Framework) was in what we thought at the time could only be a temporary ascendant. There had been so many bad experiences with ZOPP, two of them recounted below, and PRA was so enthralling and had such momentum. Many believed ZOPP and the Logical Framework would fade away and die a natural death. How wrong we were! Little did we guess that in 2011 the Logical Framework would have become a widespread norm in aid practice, and that a whole generation of young development professionals would have little idea of PRA. Little did I dream that 15 years later I would be asking whether these 1996 remarks to a GTZ-convened workshop ZOPP marries PRA? *might have become even more intensely relevant in the decade of the 2010s.*

And in the 2020s will there be more déjà vus? What are we learning about the sustainability of procedures?

First let me thank GTZ for convening this workshop. It is both timely and important. It is timely because it may help us to see good ways forward in our crisis of paradigms. It is important because since GTZ has been so much a leader in innovating with and spreading ZOPP, changes in GTZ may have big impacts in other organizations, perhaps especially the EU which I understand is currently adopting something like ZOPP for its projects.

I feel bad coming here and making the critical remarks which will follow. This is for two reasons. First, I have a disreputable past: I have been responsible for the management of a pastoral development project which was a disaster because of its top-down authoritarian style; and in the early 1970s, I was involved in the development of procedures in the Special Rural Development Programme in Kenya which some have identified as an antecedent of the Logical Framework and of ZOPP. Second, I keep on saying that old or ageing men who go around telling people what they should do are a major part of the problems of our world. And here am I doing just that. Still, if there is one field in which the English[2] can claim to be world-leaders, it is hypocrisy. So if you are generous, you will interpret my behaviour as a patriotic attempt to express and maintain my national culture.

I am not sure about this term 'marriage'. Nowadays, it is more and more the custom here in the North to have prolonged partnerships before formal union. ...Still, the imagery is appropriate in one respect, namely that ZOPP is masculine, being linear and rigid, more concerned with things and with

---

1. ZOPP is the acronym for Ziel-Orientierte Projekt Planung, a mechanistic system for project and programme planning, a close relative of which is known as the Logical Framework.
2. I do not include the Scots, the Welsh or the Northern Irish, all of whom seem to me in my stereotyped view to be less vulnerable to the evasive hypocrisies of the English. I recommend Kate Fox's wonderful book *Watching the English*, a book that illuminates as much as it entertains.

an engineering mode in action, while PRA is more feminine... and more concerned with people and processes. More than marriage, perhaps we are concerned with mutual learning and with looking for good alternatives, combinations, and sequences of activities.

Two quotations seem appropriate. The first is from Karl Popper who wrote something on these lines, 'You may be right, and I may be wrong, and by an effort together we may get closer to the truth', and the other is from a character in Tom Stoppard's play *Arcadia*: 'It is the best time to be alive, when almost everything you thought you knew is wrong'. In the spirit of these two quotations we can struggle together to find better ways of doing things.

Context

The context in which we do this is relevant. Three dimensions stand out. First, the rate of change in almost every domain seems to be accelerating. This includes the lives and aspirations of people all round the world, including those who are 'remote'. Second, we – development professionals – have a history of astonishing error. It is humbling to see how often we have been wrong. And third, a problem running through this is dominance in behaviour and attitudes. The dominance of 'uppers' over 'lowers' is part of the problem, and leads to many errors. The issue can be expressed as 'Whose reality counts?'

There are many relationships between 'uppers' and 'lowers' (Table 3.1).

'Uppers' construct their own realities and impose them on 'lowers'. When they do not fit, misinformation is generated, and development projects and other initiatives often fail. One way of seeing this is as mutually reinforcing north-south magnets. Bureaucratic hierarchies and social systems, families, relationships between professionals and non-professionals and the like can be seen as oriented between the powerful and the subordinate. The enterprise in which we are engaged in development is (I think correctly) trying to weaken these dominant north-south magnetic fields. This means that although we retain hierarchy and bureaucracy, which is necessary up to a point, the magnetism is weakened and we are freer to relate laterally, upwards and downwards, and to be adaptive and flexible in new ways.

To illustrate this, a spectacular example is that of psychoanalysts, from Freud until the 1980's and to some extent even the 1990's. They have believed that the accounts of being incestuously abused in childhood, given to them by women patients, were untrue, and reflected wish fulfilment, the repressed sexual desires of the victim. That this professional and patriarchal myth could have been perpetuated for three generations is a terrible warning to the rest of us who may be in powerful positions about the dangers of perpetuating our own fantasies in a development context. The question is 'Whose reality counts?', 'ours' or 'theirs'. As part of this we have to ask: Whose knowledge counts? Whose needs? Whose priorities/criteria? Whose appraisal? analysis? planning? Whose baseline? Whose action? Whose indicators? Whose monitoring? Whose evaluation? Is it ours, or theirs?

Table 3.1 Relationships between 'uppers' and 'lowers'

Dimension/Context	North Uppers	South Lowers
Spatial	Core (urban, industrial)	Periphery (rural, agricultural)
International Development	The North IMF, World Bank Donors Creditors	The South Poor countries Recipients Debtors
Personal, Ascriptive	Male White High Ethnic or Caste Group	Female Black Low Ethnic or Caste Group
Life Cycle	Old person Parent Mother-in-law	Young person Child Daughter-in-law
Bureaucratic Organization	Senior Manager Official Patron Officer Warden/Guard	Junior Worker Supplicant Client 'other rank' Inmate/Prisoner
Social, Spiritual	Patron Priest Guru Doctor/Psychiatrist	Client Lay Person Disciple Patient
Teaching and Learning	Master Lecturer Teacher	Apprentice Student Learner

Two Paradigms

The reality which has counted in the past has tended to be ours, top-down and related to things rather than people. Two columns can illustrate the contrast between the paradigm for things, which is top-down with planning blueprints and that of people, which is bottom-up, with participatory processes (Table 3.2).

Historically, development has been dominated by the 'things/blueprint' column. We need that side, especially when infrastructure is being constructed. The question is whether the approaches that fit there should be transferred and applied to people and processes. It will be obvious that these two columns resonate with ZOPP and with PRA respectively. The left-hand column tends to be top-down, centralized, supply driven, and with accountability upwards; the right-hand column tends to be bottom-up, decentralized, demand drawn and with accountability downwards. These may be slight caricatures and idealizations. Nevertheless, the contrast does seem to have some meaning. So a question we can ask ourselves is whether ZOPP, in practice, tends to have evolved from the modes of operation of the 'things' column and perhaps is appropriate there; and whether it is in the process of shifting, through PCM

Table 3.2 The paradigms of things and people contrasted

	Things	*People*
Mode	Blueprint	Learning Process
Key Activity/Concept	Planning	Participation
Objectives	Pre-set	Evolving
Logic	Linear, Newtonian	Iterative
Actions/Outcomes	Standardized	Diverse
Assumptions	Reductionist	Holistic, Systemic
People Seen As	Objects, Targets	Subjects, Actors
Outsiders' Roles	Transfer, 'Motivate'	Facilitate, Empower
Main Outsiders	Engineers, economists	Any/all who have participatory behaviour/attitudes
Outputs	Infrastructure Physical Change	Capabilities Institutions

(Project Cycle Management), towards the 'people and process' column which is from where PRA has evolved and to which it applies.

There is a danger here of 'four legs good, two legs bad', to use the analogy of George Orwell's (1945) *Animal Farm*, of 'people good', 'things bad'. What we are concerned with is seeing what is appropriate and what fits where. My argument is that what has been appropriate and fits when dealing with things is not appropriate and does not fit when dealing with people, society, and social processes.

PRA

If PRA has a philosophy, it is one which encourages each individual to use personal judgement. This means that any PRA practitioner or trainer who lists the commitments and principles of PRA may come up with a different list. However, seeing and trying to understand what PRA practitioners do, and how they behave, there seem to me four commitments or principles which stand out:

- *Personal responsibility*. This includes self-critical awareness, non-dominating behaviour and attitudes, and a commitment to the other three principles.

- *Equity*. A commitment to trying to enable those who are worse off to improve their lives and experiences in ways they welcome.

- *Empowerment*. Enabling them to do that, and empowering 'lowers', those who are weak, disadvantaged and marginalized.

- *Diversity*. Encouraging and celebrating diversity and pluralism in every domain.

Putting these into practice generates many questions. Among these is, 'Who participates in whose project?' Do *they* participate in *ours*? Or do *we* participate in *theirs*? And following on, the question is again and again: who are *they*? – Poor women? People who are 'remote'? Minorities? The young? The old? The poor? The rich? The local elite? Officials? Or who?

PRA is not a panacea. There is a widespread mass of bad practice in the name of PRA, often through a failure to recognize the primacy of the personal and of behaviour and attitudes. Nothing that I say here should give the impression that PRA is a universal solution to be applied everywhere to solve all problems. Nevertheless, paradigmatically it seems to fit people and process and to have potential for empowering those who are weak.

Let me illustrate how these themes come together with a practical case. Meera Shah was invited by the World Bank to facilitate some of the processes of reconstruction and rehabilitation after the Maharashtra earthquake. She found that everyone was agreeing that the best layout for the new villages would be a grid. She doubted this. But the engineers, the officials, the planners, and also the local people all seemed to agree. It was only through persistent facilitation and enabling people to express their reality through mapping and modelling that the local people were able to gain the confidence, and also to conduct the analysis, which enabled them to recognize and express that they did not want the grid layout. They wanted a more complex and varied arrangement which allowed them to live together in their familiar social groups, and to have open spaces. The point here is that there was a self-reinforcing myth, imposed by the powerful, and reflected back to them. It required commitment and an empowering mode of interaction to dispel this. It is so easy and so widespread for those who are dominant and powerful to transfer their reality to others rather than to empower others to express their own.

ZOPP

From this perspective, ZOPP in its classical form can be seen as a sequence of procedures which has tended to impose the reality of 'uppers' on 'lowers'. Seven defects (I will not say deadly sins) express and reinforce this tendency:

- The top-down descending sequence of ZOPP workshops.
- Reductionism to one core problem. Life simply is not like that. Different people have different problems, and different mixtures of problems.[1]

---

1. By requiring their partners to ZOPP

    Donors rule, with their talkers on top
    That one problem is core
    For those absent and poor
    Is agreed when thought comes to a stop

- The imperative of consensus. Divergent opinions, as surely among ourselves here, are positive. Agreement, or apparent agreement, can be a lowest common consensus, and can reflect the interests and wishes of the powerful and articulate rather than those of the weak and inarticulate, in a ZOPP workshop as in a community.
- People as targets. People are treated as objects rather than subjects. There is a 'target group', with all the imagery of us aiming and shooting and trying to hit the target, rather than of enabling people to move, choose, and determine their own destinies.
- Language. Accounts of ZOPP workshops suggest that fluency in the language used – usually English – enables some participants to dominate and marginalizes others.
- Who is present? Who participates? And on what terms? How frequently and with what degree of empowerment to analyse and express their reality, have poor women been involved in ZOPP workshops?
- The assumption that we know best.

This may not always be the case, but seems implicit in the process. A quotation from a ZOPP process in Chad comes from the World Bank Participation Sourcebook. One of the Chadians said to a Bank staff member in the middle of the ZOPP process: 'I am telling you that I have a headache, and you keep telling me that I have a foot ache and you want to force me to take a medicine for that.' (Page 30 of the Sourcebook)

There may be more. For example, ZOPP moderators may tend to be in physically dominant positions, especially in the management and organization of the cards on the wall. This contrasts with the democracy of the ground where people are free to move cards around themselves into whatever categories and relationships they think are appropriate. To what extent these points apply will be well known and recognized by many in this room who have ZOPP experience. To illustrate, let me quote from two relevant accounts.

The first is a 1995 letter from Rashida Dohad in Pakistan. She took part in a ZOPP process with an NGO. She wrote:

> ... they began developing a Project Planning Matrix. Based on problems identified by the participants at this workshop, this matrix listed the sectors in which [the NGO] would work over a certain period of time and set indicative targets. When this exercise began I protested, rather vociferously, that these decisions should not be taken in this room and argued for a more participatory, open-ended planning process. The outside facilitator tried to convince me that this exercise was in fact participatory since it involved 'representatives' of the local people! I pointed out that the 8 people – all males – from 12 'clusters' (each cluster consists of about 8–12 villages which means these 8 persons were in fact representing 49 villages!) could only represent their own view, or at best that of a certain group. I also argued that they were outnumbered by the articulate [NGO] staff and may have found it difficult to follow all the

written stuff (ZOPP makes profuse use of index cards). These so-called reps of local people had little opportunity to get in a word, leave alone participate, in deciding on the perceived problems of local people and the sectors on which [the NGO] should concentrate!

The second is from Lars Johansson, a social anthropologist, who has worked a lot in Tanzania in the Lindi and Mtwara regions. He has written (Johansson, 1995) that in the process of evolution of an on going project there was a:

> not very constructive period of trying to write up and appraise a five year plan according to the logical framework format. Making programme and project documents had become increasingly traumatic to all involved. The more we learned, the more important it seemed not to mystify development and take the initiative away from local people through abstract concepts of objectivity like outputs and indicators. The strategies that proved to work did so because they were locally intelligible and based on subjective representations of reality, so that they could be negotiated in spoken Swahili during village workshops amongst people with different perspectives and interests. Personal commitments to a coalition of people proved much more important than scientifically adequate project logic, but required a totally different approach to planning.

If these are some of the problems, the question then is whether PCM goes far enough in overcoming them and in proposing and legitimating new ways of going about things.

Ideas for action

Let me suggest three thrusts and actions: experiment, learn, share. There is much scope for trying out and adapting sequences and combinations for different conditions. Perhaps, quite radically, ideas about what a project is can be diversified. Much of this is happening anyway. Should one, perhaps, sometimes think of an ALP (Action Learning Process) rather than a 'project'. It is excellent that in the official statement of GTZ policy, diversity and experimentation are legitimated.

Some of the implications would seem to be:

- The importance of behaviour and attitudes training for staff at an early stage in any project or ALP process.
- PRA-type processes very early on involving the poor, marginalized etc., in their own analysis and identification of their needs and priorities.
- A high ratio of expenditures on staff to other items, especially in the early stages.
- Low expenditures especially at first.
- Monitoring process rather than product.
- Throughout struggling to ensure that it is 'their' reality that counts.

- Retraining ZOPP trainers. I crossed out the word 'rehabilitating' and will not use that. All the same, there is a very large and influential body of people around the world who have been trained in ZOPP. Surely, in terms of personal orientation, career pattern, dependency on ZOPP training as a source of livelihood etc., they must vary a great deal. If there is to be a shift towards more participatory approaches at field level, they could be both an obstacle and a resource. Does it make sense to institute a programme of training for them, providing them with new opportunities, stressing behaviour and attitudes (e.g. using the ground rather than the wall, handing over the stick etc.) and perhaps including 'WIN–WIN' experiences, staying with communities. ('WIN–WIN' trainings have been developed by Sam Joseph of Action Aid in India. Communities agree, in return for a fee, to host outsiders, to teach them about community life and activities, to demonstrate PRA type forms of analysis, etc. UNDP and ODA[1] are both starting to send their staff for these types of experiences).
- Recruitment: there is no-one in this room from Personnel. At a workshop of the Participatory Learning Group of the World Bank, at which almost a hundred Bank staff were present, there was also no-one from Personnel.[2] And yet recruitment and the criteria used in recruitment are critical. What are the attitudes and criteria and values of those who carry out the recruitment for organizations like GTZ? Is it critically important that those who recruit staff to join GTZ, should themselves have a participatory mode of interaction, that they should themselves share the values which go with a people-oriented process approach in development, and should recruit others who are similarly comfortable with and committed to participatory approaches?

To conclude, I sense in this meeting a wonderful openness and willingness to struggle to find better ways of doing things. I suppose that in this room we are not a representative group for GTZ as a whole. Nevertheless, it is hugely encouraging to have the sense that we are all engaged in an open learning process. It allows us to ask whether, in considering ZOPP and PRA, and the needs for bottom-up empowering modes of development, anything like a marriage makes sense. I rather doubt it. It is easy from outside an organization to urge people to be radical. It is much harder within. But this workshop provides a safe space to think radically, but also practically. Let us hope that our sharing of experiences will lead us all to insights and ideas of how to do things which are new and better, especially for those whose realities in the past have counted for little.

---

1. ODA, the Overseas Development Administration, was a predecessor of DFID, the British Department for International Development.
2. There was also no one from personnel at the final meeting attended by over 300. Or, at least, no one raised their hand when asked (see page 125).

Reversals, realities and rewards

Handed out at the GTZ workshop[1]

Here are 7 assertions. Do you agree?

1. *The realities, needs and priorities that should count most are those of local people, especially the disadvantaged* – women, the poor, the marginalized, those who are physically and socially weak and deprived. This is now conventional rhetoric, and most development professionals would endorse this statement.
2. *For those realities, needs and priorities to be expressed requires special efforts,* enabling local people, especially those who are deprived and disadvantaged, to meet, to reflect, to express and analyse their realities and needs, to plan and to act and to be sensitively supported. PRA, done well, is a way of facilitating such processes.
3. *The realities, needs and priorities expressed by local people are typically diverse, and often differ from those supposed by outside professionals.* Different communities have different needs and priorities, as do different groups (women and men, young and old, rich and poor, ethnic groups…) within communities. Outsider professionals often misread local situations.
4. *In its classic form, ZOPP has been a top-down process in which professionals' realities, needs and priorities have tended to dominate and be imposed.* This has occurred through the descending sequence of ZOPPs, the imperative of consensus, the reductionism of the method, the use of outsiders' languages, the physical and social isolation of poor women and others, and perhaps at times the assumption that 'we know best'.
5. *The challenge is for us so to organize and behave that the diverse realities, needs and priorities of the poor and the weak can be expressed and accommodated.* This requires radical reversals in project sequences, processes and procedures, in institutional cultures and rewards, and in personal behaviour and interactions at all levels. Our knowledge and values can help, but for truly empowering participation, only if they come last.
6. *To explore and implement these reversals is immensely exciting and important.* Any organization which leads can make a huge contribution, far beyond the direct impact of programmes. Precisely because it has such deep experience of ZOPP, and has promoted it so widely, GTZ is exceptionally well placed to make this contribution. The reversals require guts and vision. The rewards, for the poor, could be immense.
7. *A good way forward is for sensitive PRA to come first and inform the evolution of flexible, unhurried projects, with truly participatory processes, not blueprints or products, as the objectives to be monitored.*

---

1. The original heading was ZOPP, PCM and PRA: whose realities, needs and priorities count?

On lenders, donors, debt, and development

Verses just happen. They are therapeutic. They let off steam. Writing them is totally absorbing once they have started. In my case they balance my (incurable?) optimism. Anger, outrage, and frustration come out. Rose-coloured spectacles clear and pathologies of self-interest and greed come into sight, and disregard for poor and marginalized people who are served then only by the rhetoric. We have

- *Lenders calling themselves donors (see also page 186)*
- *Drives to lend more faster, and targets and pressures to disburse funds*
- *Spending creating dependence*
- *Good things ruined by rushing to scale*
- *Power isolated in citadels*
- *Short-term gains for the powerful causing long-term losses for the weak*

all of these combining in the perpetration of cruel and lethal tragedies. Much of the crippling indebtedness of developing countries, incurred in the 1970s and 1980s, came not only from the World Bank but from private banks following the World Bank's lead. Irresponsible lending, spawning corruption, bad projects, and massive debts, and fattening kleptocratic states, resulted. Greed ruled and greed was and remains complicit with greed. Many of the loans were 'bad'.[1] Debtor countries could not repay. So they had to be made to repay, cutting education, health, infrastructure and other services. For as we have since learnt on a vast scale, banks cannot be allowed to fail. Ordinary folk must suffer instead.

So we can ask: in Africa, Asia and Latin America, how many millions of adults and children lacked or lost health services and died or died younger, how many missed education, how many were deprived and suffered in innumerable other ways, through the structural adjustment imposed on their countries following irresponsible lending? How could those of us implicated, by what we did or did not do – we, the rich and powerful – how could we have been so blind and callous, so silent, and passive?

The Bankers' plea to poor countries

We urge you not to think about tomorrow
To prosper we must lend, so you must borrow
    Take loans all in a rush
    With money you'll be flush
Bequeath the debt to be your children's sorrow

---

1.   For an authoritative and devastating evaluation of World Bank lending for rural development 1965–86, see World Bank (1988). Recommended reading for all new World Bank staff.

The Lender's Plea to the Poor

Beneficiaries here I come
Donor with a tidy sum
Father Christmas is my name
Spending targets are the game
All will gain, that is the notion
You get cash, I get promotion

Help me be a good provider
Open up your mouths much wider
What I bring is sure to please
Sacks with stacks of free goodies
All you have to do is take'em
Evaluations? We can fake'em

Make disbursements, that's the must
Where they go we will adjust
Take a lot and quickly spend
The Financial Year is near its end
For accounting, we can fudge it
All that matters – spend the budget

Retained consultants will report
Contractors acted as they ought
None of the structures was defective
Monies spent were cost-effective
All the data that're obtainable
Show the project is sustainable

Shun the mean facilitator
What he brings is less and later
PRA is but a con
Make your map, and they move on
Their approach will make you sick
All they hand you is a stick

Participation too's a mess
You do more and they do less
What good calling you clients and actors?
Better cash from benefactors
You the poor should never spurn
Gifts you do not have to earn

[*to which the poor might or might not reply*]

Donor, we reject your song
Top-down targetry is wrong

Floods of funds as in your verse
Corrupt and spoil and make things worse.
Keep your money. We will show
True development's from below

Bankers of the World Unite!

Bankers of the world unite!
You have nothing to lose but your guilt
    For the loans that you've made
    And the debts being repaid
For the castles in air that you've built

Bankers of the world invite
All the fat cats and tycoons to dine
    Tell them greed helps the poor
    Trickling down more and more
When we're all greedy all will be fine

Bankers of the world incite
Your staff to strive harder to lend
    And send out your missions
    To add to conditions
Reinforcing your power without end

Bankers of the world indict
Debtor countries who fail to repay
    But who should blame who?
    Should the poor forgive you
For the bad loans you've put in their way?

Bankers of the world take flight
For your credit is lost in your guilt
    All's up with your game
    And transparent your shame
For the blood and the milk that you've spilt

Bankers of the world take fright
For your moral account's in the red
    The poor are your betters
    It's you who are debtors
And the reckoning's soon, when you're dead

Final Reckoning

Whose debt unpaid? Whose toll?
We can no longer hold defaulting debtors to account
We do not dare
The power we thought we had we stole
They do not fear
We cannot count or measure the amount
It has transformed. Why should they care?
The debt is ours.

Whose life is ruined? Whose health?
We can no longer structure the adjustments for their hell
We do not dare
They cursed our arrogance of wealth
Why should they fear?
We cannot lord it over them or tell
Them what is best. Nor do they care
The ruin is ours.

Who is the guilty one? Who erred?
We can no longer place the victims powerless in the dock
The dead don't fear
We have no people here who cared
Nor do they care
Our bench has gone. We stand accused. Ghosts block
Our way. We cannot flee. There is nowhere.
The guilt is ours.

Whose grave is this? Whose end?
We can no longer point our fingers southwards on the map
There's no one there
There is no message we can send
The dead can't hear
There is no plinth on which to stand. The trap
Has closed. We peer outside. Their ghosts are there.
The grave is ours.

On the World Bank

The World Bank is an organization many love to hate. Bank-baiting is a popular blood sport for academics and NGOs who do not depend on the Bank (as it is commonly referred to, as though there was no other) for funds. When power cannot harm its critics, it is a safe and easy target. There can be fun, too, at the expense of the object...

The Washington Rag

With apologies to Tom Lehrer
To be sung with piano accompaniment
to the music of the Vatican Rag

First take statistics though a mess
Clean and cook them and regress
Then you have to correlate
    And tabulate, tabulate, tabulate

Basic needs – the Bank will heed yours
If you use the right procedures
    Get your ethics re-al
    Dollars are the be-all
Doing the Washington, doing the Washington, doing the Washington rag

Get in line for quick promotion
Heavy lending is the notion
Costs and benefits, there's no thanks
If your ratios aren't the Bank's
If they're not, then hedge your bets
Fiddle with your data sets
    Two, four, six, eight
    Time to change the discount rate

Be a good Washingtonian
Have a local spending spree on
US expertise – resultants –
Contracts for DC consultants

IMF and World Bank
Washington will then thank
You for milk and honey
Yankees flush with money

Doing the Washington, doing the Washington, doing the Washington rag

The World Bank: what next?

These extracts are from an attempt to answer the What Next? question on the last day of a World Bank Workshop on Participatory Development on 17–20 May 1994. Do they show a naïve optimism? Do they apply as much today as they did then?

Such was the interest and enthusiasm in the Bank for participation that many who wanted to take part in the workshop had to be turned away. So they were invited for a final morning. For that, over 300 turned up. Strikingly, as in similar meetings in other aid agencies (GTZ, Sida, New Zealand Aid, DFID…), there was no one from Finance or from Personnel/Human Resources (at least, none raised their hands when I asked). Someone from outside the Bank had to say something. I was pressed into making some remarks. Here are the main points and thrusts.

Early points included: Reasons for pessimism: the disabilities of the Bank, with its concentration of power and isolation from poor people; the way only the like-minded came to meetings about participation while others stayed away; and the signals given by low funding allocations for participation. But there were signs of paradigm shift to decentralization, democracy and diversity. The Bank had shown it could change. Staff were being posted out to 'the field'. The Participation Learning Group had made much progress. Lewis Preston, the President, had said 'the reduction of poverty is central to the purpose of the Bank'. Primary stakeholders were now defined not just as 'beneficiaries' (which begged the question of whether they did benefit) but also those adversely affected by policies and projects, with the questions 'who gains and who loses?' firmly on the agenda. Participatory Poverty Assessments had been pioneered through the Bank and had raised repeatedly the question 'Whose reality counts?'

(Of awareness and imagination). Those in powerful positions do not realize the way in which their actions and questions can spread and be amplified downwards to have bad effects. A World Bank Board Member's question about slow disbursement, which then gets translated into signals running through the Bank, may adversely affect hundreds of thousands of people through the pressure to spend money. For it may be spent badly at the cost of participation, local control, and benefits to the poorer. Participation under pressure penalizes the poor. If only those in power would realize this, the development record for poor people would be much better.

(Of power). There are many damaging implications. One is that 'All power deceives'. The more powerful people are (and this applies especially in the Bank) and the less participatory their approaches, the more likely they are to be deceived through deference, prudence and courtesy. People in powerful positions also fear loss of control, but loss of control is essential for participation. There is a telling sentence in the account by the Task Manager, Bachir Souhlal,

on the Matruh Bedouin Project... 'Through participation we lost "control" of the project and in doing so gained ownership and sustainability, precious things in our business'. We have to realize that empowerment, which I believe is not yet a favourite word in the Bank – that empowerment for Lowers is also liberation for Uppers, that in disempowering ourselves and trusting others there is relief, satisfaction and sustainability. There are the watchwords used in participatory rural appraisal – 'handing over the stick' and 'they can do it'...

The personal satisfactions of handing over the stick, of believing that they can do it, of trusting people, are immense, but very different from those of centralized power and control. One of the satisfactions is that when a Task Manager is lying on her or his death bed – though of course I hope that all Task Managers will live to a good old age – it will be possible to think back to projects which have been sustainable and which are going on and will continue to go on in their good effects long after the former Task Manager has departed this world. A priority here is to enable more and more Task Managers and others to understand these satisfactions. They entail taking risks, being criticized sometimes within the Bank, making mistakes, and failing forwards, in order to do a good job for the poor.

(*Of personal behaviour, attitudes and commitment*). If we – the powerful – were to change, almost everything about development would change...

Who Recruits? ...As far as I know there is no one here from Personnel. Yet those responsible for recruiting are perhaps the most important... What sort of people are they? What are their values? What are their criteria? Besides skills mix and gender mix (which does not seem to have received the priority it deserves) what attention when recruiting do they give to personality, to values, to commitment, to ability to work in a participatory mode?

Changes in behaviour, attitudes and commitment can come through experiential learning...it would help if Bank staff could have unconstrained exposure to living for short periods in villages and interacting with and learning from poor people...the long term benefits for the poor in general could and should be high... Does the Bank have suitable training staff for experiential learning? Are the approaches to training themselves participatory? Who determines training policy? And perhaps as important as any of these, who recruits the trainers and according to what criteria?

(*On the Bank's culture, incentives and rewards*). Bank staff always agree that something is wrong and that major change is needed: that the incentives and rewards are for large-scale and quick disbursements, that those who are promoted are those who move most money and so on, and yet little seems to change...

What next?

What the Bank faces now is perhaps the greatest challenge in its history. It is a challenge to change its logic, to see things the other way round, and for its actions to be determined not by the habitual reflexes of professionals but by the realities of the poor. The Report of the Participatory Learning Group presents the opportunity. The question is whether the Board and the Management of the Bank will recognize its implications and seize the opportunity. The implications are a new participatory style of management within the Bank itself. Perhaps this requires a participatory action management team. Perhaps it requires that senior management themselves reflect on and experience some of the other realities – not only those of the poor, but those of current North American business practice with its stress on decentralization, trust, rapid adaptation, failing forwards, and diversity. Sven Sandstrom put it succinctly. Participation, he said, 'is the right way of doing business'. We are talking of a new professionalism. The first step is to recognize the errors and limitations of the constraining old professionalism. The second step is to learn about and to embrace and practice new ways of doing things, which are more participatory. All this is exciting and makes it a good time to be alive. In many different domains of activity and management, participation is becoming the mode. In participatory rural appraisal, which is but one of these, poor people (who are in many ways Lowers) have shown extraordinary abilities to do things and to carry out forms of analyses of which we thought they were incapable. Perhaps this is true in all Upper-Lower, North-South relationships. The spirit of the Wapenhans Report, of what one could call 'ownership for Lowers', applies in all these relationships. The Bank has shown a lead in these reversals, and we look to it now to show many more.

The context of these changes is itself changing. The world is shrinking. We used, 10–15 years ago, to talk of the global village as a novel idea. But the village has shrunk. We are all much closer together and much more interlinked than we used to be. We are now a global family in a global bed. There is the saying of the family all in the same bed, that 'When father turns, we all turn'. Perhaps I may be forgiven for noting that the patriarchal imagery may fit the Bank. Greater forgiveness will be needed for the following verse.

When Father turns

The global village had its day
But rapidly has shrunk away
So now we find ourselves instead
Together in a global bed

Enjoying patriarchal rank
We know our Father is the Bank
And up till now we had to learn
When Father turns, so we all turn.

It's hard for father with his weight
We hope he'll turn before too late
Stakeholders all, let's seize on fate
And prod him to participate[1]

What the World Bank says and does, the signals it sends out, the criteria it adopts, the way its staff behave on mission – these matter to us all. Already the Bank has pioneered on the social side with the rules about resettlement and those adversely affected by development actions, and with the participatory poverty assessments. There is also a huge negative balance with the adverse effects of structural adjustments and other policies. But let us look on the bright side. The Bank has shown that it is capable of vision and change. Two years ago, at the participatory learning workshop, it seemed right to call for guts and vision on the part of the learning group. They have shown that. It is now a question of the guts and vision of senior management. Many of us are watching that space. So much depends on what they decide and how they act. To the participatory learning group and to all those within the Bank who are working for participatory change, I am sure all of us who have been invited here from outside, would wish to say 'Go to it, and good luck'.

---

1. *A later version of this stanza was*
No more. Upend him. Master fate
And make him change before too late
Reorienting in the bed
Not side to side, but on his head.

Participation and PRA for donors

An encouraging but cautionary note.[1]

The way donors have espoused participation is encouraging. Good things have been done. PRA at its best can be empowering and exciting. And potential gains for poor people from sustained and sensitive facilitation in a participatory mode are immense.

But in these early stages there has also been terrible bad practice. For example:

- A donor staff member asks a PRA trainer to conduct training in three days in a hotel in a capital city [Kathmandu]. The trainer insists that 10–14 days are needed, in the field, and with fieldwork. The donor says that in that case he will find someone else. The responsible trainer loses the job, and her livelihood is threatened. An opportunistic trainer who has not internalized participation gets the contract. Those who take part receive certificates![2] [the person in the donor agency is promoted?]
- A donor seeks two trainers to train local consultants in two days who will then in two days in the same week conduct community workshops in four cities [yes, this *is* a real case].

Much abuse has come from requiring PRA on a large scale and fast, and as a one-off instead of a process. So all too often staff in donor agencies driven by a desire to disburse and to get quick results have been responsible for PRA which is rushed and routinized, wastes local people's time, encourages dependence, leads to plans and expectations without action, disillusions local people, and makes later efforts more difficult.

Good participation and PRA entail changes in behaviour, attitudes and organizational procedures, rewards and cultures. This applies not just to partners but if anything even more to donor organizations themselves. Not rushing, but taking time, is crucially important.

If you want to encourage and support participatory approaches and behaviours, do not expect it to be easy. It is not like pressing a button. It needs long-term commitment. It needs democratic, non-dominating and patient relationships with partners. It usually means resisting pressures within your

---

1. These remarks apply with force to the spread of Community-Led Total Sanitation, now (2011) in over 40 countries. Visit www.communityledtotalsanitation.org
2. Certificates awarded for training in participatory approaches and methods can be pernicious. Some people 'get it' with participatory attitudes and behaviours; and others do not. Certificates stuck on office walls can then publicly mislead. Kamal Singh has shown me an elegant South African solution – the pledge certificate in which the participants fill in what they pledge to do. Certificates are only signed if the pledges are judged good enough (for a specimen see Chambers, 2002: 49)

own organization. Don't expect promotion. And please don't blame me if you lose your job.[1]

We are all learning. Some advice which seems sound at this stage is:

- Find really good trainers. Ask around. They are usually the people who say they need at least 7–14 days to train anyone, and that it must be done experientially with local people in field situations. They emphazise behaviour and attitudes more than methods.
- Go for process without rigid targets. If you have to have logframes, minimize their bad effects. Stress again and again the importance of learning and sharing, flexibility, changing, and seizing unanticipated opportunities.
- Find, support and work with champions. Forge alliances. Encourage networks of those who are truly participatory.
- Set an example yourself by taking part in the field, where you can, together with colleagues from the host government. Take leave if necessary to do this.
- Take the long view. Hang in there for years if you can. Find others who can ensure continuity when you go. The handover to your successor may be critical. Try to make sure she or he is a good person for the job. Take time handing on personal contacts.

Don't be discouraged. A sea change is taking place. There are more and more people on a participatory wavelength. In some places there is already a critical mass of people who are growing participation in their bones, who understand what it is about and who want to work for change. Elsewhere there may be many places now where the mass is near-critical, and it just needs a little more support and effort to take off.

These are my optimistic views. I may be wrong.[2] But I don't think so! Above all, good participation is hugely satisfying. And its benefits last. Enjoy!

Many good people work in the World Bank. Many join it believing that they can change it. Some manage to use their powerful position to achieve good change. But a pervasive reality is the need to make big loans fast.

---

1.   I have been inscribing a book I have written *Whose Reality Counts? Putting the First Last* (Chambers, 1997) as follows:

Warning and Disclaimer
Read at your own risk

The author accepts no responsibility for damage to the career of any person reading this book.
This is not only a joke. There is a growing roll of honour of good people who have been sidelined or sacked or not funded because they have been too participatory and have promoted participation too well.

2.   I was wrong.

The Big Bank's Boast

Anything you do well acts as a trigger
Anything you can do we can do bigger
Damned with our scaling-up-instantly curse
Anything you can do we can do worse

This has often been the sad reality. A partial exception has been the Water and Sanitation Program (WSP) of the Bank. WSP was an early adopter, supporter and disseminator of Community-Led Total Sanitation (CLTS) (see pp. 196–200). It could do this because it has a small budget from Trust Funds – grants from other agencies. It is not involved in making loans. And as with the Participation Learning Process in the Bank, some trust funds from bilateral donors have been put to good use.

One example of going to scale fast was labelled Community-Based and Community-Driven Development (CBD and CDD). In the early 2000s this was evaluated by the Operations Evaluation Department of the Bank. As one of three asked to evaluate the evaluation, I found that the Bank does walk the talk, as people in Washington DC say, with its transparency. It put my critique up on its website. A cynic will say that the emperor is so powerful that he can afford to walk naked. But credit must be given where credit is due. The Bank is more transparent than international NGOs dare to be.

The reader may wish to reflect to what extent the four main criticisms do or do not apply generally or specifically to other evaluations and evaluation processes.

The effectiveness of World Bank support for community-based and -driven development

Comments on the OED Evaluation of 22 April 2005.

The OED team deserves congratulations on the effort put into the monumental task of this evaluation. The subject matter is vast, scattered and difficult to assess. The documents made available to the Advisory Committee and our discussions in December 2004 made it clear that the research was carried out with conventional rigour and care, and that the conclusions are credible, based on and emerging from careful and balanced analysis of the evidence. The extensive and valuable literature review also drew on and collated much other relevant experience. Other aid agencies would do well to conduct evaluations similar in their independence, breadth and depth as those of the OED. The conclusions, as far as they go, resonate with and are confirmed by my own experience. The recommendations, however, fall short of what the evidence implies.

I note that CD approaches with HIV/AIDS are not included and are the subject of a separate evaluation. Given the delicacy and complexity of AIDS-related issues, and my participation in a Bank-led workshop on CDD and HIV/AIDS in Africa, I expect its findings to be more negative even than those presented in this evaluation.

There is much in the report which merits endorsement, presenting aspects which are both positive and negative. Rather than list such points, let me highlight four issues which qualify the conclusions of the evaluation. I do not make these comments with any pleasure, or lightly, but given what I have experienced, and given the Bank's commitment to professionalism in the service of poor people, I have to make them. All four suggest that this evaluation is over favourable:

1. *Picking winners*. This is not a criticism of the selection of the large sample of projects where I agree with the points about this made by Norman Uphoff. There are two other points.

   First, success with 'indigenously matured organizations' is the result of no doubt rational cherry-picking by the Bank. These were outstanding organizations with exceptionally high calibre, continuity and commitment of management with charismatic and inspiring leaders and which had existed for a decade or more and already successfully gone to very large scale: for example AKRSP Pakistan, the NDDB in India, and SEWA in Gujarat. They were highly successful before the Bank became involved. They are correctly distinguished as a separate category from other CD. Their performance is irrelevant to the evaluation of other CD projects, which are by far the majority. In earlier stages of their development they did not need, and might have been hampered by, support from the World Bank.

Second, the Matrouh project in Egypt is world-renowned as perhaps the most famous Bank flagship participatory project. It is several times mentioned. We know that it benefited from exceptional continuity of exceptional staff and high-level support from James Wolfensohn. But even it, one of the most favoured and best examples that could be found, is noted in this evaluation for its serious downsides, including the effects of creating a parallel organization and overlooking changes in land tenure which harmed the Bedouin. If one of the very best cherries has such flaws, one may wonder about the rest.

2. *Positive bias.* Any evaluation of Bank projects involving interviews with Government staff and NGO beneficiaries of Bank funding is vulnerable to positive biases. The power and prestige of the Bank, the careful respect with which it is treated, and the tendency to try to please with favourable feedback, present systemic difficulties in knowing what is really happening. All power deceives (see chapter 5 of my book *Whose Reality Counts?*). However careful the research, there will always be questions about prudent, deferential and self-serving responses. It is as much as some officials' jobs are worth to say anything negative about the Bank.

3. *Hidden negative externalities.* The following negative effects are either not mentioned or understated. The fact that they are half-hidden to conventional research does not make them any less plausible or less real. Some of them are part of another and more inclusive research agenda.
   • Diversion of progressive NGOs (both INGOs and NNGOs) from rights-based and empowering activities which would do more for poor people than the provision of infrastructure which does less, and/or may even be negative, and/or may drag the NGOs back into activities they were attempting to move on from. (36 per cent of projects had some form of NGO involvement (para 4.18)). In pro-poor terms, this is likely to reduce NGO additionality, leaving poor people net losers.
   • Undermining other more participatory, less target and disbursement-driven, less infrastructure-focused, and more sustainable programmes supported by other organizations in neighbouring areas. ('Why should we do it ourselves when our neighbours are getting so much done for them or for free?')
   • Diversion of government recurrent funds, staff and materials from other places and services (schools, clinics etc.) to the new infrastructure, with hidden costs to services in those other places. With schools and clinics, for example, resources are most likely to be diverted to communities which are accessible to government and Bank staff inspection, to show success. Where government staff

and recurrent funds are, as so often, limiting, this will deprive poor communities that are less accessible.

- Risks and costs associated with top-down time-bound disbursement-driven capital projects. These include scope for petty and not so petty corruption, and the proliferation of opportunistic NGOs (as noted in para 4.20).
- The long-term disempowering effects of dependence and disillusion created at the community level (see e.g. Box 8). Communities become, as so many have, less self-reliant and more inclined to lobby, beg, and wait.

These are general tendencies. There will be exceptions. But together on balance they mean that the findings of the evaluation should be more negative. Given the goodwill, energy and commitment of many Bank staff, I regret having to say this. But it is quite possible that overall the Bank's CD initiatives do more harm than good to poor communities and people. In addition there are the opportunity costs of alternatives foregone.

4. *The comparative disadvantages of the Bank.* While the conclusions of the report follow from the evidence and analysis, they do not adequately confront the comparative disadvantage of the Bank with CD, nor the full range of what would be required if performance were to justify continuing to try to support it. This is alarming, especially when CD-related lending, far from prudently diminishing, is increasing beyond its already remarkably high level.

The comparative disadvantages are institutional and paradigmatic and related to:

- Reliance on loans, the future repayment of which may impact adversely on government services and so on poor people. If loan-based rather than grant-based projects are to be justified, repayments will be at the cost of other government expenditure. The bar therefore has to be higher.
- Disbursement pressures and the typical one-year sub-project cycle (para 3.19) with top-down one-shot interventions, an approach antithetical to participation and to assuring benefits to those who are poorer. We know and do not need to learn again how badly this works.
- The management and staff-intensity of empowering and participatory development. The extra cost of preparation of CD projects is only 10 per cent higher than non-CD. For effective pro-poor participation, it would need to be far higher than this.
- The staff incentive system of the Bank which rewards high and fast disbursements. This was a major factor which emerged from a participatory workshop for Task Managers which I facilitated a few years ago. Nothing I have heard suggests that this has changed significantly.

- Inability to learn and change. That the ratings of CD projects are stagnating suggests that institutional learning and change are not taking place. A likely reason is that the Bank is not looking hard enough at itself or is simply unable to perceive, learn and change.

These factors combine to disable the Bank, making it inherently difficult for it to do well with CD. The question then is whether they can be changed.

The report correctly points to the need for radical institutional change in Government bureaucracies: 'The literature shows that the institutionalization of a CD approach requires a radical reorientation in the way governments and bureaucracies operate.' (para 4.4.). This applies if anything more to the Bank itself, as the dominant partner, than to governments and their bureaucracies. This is not rocket science. It is common sense and common experience. In practice, the disabling culture, incentives, procedures and imperatives of the Bank are passed on 'downwards' to governments and NGOs. It is no good saying 'Do as I say but not as I do'. The Bank may not be able to become more participatory. But unless it does, it cannot expect the CD it funds to be cost-effective in empowering and benefiting poor people. This means that the Bank itself must walk the talk, and take on board 'physician heal thyself' and 'do no harm'.

The recommendations

The recommendations in this final version of the evaluation fall far short of what is demanded by the evidence. If the Bank is serious about poverty and empowerment, more radical action is required. In effect, the recommendations as they stand leave the door open to going on with more of much the same. The evidence of this OED evaluation, combined with other studies and insights, shows the CD initiatives of the Bank to be of such questionable value that the approach now should be damage limitation, intensive learning and finding out whether change is possible in the Bank. I hesitate to say what I believe the Bank should do, but the stakes for poor people and communities are so high and on such a scale that it would be wrong for me not to do so. I have agonized over this. And I recognize that there is no way I can assess fully the implications or modalities for what follows. But on the basis of the evidence of this evaluation and of other experience my own best judgement is that it the Bank should now, and decisively:

- *Rein back* on and/or slow down existing CD projects, where this is legally and ethically feasible
- Impose *a moratorium* on new ones
- Learn more about what happens and what might be made to happen by selecting on-going projects for *intensive learning through action research*, including investigating hidden externalities
- As part of this *examine the Bank itself* – its culture, procedures, norms, incentives and behaviours – *and its impact* on governments, NGOs

and communities, and analyse the contradictions between these and empowering, pro-poor community development and how these play out

- And then review *how the Bank must change* if the short and long-term effects for poor people, communities and countries of Bank-driven CD are to be positive and to justify the costs, and *whether and how such change could be achieved.*

Postscript, 2011

Change in the World Bank is, though, notoriously difficult. And others follow its lead and style. It has inbuilt syndromes of culture, procedures, imperatives, and even recruitment. In my view the procedural imperatives of the scale and speed of the lending required will continue homeostatically to sustain its culture and disabilities. The best and least harmful things it can do now seem set to continue to be dedicated, ring-fenced and limited through Trust Funds for specific purposes.

What DFID should do

In April 2007, members of IDS were asked to reflect and comment on DFID's performance. The message was 'We hope for balanced entries that are challenging but constructive'. I wrote:

DFID has much to be proud of for what it has achieved over the past ten years. The 1997 White Paper and later policy papers stressed human rights as never before. Eliminating poverty was put top of the agenda. Policies on gender and the environment have been progressive. During the ten years the aid budget has been raised and continues to rise. The PPAs (Programme Partnership Agreements) to INGOs on the basis of shared values and commitments have been a highly cost-effective use of aid money. Within DFID over this period Social Development continued to grow in numbers and clout. The proportion and influence of women staff in DFID increased sharply. DFID's standing and influence with lenders and other donors remained high. DFID quite often had a lead role in official development thinking and practice.

Aid effectiveness has, though, suffered in many ways. The abrupt abandonment of on-going projects and of projects in advanced preparation, where communities and partners had mobilized, some with years of work, was blindly irresponsible and unethical: it is a pity that senior officials did not have to face those hurt and let down, and see the damage and disillusion. The extent of the withdrawal from middle income countries, especially in Latin America, failed to understand the disproportionate gains for poor people from innovative programmes with low budgets in those countries. Decreasing staff while increasing the budget has been a pathological own goal, with aid effectiveness and poor people the losers. Combined with harmonizing with other donors, this policy has trapped and isolated in-country staff in capital cities, where they have talked policy in ignorance, not having met poor people or learnt about their realities. Moreover, the ever rising ratio of budget to staff numbers has left good NGO opportunities unfunded while large consultancy organizations move in and mop up the money because of their low transaction costs to DFID staff. Perhaps least recognized, and most damaging, the logframe, insisted on and propagated by DFID, has spread like a virus to other donors and to INGOs, reinforcing rigidity and vertical power relations all down the aid chain, the very opposite of the rhetoric of partnership and empowerment.

The hope must be that DFID, as a learning organization, will build on these experiences, increase its staff and its staff-to-budget ratio, make space for and insist on staff professional development through immersions in poor communities, and move beyond the logframe to evolve procedures which assure downward as well as upward accountability and empower partners to serve poor and marginalized people better, enhancing their well-being and achieving more of the MDGs. If it can do these things, and influence others to do likewise, it will multiply our aid effectiveness. And if not, not.

Postscript, March 2011

Since 2007, the DFID aid budget has continued to increase with cross-party commitment and staff have continued to be reduced. Reportedly the demand for cuts in staff was met in large part by reducing the number of national in-country professionals rather than those in London. The combination of a rising budget and reduced staff capacity has driven larger contributions to the World Bank, the IMF, direct budget support to countries, and very large contracts to consortia. These are all ways of reducing the ratio of DFID staff's transaction costs to money disbursed. They are by no means necessarily the most cost-effective ways of disbursing the budget. Among other things they have led to a crippling inability to make the targeted small grants which can be so highly cost-effective. Before the 2010 election the Secretary of State, Andrew Mitchell, twice publicly described cutting staff while raising the budget as 'ridiculous'. In my view it has been worse than ridiculous. It has been a gratuitous and irresponsible dereliction of duty to taxpayers and to all those who campaigned with such passion and energy To Make Poverty History. The good news in late 2011 is that national staff numbers in country are being increased, though whether this will be on the scale needed remains to be seen.

Aid and the New Bottom Billion: need for a radical rethink?

In his influential 2007 book *The Bottom Billion: Why the Poorest Countries Are Failing and What Can Be Done About It* Paul Collier wrote about the billion poor people living in the poorest countries, countries which were falling behind and falling apart, coexisting with the twenty-first century but with a reality in the fourteenth century: civil war, plague, ignorance. He identified four types of country situation – trapped by conflict, cursed with natural resources, landlocked with bad neighbours, and with bad governance in a small country. The implication for aid was that it should focus on these countries, many of them in Africa.

In October 2010 Andy Sumner (2010a, b) published a correction to the impression that the bottom billion of poor people were in the poorest countries.

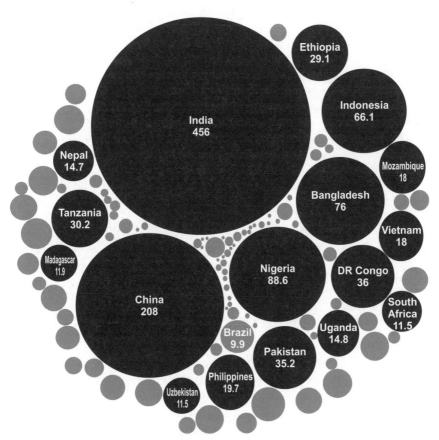

Figure 3.1 Population living under US$1.25 per day
Source: Sumner (2010b) from *The Guardian*

He reported findings that 960 million poor people, almost three-quarters of the world's 1.3 billion, were in middle income countries (MICs), 850 million of them in India, China, Nigeria, Pakistan and Indonesia, and that this was 'a dramatic change from just two decades ago when 93 per cent of poor people lived in low-income countries'. Much of the change is accounted for by low-income countries (LICs) graduating to become MICs. This has raised the question what role, if any, aid has in such countries. DFID, for instance, had been reducing its presence in Latin America. The future of British aid to India was also in question.

The point about the ratio of staff to budget is reinforced. If British aid to India, for example, is to make a difference to the third of poor people in the world who live there, it will have to be applied in a fine-pointed way. India does not need the funds. What it can gain from is collegial collaboration and resources to innovate and try new things out. This can be difficult for those working in the huge Indian administrative system. It can be easier for them on a smaller scale with an external ally. So the UK Treasury staff-cutting mindset must be stood on its head: to get better value for taxpayers' money, spend more on good, technical staff in-country, invest in relationships and continuity, and hang in there in collegial collaboration working with champions who want to innovate. The result should be more for less, more impact from more staff with less total expenditure.

Ordinary members of the public can understand this. They are not stupid. So mandarins should be able to see it too. There are signs that they are beginning to. It is proposed to use programme budgets to beef up staff in country offices. Whether this happens on an optimal scale remains to be seen.

The big push back, and the big push forward

In September 2010, Rosalind Eyben convened a one-day workshop at IDS called The Big Push Back. The context was the increasing demands made by donors in the name of accountability, and the now pervasive audit culture of development relations. What in the mid 1990s seemed a passing phase, with ZOPP and the logical framework, has permeated development practice and relations. Upward accountability expressed in numbers is now the norm, affecting the behaviour and motivation of actors at all levels.[1]

One participant in the IDS workshop mentioned meeting a high-level official who said 'I want a simple problem with a simple solution so that I can measure value for money'. A section in a donor report of another workshop was headed: 'If it can't be measured, it won't happen'. To adapt the doggerel earlier applied to economists:

> Aid agencies have come to feel,
> what can't be counted isn't real,
> the truth is always an amount,
> count numbers only number count

In the words of a note of the IDS workshop:

> many development practitioners cynically comply with the performance measurement demands, often with a nod and a wink from a sympathetic bureaucrat equally despairing of what is now required. Compliance is accompanied by secret resistance. People carry on doing what seems most appropriate according to their own judgement. But compliance and resistance consume energy and enthusiasm. The methods demanded of us to be *more accountable* are actually having the effect of our becoming ever *less responsible* for seriously enquiring of ourselves how we can most usefully contribute to transformative social change and be held accountable for our actions in that respect.

One person wrote 'My staff and my organizational partners are oppressed by the agreements I make with funders whose demands I pass on'. Even ActionAid International, for a time at least a world leader in participatory review and reflection, has had to adapt to donors' imperious demands. Of course, honest and competent financial accounting and strategic planning are needed. But the almost obsessional upward accountability now required, in excruciating detail, implies distrust, and demotivates and diverts time and attention from actually doing things, and from learning, changing and improving. It even pushes people to leave and move on to other work. Moreover, it is precisely

---

1. See Wallace with Bornstein and Chapman (2006)

those things which are least socially transformative that are most measurable and attributable, and those that are most socially transformative that are least measurable and attributable. The now dominant mindsets, methods and values are neo-Newtonian (see pp. 190–1), and fit the linear, sequential, controllable, predictable simplicity of physical things and misfit the non-linear, iterative, uncontrollable, unpredictable complexity of people and social processes. The struggle is paradigmatic. Like frogs in a heating pot, those receiving funds may not recognize how much the temperature has risen. They cannot jump out. But a time comes to recognize reality and say 'turn off the heat or you will stew us'.

The dysfunctional absurdity of what has been happening invites ridicule. Is it driven by politicians who do not understand, or who believe that taxpayers do not understand? It is against the interests of poor people. It is against the interests of taxpayers who want their money well spent. In whose interests is it then? Those of powerless cogs in the machine? And are all of us drawn into the system increasingly converted into compliant cogs? Is it like a Greek play in which the actors are principled and mean well, but when all act in their contexts according to their best lights the outcome is tragic?

The tragedy is not inevitable. If we are to transform our world, we need to fight back with new concepts, values, methods, procedures, behaviours, relationships and realism. In mid 2011 this has just begun with The Big Push Forward. This is 'a network of practitioners identifying and sharing strategies for encouraging funders to experiment with and, when appropriate, adopt additional, useful approaches to impact assessment and reporting of international aid programmes and projects'.

Watch this future space.[1]

---

1. See http://bigpushforward.wordpress.com and www.bigpushforward.net

PART IV

To provoke: For our future

Introduction

Those of us who want to act for a better world and who intervene in the lives of others face ethical dilemmas. We have to decide where we focus and what we do. Poverty palliatives are seductive low-hanging fruits; causes of poverty are more difficult – roots to uncover and dig up. H.L. Mencken, wrote: 'For every problem there is a solution that is simple, direct, and wrong'. Are many of our actions against poverty simple, direct and wrong? Do they divert us from root causes? I remember being shocked by an Indian activist who opposed eye camps, where doctors operate to give blind people sight, because they allowed supporters to feel good without tackling the conditions that create and sustain poverty and the conditions that lead to such blindness. There is the imagery of the good person who keeps fishing children out of a river instead of going upstream to stop those who are throwing them in. In the wry observation of Helder Camara, a Brazilian priest: 'When I give food to the poor they call me a saint. When I ask why the poor have no food they call me a communist'. Who are the *they*? In refusing to face and tackle root causes, am I, are we, like *them*? Should I, we, reflect on ourselves, our mindsets, motivations, hypocrisies, evasions, errors and above all omissions? And while we reflect, should we walk on two legs, both acting, and asking and reflecting, and changing our actions as we experience and as we get answers?

In the spirit of these questions, this last section is part of the struggle, a few steps, stumbles and signposts, provocations inviting you to disagree, to balance better, to be at once more radical and more realistic.

Whose priorities? and **Objectives for outsiders** are short extracts from *Rural Development: Putting the last first* (1983). They were selected by Alfonso Gumucio-Dagron for a collection he and Thomas Tufte (2006) edited on *Communication for Social Change*. I would not have thought of opening this last section with them had they not already been picked out. I do not think they provide answers. But progress has been made since 1983 in learning how to know what poor people's priorities are, as we have seen through participatory approaches and methods, Participatory Poverty Assessments, and the like. Moreover, poor rural people are generally less isolated, less powerless and less deferential than they were. The dilemmas of **Whose priorities?** and more pertinently 'whose values?' remain, but the dramatic spread of communications in rural areas over recent decades – the written word, radio, television, videos, internet, mobile phones – and the gradual decline in practices like female genital mutilation have narrowed and reduced some of the contradictions of values.[1]

---

1. This was written before the Pope had given his equivocal approval of the limited use of condoms. That long overdue narrowing is welcome as far as it goes. But tragically this slight softening of position only comes after the ignorant and authoritative dogmatism of the Catholic Church on condoms will likely have contributed to the avoidable death of hundreds of thousands if not millions of people from HIV/AIDS and the suffering of vastly many more. I wonder what Christ would have said.

Gender and participation have been two great movements in development. **The Myth of Community: gender issues in participatory development** brought them together for the first time and showed their immense transformative power when combined. The foreword to that landmark book summarizes four themes and lessons which all point to personal behaviour, attitudes, values and commitment, and concludes that gender equity and participation have, together, huge potential for enhancing well-being for all.

Power and relationships are now more on the development agenda. Radical prescriptions based on a conflict theory of social change see social movements, resistance and negotiation from strength, as in the past by Trade Unions, as essential for changing bad power relations, including those of gender. Through this lens the vision is zero sum – the powerful, rich and dominating must lose for the weak, poor and subordinate to gain. **Transforming power: from zero-sum to win–win** acknowledges the force of such arguments but points out that many solutions can be win–win. There are many ways in which 'uppers' can gain by and from empowering 'lowers'.

This leads to asking whether, if there is to be deep and lasting change, we need a **Pedagogy for the powerful** (or non-oppressed) and heightened awareness. Ideas include applying sustainable livelihoods thinking to the lifestyles of the affluent and representing poor people at meetings and the excluded and unborn in parliaments.

Oh poverty experts! poses the problem of the capital (city) trap and the partial solution of immersions. **Immersions – something is happening** is an overview with illustrations. Immersions, spending a few days and nights living in a poor community, are a potent way for development professionals at all levels to be more in touch, and to understand better the realities and aspirations of those they seek to serve. It asks whether, had immersions been widespread practice, the horrors of structural adjustment could ever have been perpetrated. Can immersions become regular practice for development professionals, so that what we do in the name of development is more fitting, focused and fair?

Much of the development agenda is set by the World Bank. That is one reason why there are some good, able and committed people who take a deep breath and go and work there. And some do make a difference. The World Development Report (WDR) 2000/2001 *Attacking Poverty* is an example. By recognizing the multidimensionality of poverty and by stressing empowerment, it marks a shift in mainstream development thinking. The report drew on the *Voices of the Poor* study in 23 countries (Narayan et al., 2000b) and the seminal immersion of Ravi Kanbur, the Task Manager for that WDR, in Gujarat. He resigned over interference and pressures but the main substance of the report was too late to change. All the same, it could have gone further. **The World Development Report: concepts, content and a chapter 12** draws together and takes further the themes of words and concepts, poverty and participation, and aid. It is a critique of the report, which illustrates its skilful use of language to gloss the true nature of much of the assistance provided by the Bank. Looking to the future, I argued, the WDR 2010 should be *Challenging Wealth and Power*. For some reason this has not happened. Do we have to wait now until 2020? Or the 22nd century? Or does some other organization, not the World Bank, have to take this up? Can I provoke someone – you? – into making this come about?

We are all trapped in our mindsets and our ways of seeing and doing things. **Development paradigms: neo-Newtonian and adaptive pluralism** delineates two contrasting paradigms. The neo-Newtonian has elements that are linear, ordered, uniform, controlling and predictable. Adaptive pluralism has elements that are non-linear, diverse, complex, empowering and unpredictable. Neo-Newtonian practice is the paradigm of the Model T Ford, of one size fits all. Development practice tends repeatedly towards neo-Newtonian practice, locked in by rules, conventions and conformist commonsense. **Paradigms, lock-ins and liberations** shows that other paradigmatic syndromes can constrain and conceal potentials. Two revolutions that have turned lock-ins on their heads are the System of Rice Intensification (SRI) and Community-Led Total Sanitation (CLTS). Multiple simultaneous mutually reinforcing flips have had astonishing results. Are similar opportunities lurking and waiting to be discovered? Should we look for them? How?

Those who will make our future, the future of our human race, are the children of today, and children yet unborn. How we treat children and bring them up has been a howling gap in the development agenda. To be sure, there are movements concerning child labour and child abuse, and massive investments in education. But what sort of people children grow into depends profoundly on their families. Love and security are fundamental. Beyond these there is believing in children's abilities, and encouraging these to flower and flourish. **Stepping Forward** is a remarkable book due for a renaissance. What it shows, not once, but again and again, is that with participatory approaches children can do more, much more, than most adults suppose. The slogan 'They can do it' applies with force to children, from birth through to adolescence, in schools, and even more in families. To paraphrase Barack Obama 'Yes *they* can'. There is a vision here of future generations brought up and empowered to realize more of their extraordinary human potential and inspired to transform our world. So, as the foreword to *Stepping Forward* concludes:

> if we adults can only change our views and behaviour, children will astonish us with what they can do, be and become, and how in time they can make our world a better place.

In August 2005 at the inaugural conference of the International Poverty Centre in Brasilia some of us were challenged to come up with a two-pager on **What would it take to eliminate poverty in the world?** As provocations go, this was outrageous. But, provoked, I banged out a note. What does this say about my mindset and orientation? And where then does this take us, in thinking through what needs to be done, by whom and how? To transform our world, for ourselves, for our children, and for other generations to come?

Whose priorities?

Excerpt from: Rural Development: Putting the Last First *(1983) pages 141–2.*

In trying to see what to do, non-rural outsiders are trapped by core-periphery perception and thinking. Looking outwards and downwards towards the remote and powerless, their vision is blurred. They see most clearly what is close by; they see action starting from where they are. The very words reflect the problem: 'Remote' means remote from urban and administrative centres, from where most of the outsiders are; and 'what to do' implies initiatives taken by them in the centres of power. However much of the rhetoric changes to 'participation', 'participatory research', 'community involvement' and the like, at the end of the day there is still an outsider seeking to change things. Marxist, socialist, capitalist, Muslim, Christian, Hindu, Buddhist, humanist, male, female, young, old, national, foreigner, black, brown, white – who the outsider is may change, but the relationship is the same. A stronger person wants to change things for a person who is weaker.

From this paternal trap there is no complete escape. A decision not to act is itself an action. A person who withdraws or who abstains from intervening is by that withdrawal or abstention still intervening by default. The weaker person is affected by what does not happen but which might have happened. There is, however, a partial remedy. Respect for the poor and what they want offsets paternalism. The reversal this implies is that outsiders should start not with their own priorities but with those of the poor, although however much self-insight they have, outsiders will still project their own values and priorities. In what follows, I too am trapped, an outsider asking what poor people want. All one can hope is that the effort of trying to find out, of asking again and again and doubting the outcomes, will check some of the worse effects of core-periphery paternalism, and that the more the priorities of the poor are known, the easier it will be to see what it is best to do.

Priorities and strategies of the poor

For those who are neither rural not poor to know the priorities of those who are both is not as easy as it sounds. The rural poor are dispersed, isolated, uncommunicative, rarely asked their views, frequently masked by others, selectively perceived, deferential. The silent cannot be heard. Direct approaches distort impressions: Replies in interviews notoriously mislead, especially when respondents believe that their replies may bring benefits. An indirect approach may help, drawing on social-science research, especially case studies of social anthropologists and social workers, and agricultural economists' understanding of the behaviour of poor farmers. On the basis of such evidence something can be said about what poor people want, inferring their priorities from what they do as much as, or even more than, from what they say.

Objectives for outsiders

Excerpt from: Rural development: Putting the Last First *(1983) page 145.*

Objectives for outsiders can, then, be expressed as a reversal, putting first the wishes of the poor themselves. But this cannot be all. Dilemmas remain; from conflicting values and objectives; from times when outsiders' knowledge is believed to be more valid than rural people's knowledge for achieving what poor people want; from trade-offs between short- and long-term costs and benefits; and from outsiders' need to be true to themselves. The question whether to give medical treatment against a patient's wishes, but in order to save her or his life, is an example of the more general problem of power and paternalism. I see no universal solution to this. But for practical purposes in rural development, a partial answer is to concentrate on those aspects of life where outsiders and the rural poor agree. Peter Berger ends his book *Pyramids of Sacrifice* (1977) with an appeal for people of different ideologies to find common ground by looking at specific situations to which there will be a common 'no': to children dying, to preventable disease, to famine, to the poor becoming poorer, to exploitation of the poor by the rich. Agreement on points such as these can provide a moral foundation for the next steps, to see what outsiders should do.

But outsiders think they know best. Some will say that rural poor do not know what is in their interests; or that with greater awareness (which is liable to mean by agreeing with the outsider), they would have other priorities; or that they should confront their powerlessness by organizing against their rich exploiters; or that they should be encouraged to have longer time horizons; or that they must be enabled to see what they would want if they knew what they really wanted. But if vulnerable people have short time horizons, who is justified in imposing long ones on them? If they have low-risk strategies, who is justified in thrusting upon them strategies with high risks? It is safer and more humane to proceed by short steps into what can be foreseen than by long leaps into the unknown, in the meantime gaining experience on the way. Changing power relations and the distribution of wealth may often be a necessary condition for major improvement.

The Myth of Community: gender issues in participatory development

The Myth of Community, edited by Irene Guijt and Meera Kaul Shah is one of those landmark books which brings together themes and experience in a manner which, once it has been done, makes one wonder why it had not happened earlier. It followed a workshop they convened at the Institute of Development Studies, Sussex, in December 1993. I hope the foreword will whet the appetite of those who have not seen the book. It remains in 2011 as insightful and relevant as ever.

Foreword

The Myth of Community fills a huge gap. With hindsight, the previous lack of a book like this appears little short of spectacular. During the past two decades, the two powerful but separate movements, of gender and of participation, have been transforming the rhetoric, and increasingly the reality, of local-level development. Each has generated much writing. Each has major implications for the other. Yet, astonishingly, to the best of my knowledge, this is the first book thoroughly to explore the overlaps, linkages, contradictions, and synergies between the two. It cannot be often that a vital gap cries out for so long to be filled; and that it is then filled so well, with such rich material and insight, and with so much of the excitement of significant discovery, as in this book.

Its importance can be understood against the background of the two movements.

First, gender and development has had an immense influence. In many ways – in rhetoric and syntax, in appointments and promotions, in organizational behaviour, in projects, programmes and policies, and above all in personal awareness and orientation – a tidal change has started and continues. At the personal level, many of us development professionals have been both threatened and liberated as we become more aware of the pervasive inequities of the socially constructed relations between women and men, and recognize the personal implications for ourselves. To be sure, there is far still to go; and whether we are women or men, we will always have much to learn and unlearn, and much to work to change. But in development thinking and action, the direction is clear. Gender awareness and equity are irreversibly on the agenda and increasingly pursued in practice.

For its part, participation has origins which go far back. It has, though, only recently come together in the mainstream of development discourse and action. Both donor agencies and governments now have policies to promote it. At the same time, methodologies for participatory development, among them PRA (originally participatory rural appraisal), have evolved and spread, presenting new opportunities and means for turning the rhetoric into reality. Participation, like gender, presents challenges and opportunities across a wide front. Not least these are institutional, to change organizations, and personal, to change individual behaviour and attitudes...

...There is here a rich and diverse harvest for the reader. Across the board, the contributions offer insights. The direct personal experiences of the writers present an immediacy and realism which carries conviction. The realities described invite reflection. They provoke review and revision of one's sense of what is right and what is doable. Each reader will draw out her or his own themes and lessons. For me, four stand out.

First, there are many *biases* to be recognized and offset. Attitudes and behaviours which are dominating and discriminatory are common among those of us who are men: to become aware of these is a first and often difficult step. Even when the application of participatory methodologies is intended to minimize biases, women are often marginalized. Again and again, women are excluded by factors like time and place of meeting, composition of groups, conventions that only men speak in public, outsiders being only or mainly men, and men talking to men. In communities, it is easier for men than women to find the undisturbed blocks of time needed for PRA mapping, diagramming, discussions and analysis. The times best for women to meet, sometimes late after dark, are often inconvenient for outsiders. When outsiders rush, make short visits, do not stay the night, and come only once or twice, it is typically difficult for local women to participate, and issues of gender are likely to be marginalized or excluded. Again and again, the cases cited in this book are, in contrast, based on repeated, sustained and sensitive contact and interaction. Recognizing and offsetting these biases requires sensitivity, patience and commitment on the part of those who are outsiders to a community.

Second, local *contexts* are complex, diverse and dynamic. The reductionism of collective nouns misleads: 'community' hides many divisions and differences, with gender often hugely significant; 'women' as a focus distracts attention from gender relations between women and men, and from men themselves; and 'women' also conceals the many differences between females by age, class, marital status and social group. Nor are common beliefs valid everywhere: female-headed households are often the worst off, but not always. Moreover, social relations change, sometimes fast. It is not just the myth of community that this book dispels, but other myths of simple, stable and uniform social realities.

Third, *conflict is* sometimes necessary and positive for good change. For gender equity, much that needs to change concerns the power and priority of males over females. Several contributions to this book strikingly confront consensual participation as a myth, at least in the short term. They show that conflict can be an essential and creative factor in change for the better. Common examples are tackling issues of power and control over resources, and dealing with aggressive and violent behaviour. Domestic violence, drunken husbands, female infanticide, discrimination against females of all ages – these are phenomena difficult to confront without conflict. This does not mean a negative sum in well-being, that for females to gain, males must lose. To cease to dominate, oppress or be violent is itself a liberation. Responsible well-being is enhanced in shared responsibilities, in good relations in the family, in social harmony, and in personal peace of mind. The key is to facilitate changes in gender relations which lead to a positive sum, in which all come to feel better off, and so in which all gain.

Fourth, issues of *ethics* are repeatedly posed by both gender and participation: whether outsiders' interventions are based on universally valid values or a form of cultural domination; whether working with those who are weak and vulnerable leads to bad results for them, as when women are beaten by their husbands when the outsider leaves; whether gender-sensitive participation leads in practice to women and girls being better off or through a backlash worse off than before. There seem to be no easy answers. The imperative is to consult women and girls, and sometimes men, and seek their views on what it is right and practicable to do; it is to recognize the dilemmas of where values conflict, to puzzle and worry about them, and in a spirit of pluralism to act according to what seems best in each context, struggling to act well through self-aware judgement which respects the rights and realities of others.

Strikingly, these four themes all point to personal behaviour, attitudes, values and commitment. This is evident in many of the contributions. It applies to all of us who seek to intervene and influence the lives of others, whether through research, facilitation, sensitization or other development actions. In offsetting biases, this means working for gender equity, reducing dominance by men, and meeting, listening to and learning from women in places and at times they find convenient. In the local context it means being sensitive to social diversity and complexity in various dimensions of social difference, including, though not exclusively, gender. In conflict it means being alert and exercising good judgement in facilitating and managing process and mediating negotiation, resolving differences and nurturing relationships in which those who lose in one way gain in others. In ethical issues, it means consulting women, girls and others who are weak, and continual self-questioning, not to the point of paralysis, but reflecting on values, combining commitment with being open to self-doubt, and learning and changing oneself.

It is in this spirit that personal sensitivity pervades this book. The insights into gender relations and into participation are nuanced. The presentations are balanced, insightful and persuasive. The experience, evidence and analysis are often fascinating, recognizing and celebrating differences. The tensions and difficulties encountered with gender have generated concepts, methods and understandings which are subtle, and which ground participation in a deeper realism.

Now that we have this book, it deserves the widest distribution and readership. For those who specialize in gender, it opens up participation. For those who specialize in participation, it reinforces the gender dimension in full measure. For all other development professionals – whether academics, researchers or trainers, whether field practitioners, managers, consultants or policymakers, and whether in government organizations, bilateral or multilateral donor agencies, or international or national NGOs it offers readable access to new development needs and opportunities.

The Myth of Community takes us – development professionals – a long step forward. After this, 'gender' and 'participation' can never be quite the same again. Let me hope that this book will be read, reread and reflected on that its insights will permeate and help to transform development practice. The editors and authors would never claim to have made a final or definitive statement. They have, though, covered so much new ground so well and so convincingly that the good impact of their work should be deep and lasting. In our world, hundreds of millions are marginalized, oppressed and made miserable by domination and exclusion. Most of them are women. May those who read this book be inspired to act to reduce their marginalization, oppression and misery and to help relations between women and men change for the better. For gender equity and participation have, together, a huge potential for enhancing well-being for all.

Transforming power: from zero sum to win–win

In 2006, my colleagues Rosalind Eyben, Colette Harris and Jethro Pettit edited an IDS Bulletin (Vol. 37 No. 6, 2006) entitled Power: Exploring Power for Change. *It brought together diverse perspectives. This piece, and the one that follows it, are edited and abbreviated extracts from the article I wrote to provoke, arguing that power can be transformed in many ways from which all can gain.*

Words, meanings and usage

Discussions with Jenny Chambers led to the concept of 'uppers' and 'lowers', common words of deceptive simplicity because of the complex, shifting, subtle and nuanced relationships they can represent, at the same time diverse, intangible and elusive. *Upper* can refer to a person who in a context is dominant or superior to a lower. *Lower* can refer to a person who in a context is subordinate or inferior to an upper.

VeneKlasen and Miller (2002: 45) usefully distinguish four sorts of power:[1]

> Power *over*: meaning the power of an upper over a lower, usually with negative connotations such as restrictive control, penalizing, withholding information and denials of access.

> Power *to*: also agency, meaning effective choice, the capability to decide on actions and do them.

> Power *with*: meaning collective power where people, typically lowers, together exercise power through organization, solidarity and acting together.

> Power *within*: meaning personal self-confidence.

Common usage shows how we think of power. First, power sounds like a commodity. Power is gained, seized and enjoyed, or lost, surrendered or abandoned. People are driven from power, deprived of it, excluded from it and stripped of it.[2] Less negatively, power can be handed over or shared. Even then the image tends to be zero-sum: more is better, less is worse, and one's gain is another's loss.

Second, power is often spoken of as bad. Power goes with authoritarianism, bossing, control, discipline, domination – and that only reaches 'd' in an

---

1. See also Gaventa (2006) for the power cube which distinguishes visible, hidden and invisible power and power which is closed, limited and claimed. See http://www.powercube.net

2. Stripping evokes the imagery of removing clothes, as in the 'unfrocking' of errant priests.

alphabetical listing. Power is abused and exploited. All power corrupts. Bad people are power-hungry, intoxicated with power, obsessed with power and use power for their own ends.

Third, the discourse about transforming power in development is mainly about bottom-up organization and action. Activists, advocates and radical academics start with the realities and interests of the powerless. Change is through those who are marginalized and powerless gaining power *with* and power *within*. These combine as power *to* influence and change the power *over* through which people are oppressed and kept down.

My provocation is to argue that power *over* does not need to be like a zero-sum commodity; that there is nothing inherently bad about power *over* – it depends how it is used; and that bottom-up power *with* and power *within* strategies, vital and often primary though they are, must not distract from win–win top-down transformations where all gain.

Reversing pathologies of power

Abuses and pathologies of power are too well known to need enumerating. They have many linked dimensions – physical through strength and weapons, legal through laws and conventions, economic through wealth, political through the state. Good change can be through change in any or all of these. But pervasively interwoven with these are bad social and interpersonal relations and experiences through domination, greed, exploitation, violence and intimidation by the powerful, and subordination, deprivation, expropriation, fear, pain and insecurity for the powerless. Good change then includes changing interpersonal power relations and the processes which mediate them. With the major exception of gender, these have been largely overlooked in development thinking and practice.[1]

The word *reversals* has been used. Reversals are implicit in the 'Who?' and 'Whose?' questions applied to uppers and lowers and to issues of power and ownership. In development, some of the more common are:

> Whose reality? Whose knowledge? Whose appraisal? Whose analysis? Whose planning? Whose action? Whose M and E? Whose indicators? Who participates in whose project?

There are many others. In *Critical Webs of Power and Change*, Chapman and Mancini (2005: 5) have this: 'We need to give a lot more attention to who is involved, who assesses, who learns, whose opinion counts and who has access to information'. For Participatory Geographic Information Systems (PLA 2006 and pp. 24–25 above), 42 of these 'who?' and 'whose?' questions have been listed (Rambaldi et al., 2006) including:

---

1.   But see for example Groves and Hinton (2004) and articles in Eyben, Harris and Pettit (2006).

Who decides on who should participate? Who participates in whose mapping? And who is left out? Who has visual and tactile access? Whose map legend is it? Who gains? Who loses? Who is empowered and who is disempowered?[1]

Where the answer is to seek to empower those who are poor, excluded, marginalized, subordinate and powerless – the three options are bottom up, top down, or combinations.

Bottom up: Starting with the powerless: a zero sum?

Many of the better-known successful initiatives in development have been bottom up, starting 'below' and spreading laterally and vertically. Outstanding examples are the Self-Employed Women's Association (SEWA) in India; Integrated Pest Management in Indonesia and now [2006] in many countries; the Grameen Bank in Bangladesh, spreading similarly; and the Reflect movement, now with at least 300 organizations in over 40 countries. These have sought to empower through *power within* and *power with*. Many inspiring social movements and women's groups have shown how oppressive and abusive power can be overcome by countervailing power from below.

The shift of balance from service delivery to rights-based approaches in many INGOs has become part of this. Thus ActionAid International in its mission statement 'Rights to End Poverty':

We believe that poor and excluded people are the primary agents of change. Poverty and injustice can be eradicated only when they are able to take charge of their lives and act to claim their rights. (ActionAid International, 2005: 17)

The means and modalities are many (see, e.g. VeneKlasen and Miller, 2002: 50): education for confidence, citizenship and collaboration; affirming resistance; speaking out and connecting with others; participatory research and dissemination; building active constituencies around common concerns; mobilising around shared agendas; litigation; voting; and running for office. Confrontation and conflict are recognised as often integral to success. Power has to be contested. Those with power *over* have to be induced to lose. It sounds like a zero sum.

Top Down: starting with the powerful: the limits of 'normal' approaches

Complementary approaches can start with closer engagement with and understanding of powerful people and organizations themselves. Chapman and Mancini (2005: 8) in *Critical Webs of Power and Change* state that 'Strengthening ... collective action, critical consciousness and leadership

---

1. A step further could be to ask: Who determines the 'Who' questions?

should always be a crucial strategy within people-centred advocacy, but will rarely be the only strategy'. In a special issue of *Participatory Learning and Action – Tools for Influencing Power and Policy*, the editor wrote:

> Many of the policy tools in this special issue aim at engaging with rather than resisting powerful bodies such as companies and government agencies, albeit engaging tactically rather than playing along with the naïve idea that if stakeholders just sit down and talk, it will be all right. (Vermeulen, 2005: 14)

The tools in that issue are grouped under three headings: build power to act; claim the tools of the powerful; take hold of participatory processes. Care is taken to recognize and warn against the armoury of the powerful that can be deployed, including co-optation, deception, reneging on agreements and resorting to force.

These and other sources[1] consulted have enough in common for their approaches and advice to be summarized as something close to consensus:

- Identifying forces, friends and foes (Veneklasen and Miller: 211–27); identifying and mapping the major players and their real and expressed interests (Chapman and Mancini: 18) who also ask: 'Who do you consider your allies and opponents?' and, 'Who in power can make the decisions that will help bring about these changes?' (Chapman and Mancini: 41).
- 'Manoeuvring on the Inside: Lobbying and Negotiating' (a whole chapter in Chapman and Mancini). Primary targets are the decision-makers with the most power to address an issue, and secondary targets are individuals who do not have the power to solve the problem but who are close to the primary target.
- Mapping the policy system and mapping power.
- Knowing about government or economic and international decision-making structures and officials.
- Analysing the short-term and long-term interests of each actor and their viewpoints.
- Understanding why opponents oppose.

In all these sources, the dominant strategy is to build countervailing power and to penetrate and influence upwards. All recognize the need for allies and friends. All also see opponents who have to be confronted and tackled. As *The New Weave ...* (VeneKlasen and Miller, 2002: 225) has it 'Rarely does anyone give

---

1. Four sources are drawn on here: *A New Weave of Power, People and Politics: The Action Guide for Advocacy and Citizen Participation* (VeneKlasen and Miller, 2002); *Critical Webs of Power and Change* (Chapman and Mancini, 2005); *Tools for Influencing Power and Policy* (PLA, 2005); and *Policy Powertools* http://www.iied.org/natural-resources/key-issues/ empowerment-and-land-rights/power-tools-for-policy-influence-natural-re and www. policy-powertools.org [accessed 30 December 2010]. This last lists 26 tools for influencing decisions and decision-making about natural resource management.

up power without a fight'. Accepting and embracing conflict, the frame tends to be zero sum. Is there scope for going further with incentives, satisfactions, and institutional cultures? From standing in the shoes of decision-makers, or sitting on their chairs, and seeing things their way round, seeing how they can gain? Are there opportunities in the realities and contexts of the powerful which we easily miss?

A complementary agenda

Seeing things from decision-makers' point of view, and analysing how they can be influenced and helped, needs a leap of the imagination. This can generate a complementary agenda. While this is not absent from the four sources, it can be elaborated further.

One approach is 'practical political economy'. For different measures or courses of action, key players are analysed for degree of gain, loss or neutrality. For 22 measures concerning water and trees in India, this was done in a matrix for the rural rich and less poor, field-level officials, and poorer rural people, enabling judgements about relative feasibility and degrees of win–win or win–lose (Chambers et al., 1989: 231–3).

Another approach is to support those of the powerful who are either allies or opponents and potential allies, for example providing them with information and arguments they can use. Treating those who are undecided, sitting on the fence, or even hostile, as allies can also be self-fulfilling. People who are assumed to be going to act well are sometimes induced to do so by the expectation. It may be harsh to describe naïve optimism as Machiavellian but it can be worth trying: face-to-face confidence and assumptions that those with power will behave well gives them an opportunity to change and without loss of face.

Three more specific activities are:[1]

- Search official statements of policy, mission statements and the like, and arm and reinforce policy-makers with the rhetoric of their own organizations, agencies or governments to strengthen their power to argue within their bureaucracies
- Provide them with information in forms which they can use, in the language suiting the style of their organizations. This may best be done by an ally who has worked in the organization or in a similar one
- Consult them informally about the most effective ways to proceed, and what pressures from outside could strengthen their hands internally.

On this last point, some NGO representatives were asked to come half a day early to a meeting on participation in a multilateral organization. They were asked not to give too much praise to the progress made in the organization.

---

1. See for example Holland with Blackburn (1998) *passim* for other actions.

Those who had invited them needed their hands to be strengthened by their colleagues hearing forceful criticism from outside.[1]

Power to empower: a win–win

There are also win–win solutions when uppers use their power *over* to empower lowers. Those with power *over* in organizations can stand to gain in three ways:

1. *Realism, knowledge and learning.* I have argued elsewhere that all power *over* deceives (Chambers, 1997: 76–101). Power exercised as punitive control feeds fear, provokes prudent concealment and dissembling, and leads to error, myth, mutual deception and tacit connivance at deception. It inhibits and distorts learning. Conversely, democratic empowerment in a non-punitive learning mode allows and encourages realism. It enables and enhances learning.
2. *Efficiency and effectiveness.* This is a commonplace of management theory and practice. Power *over* with detailed top-down controls is inefficient and ineffective. Centralization overloads uppers and the capacity of the centre, demotivates lowers, misses opportunities for lowers and peripheries to use and develop their capabilities, and imposes standardization which often misfits local diversity. Conversely, decentralized decision-making decreases pressures on uppers and the centre, motivates lowers, and allows lowers and peripheries to realize more of their potentials, fitting local diversity.
3. *Responsible well-being.* Uppers and centres of authority often suffer overwork, anxiety and stress from their responsibilities, their roles, and tense and conflictual relationships. Conversely, when lowers are empowered, stress for uppers is often replaced by satisfaction and the experiences of well-being, which flow from fair and good actions and relationships.

A wealth of common experience and case evidence could be adduced to support these points. A cameo comes from the research project *Children Decide: Power, Participation and Purpose in the Primary Classroom* (Cox et al., 2006). Children were facilitated to use PRA visual methods to analyse school and classroom decision-making, and given space to make more decisions themselves. One teacher wrote:

> One of the first things I realised … was that the children had very little opportunity to make meaningful decisions in my class … I reflected on the possibility that I was too used to making decisions for the children so I, as their teacher, could feel in control of my class and their behaviour.

---

1. In India, decades ago, together with their colleagues a senior World Bank and a senior Indian civil servant were engaged in an argument. In a tea break, the senior Indian took the World Bank man to one side, and said 'For goodness sake, you are weakening. Don't! You mustn't!' or words to that effect. He needed to be seen to be overruled.

I became much more aware of the power structure within my class and started to think of more ways of distributing it throughout the class. I began to consider how many decisions I was needlessly making for the children ... My role as educator became more focused on enabling children to make informed decisions about how and what they wanted to learn. The relationship between the children and myself became much more of a partnership with the feeling that education was not done to my students but with them. (Cox et al., 2006: 195)

The teachers reported that they '... saw the changing relationship between teacher and children in terms of leading, guiding, coaching, rather than directive teaching' (Cox et al., 2006: 49).

Some of the many actions that can empower are indicated in Figure 4.1:

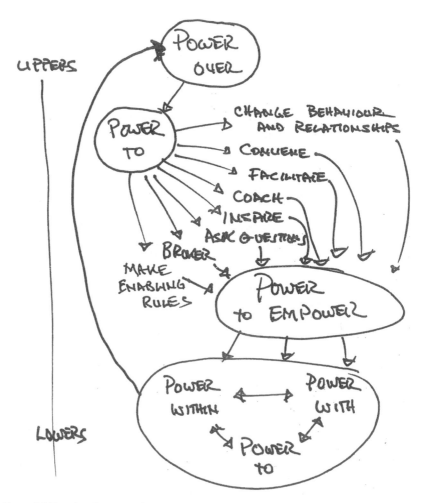

Figure 4.1 Transforming power from above

To elaborate on Figure 4.1:

Change behaviour and relationships. This covers a huge range of personal behaviour and interaction, and includes many forms of encouragement and support

Convene and catalyse. Uppers bring lowers together[1] If the other behaviours are followed, the meeting which is convened can lead to sharing, analysis, learning, solidarity and both power within and power with for those who are, or were, lowers in the situation. Convening provides opportunities to catalyse. This entails initiating or accelerating processes, sometimes described as igniting. (In chemical catalysis the catalyst does not change, so the metaphor is not wholly apposite because catalysts (facilitators) in this mode themselves are changed by the process.)

Facilitate. Uppers do not impose their ideas, or even agendas, but encourage lowers to do their own appraisals, analysis and planning, and come to their own conclusions. The slogans used in PRA apply here – hand over the stick, sit down, listen and learn, and shut up!, as do the many do's and don'ts for good facilitation (see, e.g. Kumar, 1996; Kaner et al., 1996).

Coach and inspire. A team leader, a committee chair, a teacher, a trainer or other upper sees herself less in the image of a military officer who commands and controls, and more as a football coach who trains, encourages, supports and inspires

Ask questions. Asking questions and leaving people to answer them can be an empowering way of opening up issues (for example, in transforming gender perceptions and relations (Harris, 2006 this *IDS Bulletin*) 'Ask them' in a PRA mode has been at times dramatically effective: asking lowers for their ideas and more so for their advice

Broker. This entails acting as an intermediary, connecting people and organizations, supporting negotiations, and making minimum interventions to assure fair outcomes

Make enabling rules. Minimum rules can enable complex and diverse emergent behaviour. On a computer and in human organization the resulting behaviour can be in practice unpredictable: with three simple rules random blobs on a screen can form a flock and fly around; two rules – accurate and open accounting, and rotating leadership – can make secure space for women's savings groups to decide their own norms, procedures and actions (Aloysius Fernandez, 1996, pers comm).

---

1. The others besides 'uppers' who can bring people together can include peers, strangers, even 'lowers' themselves. In this discussion we are concerned mainly with 'uppers'.

Facilitation that empowers can transform disabilities of power *over* into opportunities:

- the deceptions of power may diminish or disappear, replaced by openness and realism, with scope for learning and keeping more up to date and in touch with a changing world;
- efficiency and effectiveness may be enhanced as lowers realize more of their potentials, and act more creatively and diversely with better local ownership and fit; and
- in place of overload, stress, anxiety and hostility, there may be better relationships, fulfilment and even fun.

Beyond this, there is a realm of paradox. Aneurin Bevan said: 'The purpose of getting power is to be able to give it away', not a dictum many politicians have acted out. Going even further, one of the principles from the ActionAid workshop on Transforming Power was deliberate self-disempowerment expressed as:

We will help coalitions and networks of partners to develop the strength to challenge us.
(ActionAid, 2001: 22)

But even with that, there is a further paradox, expressed as: 'We are powerful when we question ourselves ... when we are self-critical. It is strange, but when we can really list and face our problems we have a new source of power' (ActionAid, 2001: 10).

Such reflections and actions by power-holders are scarcely on the development agenda. Yet if power is to be transformed, those actors who are powerful would seem to be crucial. In gender relations, this is recognized, with more attention paid now to working with men (Cornwall and White, 2000; Harris, 2006). We have source books for those who work with the powerless. We do not have similar source books[1] for working with the powerful, to help them act and change. Has their time come? Are such source books overdue?

---

1. I shall be grateful to anyone who can provide examples to show this statement to be false.

A pedagogy for the powerful

More edited extracts from Transforming Power: from Zero Sum to Win–win

A pedagogy for the powerful is a largely overlooked frontier in development thinking and practice. The powerful can include all who are uppers in a context, but especially multiple uppers – the staff of aid agencies and NGOs, government officials, political leaders, priests, teachers, professionals of many sorts, and pervasively men. The question is how to find ways to enable people like these to reflect and change. These are early days but there are promising practices. Five areas of activity and innovation can be proposed.

Workshops, retreats and reflection

Reflective practice, as Pettit (2006) has pointed out has been increasingly accepted as a professional norm. Yet for people in powerful positions in development organizations, times and spaces for personal and joint reflection and learning, in quiet places far from offices, are astonishingly rare. If they do go to retreats or workshops, it is often only for part of the time, and Blackberries, Iphones, mobile phones and the internet will not give them peace. Yet the irony is that such experience may matter more for them than for others.

A pioneering attempt to do this was as an 8-day ActionAid workshop for 40 people convened in Dhaka in 2001. We thought we had gone to share our experiences with participatory approaches and methods. Had we known it was going to be about power and relationships, we might have been less willing to take part. Some who were more powerful might have felt this would be a waste of their time, or a challenge to their authority. The experience was both traumatic and transformative. Those of us who were usually multiple uppers were repeatedly induced to acknowledge and offset our power. While there can be no substitute for the personal experience of such a workshop, the record and review of this one (ActionAid, 2001) is an eloquent and challenging source of insight.

Training to facilitate

Arguably, all development professionals should be facilitators, and all should be trained in facilitation. The 3 days of training in facilitation for staff from International Agricultural Research Centres were inspiring and seminal, and reportedly led to changes of behaviour, the way meetings were held and

---

For an earlier and fuller treatment, under the rubric 'A pedagogy for the non-oppressed' (with apologies to Paulo Freire), see Chambers (1995).

relationships.[1] Training may, indeed, be an inappropriate word, for it can carry associations with didactic teaching and even Pavlov's dogs, while processes of learning and changing are more personal, experiential and evolutionary. Neither should this be limited to one or a few categories of people. It is in the spirit of participatory and non-dominating relationships that in some sense, everyone is a facilitator, everyone including, and especially but not only, the powerful.

Face-to-face direct experience

Approaches have been evolving to enable senior and other development professionals to listen and learn from poor and marginalized people, and to experience and understand something of their lives, realities and priorities. Participatory action research (Jupp, 2004) and week-long periods in the field listening to and learning from 'people of concern' (Groves, 2005; UNHCR, 2006) are two examples. The most common and spreading are immersions and facilitated immersion workshops, typically with a few days and nights in a community (see below pp. 171–180). These have already proved valuable for general exposure, and have also been tailored for specific contexts and purposes. There is a potential here for empathy and insight, for feeling as well as thinking, and for direct experiential learning.

Peer influence between the powerful

To gain the attention of the very powerful and influence them can demand prestige, credibility and courage. These have been characteristics of Bono and Geldof. Bono has been remarkably successful with some of the world's leaders. In 2002, he took the US Treasury Secretary, Paul O'Neill, on a four-country tour of Africa (Vallely, 2006). Geldof remains prominent in trying to hold the G8 nations to their 2005 Gleneagles commitments. Both continue to challenge governments, not just on debt and aid, but especially on trade. It is now for other individuals, and for more organizations, to 'do a Bono' and 'do a Geldof' and affirm ideals with actions.

The same applies to philanthropy with the examples of George Soros, Bill Gates, Warren Buffett, and many others on a lesser scale, some of whom seek to remain unknown. Whatever reservations and criticisms there may be of the origins of the money or its uses, even a cynic accomplished in casuistry would find it difficult to argue that the world would be a better place without, for example, the Bill and Melinda Gates Foundation. And the best people to encourage others among the wealthy to do likewise are precisely those who are philanthropists already.

---

1.   The training was conducted by Sam Kaner, the author with others of *Facilitator's Guide to Participatory Decision-Making* (1996).

Well-being

Acknowledging and transforming personal power as an upper can be difficult and painful, but also liberating. The resulting changes in behaviour and relationships can bring long-term gains to well-being and fulfilment for uppers as well as lowers. The opportunity is then for win–win solutions with better relationships for all, reducing their disabilities and realizing more of their potentials. For uppers, with the exercise of less controlling power *over* can come a better experience of life.

If the bottom line in development is equity and the good life, a key power-related question to ask is what is a good life for a powerful person.

Arguably, this can be applied to all exploitative upper–lower relationships. Much of the material well-being of those who are 'better off' is based on the ill-being of others. But the other side of the coin is the scope for offsetting that ill-being when those who are better off use their resources and power to work on the side of the poor, marginalized and weak. They then gain the well-being that comes with responsible action. A man who beats his wife is not a happy man. If he changes, he stands to gain, as does the woman he beats, in many social and psychological ways.

On these lines, for Jung (1916) there was a dialectic of power and love. At the personal level:

> Where love rules, there is no will to power, and where power predominates, love is lacking. The one is the shadow of the other.

Is Jung's opposition of power and love a profound aspiration and challenge? In gender relations, between parents and children and also more widely in family, community, society, organizations and politics? And can a will to power be transformed, in a spirit of love, into a will to empower?

Answers to these questions may usually be affirmative but they have to be conditional to context. In organizations, in politics and in conditions of danger and insecurity, the will to power cannot be so clearly opposed to love: for some, exercise of power and control are needed. The key distinction is between the will to power and the responsible exercise of power. We need organizations with structures of power, political leadership, which exercises power on behalf of citizens, and power and control as one means of providing protection in danger and insecurity, but in each case exercised with humane responsibility.

So we are brought to asking whether power and relationships are central to development, as argued by Rosalind Eyben in *Relationships for Aid* (2006). Power and relationships are pervasively implied by concerns with gender, empowerment, participation, ownership, accountability, transparency and partnership. As I have noted (pp. 8, 22–23) all these words have been mainstreamed in the development lexicon. But this has been largely without realizing their implications for mindsets, behaviour and attitudes. The Paris Declaration on Aid Effectiveness (OECD, 2005; pp. 31–2) used the words 'partner' and 'partnership' 96 times but neither 'power' nor 'relationship' once. What is going on? Are power and relationships, and what these two words represent taken together, an elephant in the room, so large, occupying so much space, that it is not seen? Is one of the biggest challenges for the twenty-first century to recognize, tame and transform that elephant? And if so, is the place to start with a pedagogy for the powerful, enabling them to understand how they are disabled by power, and how in many ways they find fulfilment and can gain if they use their power to empower those weaker than themselves?

21 ways to move[1] an organization towards participation

For good change, there is usually organizational context. Where to start and what to do? Participatory changes in organizations and in institutional culture are not easy. They can need long campaigns. They take commitment, time, patience, persistence, resilience... They can be painful. You may make steady progress and then with a new top-down boss much ground is lost. Snakes as well as ladders. At the same time, it can be a bit of a game, with collegiality, convivial conspiracy, solidarity, jokes and fun. Even the dreary drudgery of form filling can become personally fulfilling. So why not consider and try some of these?

1.   Search out others who are like-minded. Build alliances. Find champions
2.   Meet informally outside office hours
3.   Search for, invent and introduce participatory methodologies for routine or regular activities
4.   Democratize meetings. Rotate those who chair meetings. Review seating patterns and how people interact
5.   Train staff in facilitation
6.   Organize space for informal and chance meetings (common room, coffee room...)
7.   Prudently and sensitively move to more informal dress
8.   Reduce formal written reports
9.   Make budgets transparent to all stakeholders
10. Draft job descriptions. Get on appointments committees
11. Recruit women (but beware of Thatcher clones) and enhance diversity
12. Work for a participatory process to produce or revise your organization's strategy and mission statement including accountabilities
13. Ask: what are our principles, our non-negotiables? List them and try to stick to them
14. Hold staff retreats, staying overnight (where allowed, a bar helps some of us)
15. Start regular review and reflection meetings (perhaps quarterly, twice a year or annually)
16. Get support and funding for participatory activities and relationships with clients and partners

---

1.   I originally used the word 'nudge' but this has a technical meaning, with 'choice architects' identifying nudges – small actions and guidance often stressing social norms – which are designed to change behaviour. The British Cabinet Office has a Behavioural Insight Team working on this, advised by Richard H. Thaler, the senior author of the book *Nudge* (Thaler and Sunstein, 2008). 'Move' is stronger and more proactive.

17. Invite and encourage senior staff to meet clients (poor people, lowers in any sense) informally and unhurriedly in their own environment, and to know them as people (as with immersions)
18. Start a pantomime for fun and effect in holding up mirrors, not least to power[1]
19. Set an example. Treat others not as you are treated but as you wish to be treated
20. Remember Gandhi: We must become the change we wish to see in the world
21. Work out your own strategy and methods. Innovate. Be bold. And share.

---

1. A Christmas pantomime is a long tradition at IDS. It has wickedly taken the mickey (e.g. 'I can now confirm that it is indeed true that (the always well dressed former director) does wear his tie in the bath') and the older scripts have been published. The lyrics of the pantomime are still clever and relevant, but just as we now disagree and argue less in seminars so too the pantomime has become nicer... does it mean that we now have less to be sharp about, are students on one-year courses more deferential, and less frustrated, informed, confident and critical than those on the previous two-year M Phil, or what? Or is this a cost of having become more participatory, friendly and consensual?

Livelihoods: sustainable in what sense, and for whom?

Sustainable livelihoods thinking has been widely applied to *them* – poor and marginalized people living in the global South whose livelihoods are inadequate and insecure. It has been little applied to the North and those who are rich in the South. We conveniently overlook that the least environmentally sustainable livelihoods and lives are *ours*; those of the relatively affluent who are most likely to read this. For us, the challenge is discomforting. Are we prepared to adopt a wider definition of sustainability for our livelihoods and lifestyles? One which includes effects on the sustainability of livelihoods of others today and of others unborn? Economically, through fairer trade relations today, and environmentally for the future? I cringe to ask: what degrees of short-term irresponsibility, inconsistency and hypocrisy do we allow ourselves in disregarding the interests of future generations? Does anyone speak for them?

The proposal that follows is serious and feasible.

We know that to include and empower those who are excluded, marginalized, weak and subordinate, there is a repertoire of positive discrimination such as quotas and reservations; but quotas and reservations have not yet been applied to future generations. There have been instances of silent representation at a meeting of those who are poor and excluded through an empty chair at the table. But this has not yet to my knowledge been done for the unborn. The Kenya Constitution for the Second Republic provides a lead by filling such chairs for some of the living. The National Assembly of 350 members includes 12 members nominated 'to represent special interests including the youth, persons with disabilities and workers'.[1] This principle can be extended to others who cannot be present and who cannot speak for themselves. Members could then be appointed to represent and speak on behalf of them, of generations unborn. Short of a future cataclysm, the number to be represented would spectacularly outnumber us who are alive today. Yet they have no voice. There is no one designated to speak for them. In the interests of equity, reflecting on and arguing for their interests could, and in my view should, be the responsibility of specially nominated members of all national democratic assemblies.

Why not? It seems so obvious.

Who will be first?

---

1. ROK (2010) *The Proposed Constitution of Kenya* section 97 (1) (c).

Oh poverty experts! Time to stand on our heads

To everything there is a season, and a time to every purpose under the heaven
The Bible, Ecclesiastes chapter 3: verse 1

A time to stand on our heads, a time to escape the capital (city) trap...

> We poverty experts sit pretty
> Snug and stuck in the capital city
> > For we know what is right
> > As we meet, talk and write
> And bestow on the poor plans and pity

> We poverty experts are caught
> In conceit and cannot be taught
> > From poor people we turn
> > We have nothing to learn
> Doling out direct budget support

> We poverty experts don't know
> What it's like for those living below
> > We look up with our eyes on
> > A distant horizon
> Not poor people but what numbers show

> But the experts aren't us but the poor
> It is they and not us know the score
> > We must learn from them, hear
> > What they say loud and clear
> So their voices can count more and more

> Oh poverty experts get real
> Your condition is far from ideal
> > Beat the capital curse
> > Get out and immerse
> Don't just think. Open up. Learn to feel

> Yes, immersions can threaten, it's true
> You don't know what will happen to you
> > But relax, let it flow
> > Let relationships grow
> Be surprised how the insights are new

Immersions: something is happening

Issue 57 of Participatory Learning and Action – Immersions: learning about poverty face-to-face *was without precedent. There had been earlier issues devoted to special topics. But not one of its 56 predecessors had focused as Issue 57 did in 2007 on the heart of development awareness, commitment and practice. The experiences described there inspire and disturb. They challenge us professionally, institutionally and personally. They show that, quietly, something with immense promise has been happening and gathering momentum. They drive us to ask how much immersions could transform the quality of what is done in the name of development.*[1]

What are we talking about?

Immersions can take many forms. There is no template or formula. Some are self-organized or even spur-of-the-moment. Some are organized with a programme. Some are open-ended for experiential learning; others are thematic, designed to focus on and learn about a topic or sector. Some are personal and individual. Others more usually are in groups. An almost universal feature is, though, staying in a poor community, as a person, living with a host family, helping with tasks and sharing in their life. This can be for any number of days or nights, often between one and ten, with three or four perhaps most common. The overnight stay is vital for relationships, experience, and relaxed conversations after dark and talking into the night. Even when immersions are thematic, they are usually quite open-ended. There may be activities like working with and helping the family, listening and dialogue, learning a life history, keeping a reflective diary or trying to explain your work and its relevance, but the essence is to be open much of the time to the unplanned and unexpected, to live and be and relate as a person. The unplanned incident is so often the most striking, moving and significant. Much is experienced and learnt, but what that will be is hard to predict.

For all this the term *immersion* has come to be used: the visitor is immersed in daily life, having left behind her baggage of role, organization and importance, and staying days and nights in a community. There is room for other related activities and ways to express them. For Sida in Bangladesh (Jupp et al.) *reality check* is used for a listening study that gathers information from structured dialogues with poor people (see p. 173). Different activities and expressions are fine as long as we say how we are using them. In this editorial, I shall stick to *immersion*, including within that term activities with other names

---

1. PLA 57 can be accessed at http://pubs.iied.org/pdfs/14558IIED.pdf. Names in brackets in this section refer to contributions to PLA 57, the contents of which are in the appendix on pages 179–80.

such as *EDPs* – immersions of the Exposure and Dialogue Programme (Hilgers) and Ashish Shah's (Shah) *reality check* of 'checking your work, ideology and practice against the realities that poor citizens face.'

A gathering momentum

Immersions have been evolving quietly and gathering momentum. The build up has been slow but steady. Antecedents include the participant observation of social anthropologists. During recent decades, more and more organizations have promoted and adopted immersions. Some of the more visible and prominent ones are represented in PLA 57.

The major early initiative was taken by Karl Osner who pioneered the Exposure and Dialogue Programme (EDP). Since 1985 there had by mid-2010 been 80 EDPs in 20 host countries with 1,364 participants (German parliamentarians, senior officials, leaders of NGOs and the private sector, aid agency and government staff…) in 20 host countries in Latin America, Asia, Africa, Europe and the former Soviet Union. For more than a decade SEWA (the Self-employed Women's Association), a very large trade union of poor women in India, has been hosting EDPs for others. After he became President of the World Bank in 1995, James Wolfensohn introduced immersions as part of the Harvard executive development programme for senior staff at the World Bank. The EDP, SEWA and World Bank streams came together in Ravi Kanbur's seminal immersion when he was leading the preparation of the World Development Report 2000 on development and poverty (Kanbur).

Others have been active. In Sweden, the Global School has for years had a programme of six annual Global Journeys each for 20–25 teachers with 10 days with a rural family in various countries including Bangladesh facilitated by the national NGO Proshika (Kramsjo). In several countries including India and Kenya, staff of ActionAid International have over the years practised immersions and now organize them for others. Among bilateral donors, a few DFID staff have taken part. SDC pioneered an intensive form of participatory research for staff in Tanzania, living and working with a very poor family for a day (SDC, 2003; Jupp, c.2004). Sida for a time took the lead: with senior staff backing, Sida officially endorsed and promoted immersions for its staff (Nilsson et al.). But Sida's new leadership has not followed through, and it is now DFID that looks set to lead the field. Before the 2010 general election in the UK, the Conservative party published a Green Paper of policies it would introduce with this paragraph:

> The present government has been criticised by the National Audit Office for failing to ensure that DFID staff spend time in rural areas, where many poor people live. We will introduce 'poverty immersions', similar to those of the World Bank and the Swedish development agency SIDA. DFID staff in poor countries will spend a week living with a poor family, sharing their experiences, listening to their views and learning from their

insights. Senior London-based members of DFID will also be expected to undertake such immersions. We are working with the world's poorest; we must understand their lives in order to serve them well.

What immersions give

Some immersions have specific purposes. There are thematic immersions designed to focus on one sector or aspect of development, sometimes with organized programmes. There are immersions used for:

- project monitoring (Isa)
- familiarization in a new post, as when ActionAid India organized one for a newly arrived British High Commissioner
- experiential realism as part of a conference, as organized by SEWA for WIEGO (Women in Informal Employment: Globalizing and Organizing)
- the selection, induction, and capacity building of staff in India by a movement (SEWA) (Nanavaty) and by NGOs (Kumar and Haridarkee, PRADAN HRD Unit; Shroff)
- programme development at the community level as by Plan Bangladesh (Yakub and Islam)
- systematically and regularly learning about and keeping in touch with local realities by sector and how they are changing (Jupp with others; Sida, 2008, 2009, 2010)

This last is a major breakthrough initiated by Sida in Bangladesh as a way of keeping in touch and up-to-date with ground realities in primary education and primary healthcare, sector programmes which Sida supports. Fifteen participants spend five days and four nights with the same poor family each year in the same season and informally meet, discuss and observe. The three annual reports so far published (Sida, 2008, 2009, 2010) give remarkable, readable, credible, insightful and at times (to me) startling insights into change and its speed. AusAid has followed suit with education in Indonesia (AusAid, 2010).[1]

Agreement seems universal that immersions give insights and experiences that are not otherwise accessible. Those who participate learn in a personal way about people's lives, livelihoods and cultures and the conditions they experience. The world can be seen the other way round, from the perspective of people living in poverty. It is expressed in many ways and by many phrases – 'face to face' 'walking in their shoes' 'putting a face on poverty'… This ground truthing provides a touchstone to refer to, and a source of confidence and the conviction of authority based on personal experience. On her return to IDS Rosalind Eyben asked how discussions in a programme review connected with the lives of her hosts in a village in Ghana. This led her to make points she

---

1. A further Reality Check is proposed in 2011 in Mozambique

would not otherwise have made. Personal witness statements can often work to build up credibility and convincing ideas, communication and arguments (Nilsson et al.). Katy Oswald said that her immersion in China gave her:

> the confidence to talk about poverty in rural China with some personal authority. You often come up against people who are ignorant of the level of poverty that still exists in rural China and now, as well as referring to the statistics, I can refer to my own personal experience.

Quite often there are stark and startling insights and impacts. Ravi Kanbur had an immersion with SEWA in India as part of the preparation for the World Development Report 2000/2001 (World Bank, 2000) for which he was Task Manager. He spent three days in a remote village, Mohadi. Parents were keen for their children to learn to read and write but the schoolmaster only came once a month. But he turned up on the second day when he had heard there were visitors. He launched into a litany of the difficulties of teaching the village children whom he described as 'junglee' (from the jungle). This 'Master of Mohadi' incident, Kanbur wrote, 'encapsulated for me the gap between macro-level strategies and ground-level realities'. Later, immersion participants tried to make sense of what they had experienced. He wrote:

> Alongside the emotion of the experience (the quiet dignity of our host ladies, and the utter commitment of our SEWA facilitators, moved most of us to tears as we told our stories) we tried to analyse what we had seen and to relate it to the more conventional discourse on poverty reduction strategies. For my part, I tried to relate what I had seen to our proposed *World Development Report* themes of Empowerment, Security and Opportunity. These themes have considerable resonance in Basrabai's [his host lady's] life, but what also came out was the interrelationship between them and how one fed into another.

There have been many other cases of personal, professional and policy impact: Olof Sandkull and Goran Schill (2007) of Sida coming to realize through their immersion with a tsunami-affected family in Sri Lanka that in a 'second tsunami', of foreign funds, those who had lost most received least. Gary Fields (2007) revising his professional economist's view of the impacts on poor producers of the minimum wage; Leonard Okello in an HIV/AIDS-related immersion in Western Kenya who said 'I've learnt more about HIV/AIDS and its impact in the last 24 hours than I have in the last six years that AIDS affected my family'. I know of no case where someone has come back from an immersion without new insights and experiences that have affected them.

Major impact on policy is also noted. 'The experiences gained from the immersions made a crucial impact on the direction of the forthcoming country strategy, steering it towards a sharpened poverty focus and a commitment to participatory research (reality checks) as a means of gaining insights into the perspectives of people living in poverty' (Nilsson et al.).

All this is enough to justify immersions over and over again. If this were all, the case would already be overwhelming. But people repeatedly say they gained much more than just useful insights and knowledge. They stress, and often give more importance to, the experiential learning, the personal and emotional impact. This resonates with other expressed purposes. Fred Nunes writes that Jim Wolfensohn 'wanted managers who had heart as well as intellect'. The aim was to 'rekindle the staff's passion for poverty reduction'. Bo Kramsjo asks how thinking and intellectual shifts can happen without complete involvement. Goran Holmqvist (in Nilsson et al.) says that his immersions offered what he most hoped for 'an alternative way of learning, through emotional exposure rather than conventional intellect'; he had been given a 'gut feeling' of the life and perspectives of the people he lived with. John Samuel writes of his immersions as intense personal moments: 'They make me restless but hopeful. They disturb me deeply, but at the same time recharge me. More than anything they challenge me'. For Koy Thomson having the time and space for unlearning was important. For Taaka Awori:

> The immersion has helped me grow as a development practitioner, but more importantly as a person. It was a very different learning for me because I learnt experientially. In that sense, all of me was learning, not just my mind, as is usually the case. The immersion allowed me to stop analysing people living in poverty as objects of development, but rather just to be with them and allow the learning to emerge.

The best should not be the enemy of the good; and many immersions may not be such deep experiences, or so transformational. No one should feel they have somehow failed if their experiences seem less remarkable or moving than those described in this collection. Immersions can be serious but also inspiring, and can have their light side, with laughter, fun, singing and dancing. What matters, the accounts that follow suggest, is heart as well as mind, an open and learning frame of mind and being. For Qazi Azmat Isa 'Immersion allows profound learning'. Of the SDC participatory research with poor families in Tanzania, Dee Jupp wrote:

> The outcomes of the exercise were extraordinary. Not only was a wealth of insights into the life of poor households gathered, but the experience turned out to be transformational for many of the research team.

Why did immersions not take off earlier?

If these experiences mean so much, and can make such a difference, why have they not spread more and been more widely adopted? It seems so evident that they should be part of responsible personal and professional practice. They cost less than going to a workshop. They take little time – usually not more than a week. It is not as though most organizations lack money: training and capacity building funds for professional development are frequently underspent.

Three clusters of forces stand out.

The first is personal. It is easy to make excuses, especially being too busy with important work. There is time for a workshop, within our comfort zones, but not for an immersion which is outside, unfamiliar, threatening (Ruparel). For myself, I am reluctant to give up what is known, cosy, and controllable for the unknown, perhaps uncomfortable and uncontrollable. I fear behaving badly and making a fool of myself. And here I and others must thank Ravi Kanbur for his 'I don't think I want to go to that temple any more' (in Birch et al.): he asked twice to visit an inviting looking temple before realizing that his host family were excluded from the temple because they were lower caste. This makes it easier for me to acknowledge my own shameful mistake, so hurtful to our host lady in Gujarat, of going to bed instead of meeting the people who had come across the desert to meet us. And then there are other arguments that can be mustered: 'I know all about that. I grew up in a village (or slum). I don't have anything to learn about that' (Shah). Against this can be set the reflections of a participant in 'Views of the Poor' (Jupp, c.2004: 4):

> I thought I knew about village life as my roots are in the village and I still visit family in my village from time to time. But I know nothing about what it is like to be poor and how hidden this kind of poverty can be.

The second cluster of forces is institutional. These are so many: values and incentives that reward writing good memoranda and reports and speaking well in meetings with important people; and the low value given to listening to the unimportant poor. There are senior staff who regard immersions as frivolous, useless or voyeurism, and/or feel personally threatened by them. There are normal pressures of work and other perceived priorities. Bureaucratic culture looks inwards and upwards, not downwards and outwards.

A third force is rhetoric about development relations. For staff of lender and donor agencies, there has been the convenient political correctness of government ownership. For international NGOs there has been increasing reliance on the insights of partners who are supposedly close to poverty. To seek direct personal experience through immersions could then be thought of as untrusting and interfering.

These personal, institutional and rhetorical forces combine. Any organization or individuals who want excuses for not pressing for immersions have no difficulty finding them. It is not difficult, then, to understand why until recently effective demand for immersions has not been strong.

Why now?

The evidence and examples in *PLA* 57 make a strong case for immersions as standard practice for development professionals.[1] The case is stronger now than ever for three reasons.

---

1. See also Eyben (2004), Irvine et al. (2006) and ActionAid International (2011).

First, the conditions, awareness, priorities and aspirations of poor people are changing faster than ever before. Almost everywhere, social change is accelerating. There is a continuous and intensifying challenge to policy makers and practitioners to keep in touch and up to date.

Second, a new simplistic certainty has been infiltrating development thinking and practice. The downside of the Millennium Development Goals and of the inspiring movement to Make Poverty History, has been the belief that 'we know what needs to be done' (especially on the part of non-Africans about Africa) – and that the solution is more money. The issues are not so simple; nor in most cases are the solutions. For vital ground-truthing, immersions provide one means of checking against the complex and diverse realities of poor people.

Third, the grip of the urban offices, capital traps and elite activities has tightened – for government, aid agency and NGO staff alike: more and more emails, meetings, negotiations, reports, often with fewer staff; participation in the pandemic of incestuous workshops, many of them about poverty; donors' budget support, sector-wide programmes, and harmonization on policy issues, all of this in what Koy Thomson calls our 'self-referential universe'. Qazi Azmat Isa speaks for other agencies too when he notes that 'increasingly World Bank staff are confined to government departments in capital and provincial cities, removed from the reality of poverty and from our ultimate clients – the poor of the country'.

Immersions are means to offset these biases and trends: to keep up to date; to be in touch; to escape the self-referential trap. It is fitting and fortunate that they are rising fast on the agenda. They are now better understood, more talked about and easier to arrange. More organizations – EDP, SEWA, ActionAid International, Praxis, Proshika – are providing them for others. More people and more organizations are setting them up for themselves. The increasing numbers of those who have experienced immersions and the conviction, commitment and authority with which they can speak, encourage others. We appear to be approaching a tipping point of a critical mass of stories, buzz, communications and enthusiasm. Immersions are increasingly recognized as good professional practice that must be encouraged as more and more people are making them a regular practice (Kanbur, Fields, Samuel, Ruparel, Shah...)

So what?

The implications are quietly revolutionary. After reading others' experiences of immersions, we have to ask: what would have happened if the experiential learning and reflection of immersions and reality checks had been the norm of good practice of development professionals over past decades? Would the deprivations, suffering and death inflicted on poor people by structural adjustment have been perpetrated if those responsible had spent a few days and nights immersed in a poor affected community? Might those responsible have put a face and a person on the human price and sought other policies?

To be more realistically pro-poor, could there conceivably have been any more cost-effective use of their time than an immersion? The gratuitous suffering that might have been averted blows the mind.

And what about us, now?

What would those living in poverty want us to do? Would they, as Koy Thomson has asked 'express their amazement that people who are experts in poverty don't even bother to spend time with them'. As he observes 'For a development organization to see four days simply being with people living in poverty as a luxury is a sign of pathology'. The question is not whether the direct experiential learning of immersions and reality checks can be afforded. It is whether anyone in any organization committed to the MDGs, social justice and reducing poverty, can justify not affording and making space for them. Should they follow Goran Schill who began as a sceptic, and then after three nights with a tsunami-affected family exclaimed 'Everyone at Sida should do an immersion!'?

The cumulative evidence drives us, however reluctantly and with whatever discomfort, to see personal experiential learning, face-to-face, with those we seek to serve as a key missing link in development practice. Wriggle though we may, the conclusion, the message, is there: to be serious about poverty, we have to be serious about immersions.

This demands vision, leadership, guts and priority. It means that ministers,[1] permanent and principal secretaries, chief executives and senior managers, in aid agencies, governments, and NGOs must set examples through their own immersions and make space for others to do likewise. It means that organizations must make immersions policy and encourage staff to undertake them. It means that the time for them must be ring-fenced to avoid postponements or cancellations, and that resources must be made available. In sum, politically and as policy and practice, immersions have to be given priority.

So the final discomforting question is this. Can anyone make a credible case for not doing immersions? And if we cannot, what are we going to do about it?

Will we, can we, rise to the challenge and seize the opportunity? ? And if we do, more and more, might that over the years transform the quality of what we do and what happens in the name of development?[2]

---

1. Andrew Mitchell, the British Minister for Overseas Development, soon after taking office, himself set an example with an immersion organized by ActionAid Ethiopia, and the Permanent Secretary has done the same in India.
2. I am embarrassed to ask these questions when I do so few myself, and in March 2011 have been shamed and inspired by the example of Lenny Henry, Samantha Womack, Reggie Yates and Angela Rippon whose immersion for three days and nights in Kibera in Nairobi, during which they had to work and earn the money for living, was the subject of a much-praised BBC television programme.

The World Development Report: concepts, content and a chapter 12

World Development Report (WDR) process set new standards for openness and consultation. Its concepts and content are a major advance on its 1990 predecessor. The intention that its concepts and content should be influenced by Voices of the Poor *was partly fulfilled. Conceptually, the* Voices of the Poor *(Narayan et al., 2006) findings support the multidimensional view of poverty as 'pronounced deprivation of well-being', and the use of income-poverty to describe what is only one dimension of poverty (though this welcome usage is not consistent throughout in the WDR). Two concepts or analytical orientations were not adopted: powerlessness and disadvantage seen as a multidimensional interlinked web; and livelihoods. On content, three areas where the influence fell short were: how the Police persecute and impoverish poor people; the diversity of the poorest people; and the significance of the body as the main but vulnerable and indivisible asset of many poor people.*

A weakness of the WDR is its lack of critical self-awareness. Chapter 11 is self-serving for the International Financial Institutions: it lumps loans with grants as concessional finance; it makes liberal use of the term donor, but never lender; and it does not consider debt avoidance as a strategy. The Report ends abruptly, a body without a head. Its multidimensional view of poverty is not matched by a multidimensional view of power and responsibility. A Chapter 12 is crying out to be written. This would confront issues of professional, institutional and personal commitment and change. It would stress critical reflection as a professional norm, disempowerment for democratic diversity as institutional practice, and personal values, attitudes and courageous behaviour as primary and crucial if development is to be change that is good for poor people. A new conclusion is suggested for the WDR, and a title for the World Development Report 2010.

The WDR 2000/01 is a major advance on WDR 1990. Like the Bible,[1] it is long and diverse enough to be a cornucopia of quotations with which to agree or disagree. And like the Bible, its length (204 double column large pages) makes it hazardous to assert that a particular point is not supported or made in it somewhere. What follows is a selective personal view, with no pretence to be comprehensive. Some achievements and limitations of the WDR will be reviewed in terms of process, concepts and content, examining the words used in the report and asking to what extent the realities and voices of poor people may have had an influence.

For useful comments on a draft of this article I am grateful to Karen Brock, Simon Maxwell and Howard White. The usual disclaimers apply.
1. I owe this analogy to Mick Moore.

Process

The open process. The way the drafts were shared on the internet, including the first outline as early as January 1999, and the electronic debates which were encouraged and took place, set new standards for openness and participation for which Ravi Kanbur, as director of the team, and those who supported him, deserve high praise. True, many could not and did not take part: the medium was the internet to which many did not have access; and the words were numerous, deterring those with little time. All the same, an important precedent of openness and consultation was set. The chapter a week, e-discussion hosted, moderated and summarized by the Bretton Woods Project received contributions in English, French and Spanish, with weekly summaries in all three languages, and was a model to inform and inspire future debates.

Voices of the Poor. From the inception of the report, it was intended that the voices of poor people should be heard and the realities they expressed should influence the WDR. Three initiatives were undertaken: a search for, and review of, participatory studies of poverty by Karen Brock, at the Institute of Development Studies, Sussex published as *A Review of Participatory Work on Poverty and Ill-being* (Brock, 1999); an analysis of Participatory Poverty Assessments by a team at Cornell University under the direction of Deepa Narayan published as *Voices of the Poor: Can Anyone Hear Us?* (Narayan et al., 2000a); and the Consultations with the Poor undertaken in some 272 sites in 23 countries, published as *Voices of the Poor: Crying Out for Change* (Narayan et al., 2000b). The Cornell and Consultations studies taken together have come to be known as *Voices of the Poor* (VOP).

These studies were without precedent in their combination of range, their participatory nature, and the intention that they should influence the WDR. In the words of the Process Guide (World Bank, 1999) for the Consultations:

> The purpose of the Consultations with the Poor study is to enable a wide range of poor people in diverse countries and conditions to share their views in such a way that they can inform and contribute to the concepts and content of the WDR 2000/01.

Concepts

The main text of the WDR opens with the dramatic and conceptually radical sentence: 'Poverty is pronounced deprivation of well-being.' This does not just broaden the old reductionism of poverty defined as low income or consumption. It does not just add other dimensions. It goes further. It makes every dimension of human experience which can be considered deprivation of well-being potentially relevant. Further, it provokes the question: who defines well-being and deprivations of well-being? In the Consultations, it was poor people who were invited, through participatory analysis, to express their ideas of well-being and ill-being, of the good life and of the bad (see Narayan et al., 2000b chapters 1 and 2). Did these ideas influence the WDR?

To what extent the multidimensionality stressed in the WDR was influenced by the *Voices of the Poor* is difficult to assess. Of the six boxes in the WDR which present evidence from the VOP, those most relevant to multidimensionality are the first three: Box 1 *The voices of the poor*, Box 1.1 *Poverty in the voices of poor people*, and Box 1.4 *Measuring voice and power using participatory methods*. These include such aspects as powerlessness, suffering rudeness and humiliation, anxiety and having bad feelings about oneself. More generally, other words and concepts widely used in the WDR resonate with and are supported by the VOP. Most obviously these include empowerment, security, vulnerability and assets.

The radical flip implied by defining poverty as 'pronounced deprivation of well-being' is framed and supported by much of the structure and language of the WDR in the sections on empowerment, security, and opportunity. The word ill-being appears several times[1] as a newcomer to the development lexicon. It is commendable and encouraging that the reductionism of much past analysis is recognized by using the term 'income-poverty' where the reference is to that dimension of poverty measured as income or consumption. This is sustained, almost valiantly, through the first pages and tables of Chapter 1, but the effort was evidently too much for the authors (or editors). From page 18 onwards they fall from grace and largely lapse into the old usage, for example in Box 1.8 'Tracking poverty in India during the 1990s'. For all that, by emphasizing and elaborating multidimensionality, and by adding its authority to establishing the terms income-poverty and income-poor, the WDR reaffirms and consolidates a conceptual ratchet effect from which it would be difficult now to go back, even if the mindsets of many in Washington remain largely unaffected.

In two respects the WDR could have gone further conceptually in the light the findings and analysis of the Consultations.

First, analysis of the Consultations sources drove the authors of *Crying Out for Change* to identify a web of disadvantage, powerlessness and ill-being (see e.g. Narayan et al., 2000b: 249[2]). Beyond the old vicious circle of poverty, ignorance and disease, and beyond the interactions of the five dimensions (Narayan et al., 1999: 5) of:

- material poverty
- physical weakness
- bad social (including gender) relations
- insecurity and vulnerability
- powerlessness

other linkages were identified with:

- places of the poor – isolated, risky, unserviced and stigmatized
- livelihoods and assets – precarious, seasonal and inadequate

---

1. "Ill-being" is used, for example, on pages 3,16,18,and 29.
2. See page 61.

- incapabilities – lack of information, education, skills and confidence
- institutions – disempowering and excluding
- weak and disconnected organizations of the poor
- behaviours – disregard and abuse by those with more power and wealth

Together these were seen as connected in a many stranded web.

Multidimensionality in the perspective of a linked web does more than just add dimensions: it points to their interconnections, and how each compounds others. This concept of a web is not to be found in the WDR.

Second, in the WDR old categories and mindsets of traditional economics do persist, or to put it more generously, provide continuity. The discourse is about work and jobs: there is 'an urgent need to get countries into dynamic *job*-creating development paths' (WDR: 76, my italics). It is hardly at all about livelihoods. This is despite livelihood, recognizing a diversity of sources of food, income and other resources, being broader and closer to the realities of most poor people than employment in jobs, and despite sustainable livelihoods being well established now as both concept and practical tool for analysis and action. Half of Brock's (1999) monograph[1] is concerned with managing livelihoods. *Crying Out for Change* has a whole chapter on 'The Struggle for Livelihoods' (Narayan et al., 2000b: 46–70). Livelihoods are implied in parts of the WDR, but the concept is not adopted and the word rarely used.

Content

The extent to which quotations and insights from the *Voices of the Poor* were incorporated in the report must surely help to shift the development discourse further towards listening to poor people, learning from them, and respecting their realities and priorities. 30 quotations stand out at the heads of sections of the Report, highlighted in green. Of the six boxes derived from the *Voices of the Poor*, the latter three:

2.1 On interacting with state institutions: the voices of the poor
5.4 Locked out by health and education fees, and
6.1 Poor people are often harassed by public officials

point in painful detail to areas where changes in policy and in the behaviour of officials could make a big difference to the well-being of poor people. These put a foot in the door, opening the way for the behaviour and attitudes of those with power to move to the centre of the development agenda.

That said, there are three notable areas where the WDR could have picked up more on insights from the *Voices of the Poor*, and from the Consultations in particular:

- *The Police*. From the time when the earliest Consultations site reports came in it was evident that the Police were often a problem for poor

---

1.   It is a strange omission that Karen Brock's work, although published by the World Bank, is not cited in the voluminous references to the WDR.

people. There were exceptions, like the Superintendent of Constant Spring Police Station in Kingston, Jamaica, and the Police in Sri Lanka generally. Commonly, though, the Police were reported to persecute and exploit poor people in many ways. The India National Synthesis Report (PRAXIS, 1999: 35) had a box 'Police: a Licensed Evil?': 15 out of 18 groups of poor people in India were said to have considered Police to be a burden on society. Over four pages (162–6) of *Crying Out for Change* present evidence of abuses by Police. Police reform came out as a very high priority for pro-poor policies. Yet this is barely mentioned in the WDR. 'Honest police and a fair legal system' are one of eight factors noted as reducing vulnerability for poor people (WDR: 37). Also 'An effective modern police force is needed to maintain order by enforcing the law, dealing with potentially disorderly situations, and attending to citizens in distress' (ibid.: 103). But these passing observations come nowhere near the radical Police reform that so many poor people implied was needed.

- *The Diversity of the Bottom Poor.* The Consultations identified a diverse group of people whose multiple disadvantages made them more than just poor. The WDR does refer to the poorest of the poor (e.g. on pages 145–6,154,156) but perhaps it could have gone further. It mentions for example people with disabilities, widows and the elderly. Besides these others were identified in the Consultations – women divorced or deserted by their husbands, the physically weak, the mentally disturbed, orphans, street children, the homeless, sex workers, scavengers, beggars, drug addicts, the chronically sick, those who are very old, poor and isolated, those who in desperation steal to survive, and the very, very poor or destitute.[1] These marginal and often unseen people, many of them forced to live on the fringes of the law, were estimated in most of the Consultations sites to have increased in the past decade. It is their *diversity*, and the diversity of the challenges which they present that the WDR could have gone further in recognizing.
- *The Body as Asset.* The Consultations illustrated the importance of the body as the main asset of many of the poorest (Narayan et al., 2000b: chapter 5). As an asset it can flip, through sickness or accident, from being major asset to major liability: whoever is injured or ill cannot work and earn, but has to be fed, and most treatment is costly. This insight is a commonplace of the experience of many poor people. Chapter 5 of the WDR on expanding poor people's assets and tackling inequalities does deal with health, and chapter 8, on helping poor people manage risk, does discuss injury and illness, the importance of preventive health measures, and the potentials of health insurance. But

---

1. I do not imply that none of these are mentioned in the WDR. The point is about the *diversity* of the bottom poor.

neither goes all the way in recognizing the body as the most precious, and yet vulnerable and indivisible, *asset* of many poor people.

The irony and evasions of Chapter 11

In its early incarnation, the draft of the WDR had 10 chapters. The authors were challenged to add a Chapter 11 on Professional, Institutional and Personal Commitment and Change, as being necessary if the report were to go beyond rhetoric and make a real difference in the world. In declining the challenge, the whimsical point was put that in the United States Chapter Eleven is the law on insolvency. Any chapter 11 in the WDR would carry this unfortunate, if culturally specific, stigma by association. The final version of the WDR found a fitting solution. An earlier chapter was added to the Report. So the former Chapter 10 became 11, and it was international aid and debt that acquired the aura of insolvency.

One has to admire the skilfully evasive choice and use of words and categories in this last chapter. The words 'grants' (twice) and 'loans' (four times) appear only in the context of rescheduling debt (pages 202 and 203). Nowhere else are grants and loans distinguished or the words even used. They must have been ruled out of order. Nor can I find any indication that World Bank or IMF loans can be for purposes other than rescheduling debt. Instead of loans, we read repeatedly of 'donor funds', 'aid money', 'resource flows', 'concessional funds', 'concessional financing' and 'concessional assistance'. All these terms conflate grants which do not put countries in debt and loans which do, however concessional they may be. Similarly, the word 'lender', which one might suppose would describe Banks which make loans, is never used. Anyone coming fresh to this subject could be forgiven for supposing that the World Bank and the IMF were givers not lenders. With rigorous consistency the discourse is couched in terms of 'donor' and 'donors' (words used over 100 times in the chapter). It is scarcely necessary to point out that in common usage and understanding a donor is a person who gives or who makes donations. Anyone in Washington who characterized money-lenders in developing countries as donors could expect howls of derision. But then consistency is rarely a vice of the powerful.

The treatment of debt presents further evasions. There is no acknowledgement that lenders might bear any responsibility for bad loans. The loaded term 'debt forgiveness' has been avoided (for who forgives who?) but 'debt relief' which is 'granted' (page 203) is common. Frequently, though, the more neutral 'debt reduction' is the usage. The importance is recognised of ensuring that countries that receive debt relief do not have policies that will lead them deeply into debt again but this does not go as far as mentioning, let alone stressing, the responsibilities of lenders to minimize lending. 'Debt avoidance' is not mentioned or considered as a strategy.

A clue to understanding this omission can be found in Box 7.10 which refers to 'Breaking the grip of moneylenders...', concluding that 'powerful vested interests can be expected to mobilize against reforms that seek to erode their position in the name of poor people. Development researchers, policymakers and practitioners must recognize these tensions and respond appropriately'. We can ask: as moneylenders, are the World Bank and the IMF also powerful vested interests? Do development researchers, policymakers and practitioners, including those of the World Bank and IMF themselves, recognize these tensions? Do they respond appropriately?[1]

Good dentists undermine their livelihoods by promoting dental hygiene. Should good lenders do the same with debt hygiene? But then that would be self-destructive. So lenders are donors, and loans and grants alike are concessional assistance. Bank staff sustain their livelihoods by labelling. By calling Christmas vegetarian, the powerful turkeys survive.

Self-critical reflection and a Chapter 12

As chapter 11 illustrates, self-critical reflection is not a consistent feature of the WDR. As a critic I must also examine myself, and recognize, and try to offset, drives within myself which distort the lenses with which I see the WDR, the World Bank and the IMF: for example, the twinges of mischievous glee I felt in writing the two paragraphs above. More generally and seriously, I believe that extreme power is disabling, and that the World Bank and IMF are victims of their power (see e.g. Chambers, 1997: 97–100). In contrast, the WDR, under the direction of Ravi Kanbur until he resigned, broke new ground in transparency and consultation. Perhaps it went as far as it could at the time.

Still, there could have been more critical reflection. At the outset the Report might have maintained an acknowledgement of the wide diversity of sincerely held views about how to fight poverty and then gone on to ask:

'How do such widely different – and often strongly held – views arise when the common objective is poverty reduction? The answer is that people differ in their understanding of poverty and its causes. Critical reflection and self-awareness suggest that personality, social background, education, profession,

---

1. Differences between poor people borrowing from moneylenders and poor countries borrowing from the World Bank and the IMF are several. The concessionality of IDA loans, including their long moratoria and low interest rates, stands out. This reinforces the point about vested interests. Poor people borrowing at high rates suffer immediately. In contrast, with the Banks' loans, borrowers as well as lenders can be big gainers – politicians, officials, and contractors as well as the Banks and Bank staffers. Unless the uses of the loans are very good, and neither grants nor revenue were available, the losers are future generations. They may suffer as so many do today from the big and often bad loans of past decades. Is there more than whimsy in an appeal of the Banks to poor countries which runs:

    We urge you not to think about tomorrow
    To prosper we must lend, so you must borrow
        Take big loans in a rush
        With money you'll be flush
    Bequeath the debt to be your children's sorrow.

organisational culture, and personal interests and mindsets all contribute to the formation of views. No analyst or observer is immune. Nor is anyone likely to be completely correct or completely wrong. Our current understanding is that the realities of poverty are multidimensional, complex, diverse and dynamic. So too are the perceptions of those realities. The best way forward to better understanding and practice is then a self-doubting pluralism. This is to be aware of, reflect on and offset personal and professional predispositions and biases, and to invite and be open to other perspectives. Among the perspectives that inform this Report, and of crucial significance, are those of poor people themselves. It is then in an open and pluralist spirit that this report has been undertaken, beginning with a discussion of poverty and its measurement...'

To conclude the Report, a chapter 12 could and should still be written. This would confront the issues of power, and the professional, institutional and personal commitment and change needed for the recommendations of the WDR to bite and make a difference in the real, messy world. But even without or before a chapter 12, the present chapter 11 could be given a conclusion. It ends in the air, as if space had suddenly run out, a body missing its head. Other development professionals may wish to reflect on what conclusion they would give the Report. My final paragraphs would be as follows:

'The international community has set ambitious goals for poverty reduction. The framework for national action and international cooperation outlined in this Report can help make these goals a reality. We must not fail.

To succeed demands action. In itself this Report will make no difference to poor people. To translate it into policy, and into practice on the ground, requires professional, institutional and personal commitment and change. Professionally, this means critical epistemological awareness, examining and reflecting on how power, wealth, knowledge and beliefs are related. It means an open and evolving pluralism, valuing the multiple perspectives and realities of others, especially those of poor people. Institutionally, it means decentring and decontrolling for democratic diversity, transforming top-down hierarchies of domination into cultures of participatory interaction which empower. Personally, it means self-critical reflection, with continual learning and unlearning, changing behaviour and attitudes, and courageous commitment to action. It means recognizing personal values, responsibility and action as primary and crucial if development is to be change that is good for poor people. Professions, organizations and persons with power and wealth, in all countries and contexts, are then profoundly challenged. There is an opportunity to seize. We need not fail. The question is whether, as individuals and together, we have the vision, guts and will to change and make things change. It is whether in actions, not just words, we can and will resolutely put poor people first. Future generations will be our judge.'

Why did the authors and editors of the Report not end on such a note? It was suggested. Would it, perhaps, have pointed too clearly to our personal and collective hypocrisies? Do we now have to wait until 2010 for the next WDR on Poverty and Development to focus on *'us'*, the powerful, the less poor, the wealthy? With attention not only to the needs of have-nots, but more potently to the greed of haves? On how *we* need to change? On pedagogies for *us*, the non-oppressed, or as some would say, the oppressors? On professional, institutional and personal disempowerment and change? Could the Voices of the Poor be followed now by Choices of the Rich? Could the deprivations of poverty and powerlessness confront the responsibilities of wealth and power? Dare we hope then for a new reflective self-critical awareness and a redefinition of the goal of development as responsible well-being for and by all, stressing the well-being of the poor and weak, and the responsibilities of the rich and strong? And could this lead to:

WORLD DEVELOPMENT REPORT 2010: CHALLENGING WEALTH AND POWER

But then, why wait until 2010?

Postscript

Time flies. We are into 2011 as I write, and no one has produced this report. In the meantime, the greed of bankers for bonuses in the UK and elsewhere almost passes understanding, continuing moreover after massive bail-outs by the taxpayer. Written in a novel, this might have been dismissed as a dismal fantasy. But no, it has happened, and is but one example of the many dimensions in many countries where inequalities continue to magnify.

It is sobering to set this against the impeccable research and argument of Wilkinson and Pickett in *The Spirit Level: Why more equal societies almost always do better* (2009). They have found that the curves for both happiness and life expectancy flatten off at around $25,000 per capita. Well-being is then related to inequality. To quote:

> Across whole populations, rates of mental illness are five times higher in the most unequal compared to the least unequal societies. Similarly, in more unequal societies people are five times as likely to be imprisoned, six times as likely to be clinically obese, and murder rates may be many times higher. The reason why these differences are so big is, quite simply, because the effects of inequality are not confined just to the least well-off: instead they affect the vast majority of the population.

So it is not a zero sum. It is a tragedy of the commons. It is in the interests of all that our societies should be more equal. From greater equality, everyone benefits. To enhance human well-being, economic growth remains vital in the poorer countries. In countries that are better off, the path to a better life for all is not more economic growth but more equality. So today the case for that World Development Report is stronger than ever. It is needed urgently now!

Development paradigms: neo-Newtonian and adaptive pluralism

Paradigm can be defined as a coherent and mutually supporting pattern of:

- concepts and ontological[1] assumptions
- values and principles
- methods, procedures and processes
- roles and behaviours
- relationships
- mindsets, orientations and predispositions.[2]

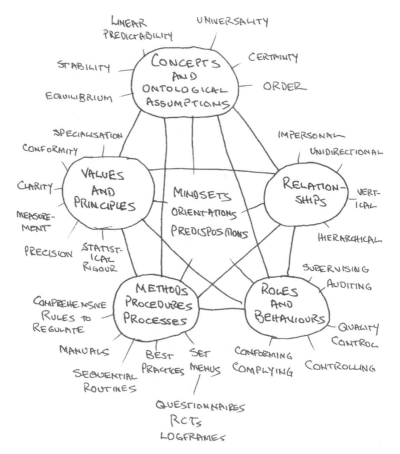

Figure 4.2 Elements in a paradigm of neo-Newtonian practice

---

1. Ontology refers to the nature of things and being
2. For a fuller treatment and argument see my paper *Paradigms, poverty and adaptive pluralism*, Working Paper, 334 IDS, 2010.

The polarized paradigms of things and of people (see ZOPP pp. 111–118) can be evolved into paradigms of neo-Newtonian practice (from things) and adaptive pluralism (from people). Rather than elaborate these, let me invite you to examine and critically reflect on the figures. They are on opposite pages to make comparisons easy to see, reflect on, disagree with, and change.

The neo-Newtonian paradigm has always been powerfully present in development practice. To a degree it weakened in the 1990s and adaptive pluralism had more space to flourish. But then its pervasive and persistent magnetism reasserted itself. Perhaps this should not be surprising. For it is the paradigm of normal professionalism in engineering, in medical research,

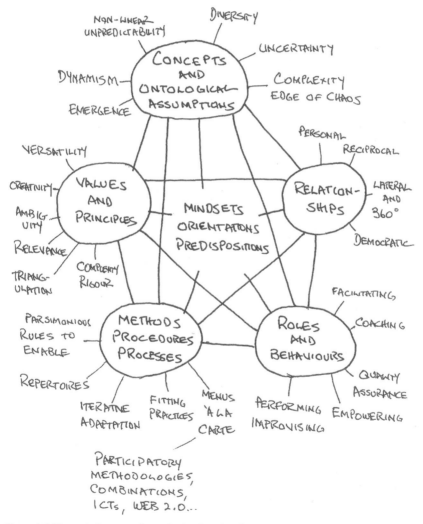

Figure 4.3 Elements in a paradigm of adaptive pluralism

in economics, in digital technology and in laboratories round the world. 'Measurement matters' blurs regressively into 'What is measured is what matters' and then 'If it can't be measured, it can't be important', 'If it can't be measured it isn't real', and finally 'If it isn't measured it won't happen'.[1] This is the basic paradigm of the logframe and of results-based management (RBM), of top-down targets, of 'upward' accountability to those with the power to allocate funds – donors, lenders, INGOs, parliaments, Ministries of Finance, auditors, watchdogs of one sort or another. It is the paradigm of hierarchical control-oriented Weberian bureaucracy, of Taylorism and Fordism in which people have to be machines, of silver bullets, of simple preset solutions, of one-size fits all, of Henry Ford's mass-produced production line Model T.

Long Live the Model T (see notes at the end for explanations)

Old Henry Ford the First, now dead
Reputedly, while living, said
Americans should never lack
Their Model T, so long as black

This way of acting still persists
Professionals are reductionists
while bureaucrats embrace the norm
that programmes should be uniform*

The poor are look-alikes and weak
We know their needs. They need not speak
Our mass production's sure to please
Let's make our programmes Model Ts

To help the poor from high above
Takes more than charity and love
We'll motivate them well to try
To want what we plan to supply

(The rich are different and nice
for they have cash to pay our price
we listen, keen to hear their voice
and give them wide Toyota choice)

---

1. This was a heading in a workshop report. Surely ironic, I thought. But no, experience suggested it was probably serious.

*   And teachers tend to standardize
    'Our lecture notes we'll not revise'
    Obedient students have to please
    becoming regular Model Ts

The World Bank, highest of us all
Looks down to see poor people small
Like atoms all the same, a size
For which it's right to standardize

In Benor's model T and V
Conveyor belt machinery
Presents its stock delivery
Of packages by TOT

Your field's eroding with the rain?
It's gullied? We will doze it plain
Then plant the grass that you prefer
As long as it is Vetiver

You irrigating farmers may
Distribute water any way
You like, weeklong, including Sunday
As long as it is *warabandi*

You're landless, deep in debt, and poor?
IRDP will lend you more
Choose any asset that you know
As long as it's a buffalo

You want to grow trees on your land?
We have the seedlings right at hand
Plant what you like, all trees the same
As long as Eucalypt's its name

And if the package does not fit
No matter. We can handle it
Reports are doctored, visits planned
The good we see; the bad is banned

For many years yet, I believe,
Psychotic States will self-deceive
Historically Ford's Model T
Achieved sustainability

But don't despair. However long
We have to wait Henry was wrong.
History's not bunk. His public's voice
Insisted that it wanted choice

Enough, it said, of Model Ts
Give us variety, if you please
Today Toyota timely, topical
Colours cars kaleidoscopical

So act for change. The world awaits
reversals for psychotic States
In search of long-term therapy
seek truth, trust and diversity

'Model T', is a reference to the Ford Model T motorcar of which Henry Ford is supposed to have said something like 'Americans can have their Model T any colour they like as long as it is black.' T and V was the Training and Visit system of agricultural extension imperiously promoted in many developing countries through World Bank loans and now of only historical interest. TOT refers to the transfer of technology approach to development. Vetiver grass was at one time widely recommended by the World Bank in many countries. Warabandi is a rigid system of weekly water distribution the Indian Government sought to introduce on a huge scale. The IRDP is the Integrated Rural Development Programme in India, a favourite asset in which was the milch buffalo. Stands of eucalyptus were at one time very widely promoted on farms in India. And Henry Ford did eventually produce cars in different colours.

Paradigms, lock-ins and liberations

A lock-in is a paradigmatic syndrome in which there is strong mutually-supporting inflexibility.[1] The neo-Newtonian paradigm shows some such rigidity. And that sounds bad. But there is nothing inherently bad about it. Neo-Newtonian practices are needed for much engineering and for much financial accounting. The neo-Newtonian paradigm has good applications in much physical, medical and scientific research. In appropriate contexts it is effective, often dramatically so. If it were limited to where it works and makes sense, there would be little problem. But precisely because it is so effective in some contexts and for some purposes, and because those whose training, mindsets and practice have given them that orientation are often both powerful and confident (and sometimes unreflexive), the neo-Newtonian colonizes domains that are non-linear, unpredictable and diverse, where it does not fit and where instead the non-linear unpredictabilities of complexity science apply. And it is these domains that prevail in most development practice. The challenge is to find, adopt and adapt better alternatives.

Let us examine two examples of paradigmatic lock-ins which have been comprehensively turned on their heads to create new counter-intuitive, counter-commonsense, syndromes of startling potency. They raise questions about what Donald Rumsfeld famously described as 'unknown unknowns'.[2] Looking back at the lock-ins which they have transformed, they can be seen as liberations.

The first liberation concerns rice cultivation and the second rural sanitation.

The rice plant can tolerate flooding, but grows better in mainly aerobic conditions.[3] Farmers flood their fields to control weeds, substituting water for labour. Scientists have taken this as a norm. Conventional paddy growing practices are relatively management sparing. Seedlings are grown in a flooded seed bed, uprooted quite roughly when 21–40 days old and transplanted by being pushed down in clumps of 3, 4 or more into flooded, puddled soil, either in lines or at random and close together. Fields are then kept flooded throughout the growing cycle.

---

1. There is some analogy with a strange attractor in complexity science, where a pattern is inescapably repeated with minor variations.
2. This provokes reflection on extending the following (questionable on several grounds) saying: he who knows not, and knows not that he knows not, is a fool, shun him; he who knows not, and knows that he knows not, is a child, teach him; he who knows and knows that he knows, is a wise man, hear him; he who knows and knows not that he knows, is a prophet, follow him. The contemporary extension might be: She or he who knows that she or he does not know what she or he does not know is a seeker, fund her or him. Providing she or he has commitment, energy, creativity, realism, a significant concern and some credibility.
3. I am proud to be able to name drop by mentioning that my former colleague, B.P Ghildyal, with whom I worked closely in the Ford Foundation, Delhi, was an author of a research paper that established this some four to five decades ago. As so often with seminal research, its significance was not recognized.

The System of Rice Intensification (SRI)[1] simultaneously changes all these practices. Seedlings when still very young and small, 8–12 days old, are transplanted carefully (the principle is TLC – tender loving care), 1–2 plants per hill and widely spaced in a square pattern: this reduces plant population by two-thirds or more. The paddy soil is kept moist with mostly aerobic conditions, with intermittent applications of light irrigation. Manual push-weeders control weeds and churn up and aerate the soil. There are many benefits and few disbenefits from this set of practices: plants are supported above ground by more extensive longer-lived root systems, are stronger and healthier and more resistant to pests and diseases and to drought and storms, and produce many more tillers (each of which bears a head of grains) which also give better outturns in milling. Across many rice varieties, on-farm evaluations in eight countries found yields raised by an average of 47 per cent, with water savings averaging 40 per cent.[2] Costs of production per hectare were reduced by 23 per cent and farmers' net income per hectare was boosted by 68 per cent.

Traditional rice research, notably that of the International Rice Research Institute (IRRI), has been locked into a paradigm of crop improvement through breeding higher-yielding varieties, responsive to chemical fertilizer, and dependent on large amounts of water for flooding.[3] This genocentric strategy led to the Green Revolution. There have been other successes particularly with some disease resistance, and recently with developments in GM breeding for beta-carotene (for Vitamin A).[4] But despite huge investments there have been no broad improvements which work with all varieties equivalent to those with SRI management. Nor which bring such multiple benefits. SRI is a green revolution of a different sort.

---

1. See the Cornell website http://sri.ciifad.cornell.edu and the India one www.sri-india.net A recent source for SRI which lists source materials and videos is Africare, OXFAM America, and WWF-Icrisat Project *More Rice for People, More Water for the Planet* (Africare, Oxfam America, 2010). I am grateful to Norman Uphoff for personal communications on which some of the text of this section is based. As ever, responsibility for any errors is mine.
2. The range of yield increases in on-farm evaluations in eight countries was 17–105 per cent with an average of 47, with water savings between 24 and 50 per cent with an average of 40. The Ciifad Cornell website (June 2011) summarizes as follows: The benefits of SRI, which have been demonstrated in over 40 countries… include: increased yield (50–100% or more), a reduction in seed requirements (up to 90%) and water savings (50% or more). Many SRI users also report a reduction in pests, diseases, grain shattering, unfilled grains and lodging. As a climate-smart agricultural methodology, additional environmental benefits stem from the reduction of agricultural chemicals, water use and methane emissions that contribute to global warming.
3. Recent research has re-focused on alternative wetting and drying to reduce water requirements but the strategy remains preoccupied with breeding for varietal improvement.
4. On GM I am an uneasy agnostic. I believe extreme caution is right and hold to the Precautionary Principle (see Chambers, 2005: 23–5). The apparent or real irreversibility of GM is daunting. Counterbalancing the dangers in that, if thousands of children who would have died from Vitamin A deficiency will live as a result of GM, one can ask: who is willing to sign their death warrant by default? But it is not so simply polarized. There are alternatives…Sitting on a fence hurts a sensitive area…

Turning to rural sanitation, the conventional approach worldwide has had two thrusts: first, to teach and educate, seeking to induce changes in behaviour (software); and second, to subsidize the installation of facilities (hardware) designed by engineers. The reasoning has been that poor people need to be taught the importance of hygienic behaviour, and that they deserve decent sanitation but cannot afford it. However, didactic strategies of behaviour change have had rather limited effect, and the commonsense approach of hardware subsidies has not worked: the experience in many countries, with both Government and NGO programmes, has been that about half of the toilets constructed are not used or are used for other purposes.

Community-Led Total Sanitation (CLTS),[1] like SRI, turns conventions on their heads, with radical, simultaneous, mutually-supporting changes. Instead of teaching people, there is facilitation of people's own appraisal and analysis of their own open defecation and its effects. Instead of subsidies for hardware for individual households, people dig their own pits and construct their own latrines. Instead of being handed down engineering designs, people make their own designs. Instead of outside interventions for those least able to construct their own latrines, community members are encouraged to help them. Instead of the number of latrines constructed, the focus is more on how many communities have been verified as open defecation-free.

SRI and CLTS have met with similar resistances from the respective professions. Both confront the stasis of accepted commonsense conventions: these stem from and are locked in by professional training and norms – of rice research scientists and of engineers and others who promote rural sanitation. The lock-ins are reinforced by funding. Funding streams and budgets, and related institutional commitments, have had conservative effects. IRRI has been locked into its funding of multi-year long-term research and the need to justify this, and has variously denied, ignored and declined to evaluate SRI. The 30–40[2] organizations worldwide listed as having worked with SRI do not include IRRI, reputedly the premier rice research institute in the world. As for CLTS, in many parts of India and elsewhere, big budgets once allocated are difficult to turn down, and bring political patronage and bureaucratic incentives, and maintain policies of hardware subsidies inimical to CLTS. With both SRI and CLTS, these forces have combined in resistance, denial and sometimes rubbishing the new approaches.

Both SRI and CLTS entail multiple simultaneous changes of concepts, principles, methods, behaviours, relationships and mindsets. Both are, in a full sense, shifts or flips of paradigm taking us into new spaces with dramatic new potentials. Neither cost much to develop. Both were evolved by doing, hands-on, in local conditions. Both are close to the lives and realities of

---

1.   Kar (2003), Kar and Pasteur (2005), Kar with Chambers (2008), Bongartz and Chambers (2009). Website www.communityledtotalsanitation.org

2.   The listing is in Africare et al. (2010: 35). The imprecision of 30–40 is because some organizations work in several countries and so can be counted in different ways.

poor rural people. Both were discovered by remarkable innovators – Father de Laulanié with SRI in Madagascar in the mid-1980s, and Kamal Kar with CLTS in Bangladesh in early 2000. Both have been spread internationally by champions fired with well-informed enthusiasm – Norman Uphoff with SRI, and Kamal Kar himself with CLTS, both of them quickly joined by many other champions energized through the wonder and excitement of 'seeing is believing' personal experience of dramatic transformations.

These two movements are unstoppable and spreading on a remarkable scale. By mid-2011, the merits of SRI practices have been shown in over 40 countries. The Governments of China, India, Indonesia, Vietnam and Cambodia, where together two-thirds of the world's rice is produced, are promoting SRI methods, based on their own evaluations and results. Worldwide, the number of farmers benefiting from SRI practices is in the range of 2 million and growing rapidly.

In mid-2011, CLTS practices are also found in over 40 countries. Spread has been most extensive in India, Indonesia, Pakistan, Bangladesh, and Ethiopia, with other African countries following hard on their heels. It is increasingly endorsed by governments as policy or approved practice. After quite brutal discounting for over-reporting, and allowing for some negative effects, I have estimated the number of people in communities that have been, with reasonable credibility, been declared open-defecation free as a result of CLTS. By mid-2011 this may have risen as high as 15 million, while millions more should be benefiting in communities which are not yet ODF. And there are indications that the spread of CLTS is exponential.

Both SRI and CLTS have discovered principles with wider applications. SRI principles and practices have been applied to sugarcane, wheat, finger millet, teff and other crops.[1] Some have renamed it SCI, the System of Crop Intensification. CLTS principles and practices have been applied also to solid waste management, for example in Cairo, and to sanitation in urban slums.[2] Further applications in yet other domains may well be discovered. These are early days.

SRI and CLTS raise acute questions. I pose these as challenges to you and to all development professionals:

- Are we disabled by lock-ins to paradigms and mindsets which narrow, focus and frame our vision so that, as with traditional rice research and rural sanitation, we fail to see and find breakthroughs?
- Are there other development liberations from lock-ins waiting to be discovered and promoted?
- If there may be, how should we set about looking for them? How in other words can radical, revolutionary, innovators and disseminators – de Laulanié's, Uphoffs, and Kamal Kars – be found, supported and encouraged?

---

1. See http://sri.ciifad.cornell.edu/aboutsri/othercrops/index.html
2. See http://www.communityledtotalsanitation.org/resources/results/taxonomy%3A19

- Do we need to take more risks and to celebrate failures in development, as Engineers Without Borders[1] do? Should we judge harshly any organization that cannot boast of the risks it takes, and of its failures to prove it? Is lack of failures itself a failure?[2]
- Is one creeping, tightening lock-in the application of neo-Newtonian practices to the local, complex, diverse, dynamic, uncontrollable and unpredictable conditions experienced by so many people living in poverty and prevailing in so many domains of development? Through logframes, inflexible planning, standardized top-down programmes, and target-driven development? And if so, who and where are the liberators?

There may be clues in the commonalities of SRI and CLTS. Both were counter-intuitive. Both confronted and upended unquestioned commonsense and conventions of deeply rooted neo-Newtonian best practice. Both originated from grounded hands-on innovation, observation and awareness. And both followed many years of applied experimental experience – de Laulanié's growing rice and Kamal Kar's in participatory facilitation and development. So does this mean that such people and such conditions should be sought out and supported? The MacArthur Foundation's Fellows Program gets close to this by awarding unrestricted fellowships to talented individuals who have shown extraordinary originality and dedication in their creative pursuits and a marked capacity for self-direction, allowing for bold new work, changing fields or altering career direction.[3] Apart from being restricted to residents or citizens of the United States, the terms of the fellowships resonate with the paradigm of adaptive pluralism. The question is whether they have led, or could lead, to SRIs and CLTSs in other domains.

So finally – are these transformative international movements of SRI and CLTS one-off phenomena? Or are they forerunners of much else waiting to be discovered and spread? Are there similarly paradigmatic flips lurking latent in other improbable domains? And will future generations look back and marvel at how we could have been so timid, unimaginative and lacking in hands-on creativity, that none of us discovered them earlier?

---

1. See http://www.ewb.ca/en/whoweare/accountable/failure.html
2. See http://www.admittingfailures.com
3. See http://www.macfound.org/site/c.lkLXJ8MQKrH/b.4536879/k.9B87/About_the_Program.htm

Stepping Forward: children's and young people's participation in development

Adults underestimate what children can do. And children have capabilities and creativity that most adults have lost: they play, they fail forwards and they learn fast in ways which decline with age. We owe to Dr Zeuss the observation that 'Adults are obsolete children'. Stepping Forward: Children and young people's participation in development *(Vicky Johnson, G. Ivan-Smith, Gill Gordon, Pat Pridmore and Patta Scott eds 1998) is an inspiring and insightful book that illustrates children's often unrecognized abilities and potentials. The book deserves renewed attention. I am puzzled that it has not been read and cited more. I warmly commend it, as you will see from this foreword. Its evidence gives hope that the children and young people of today can help to transform our world for the better.*

Foreword

Participation has entered the mainstream vocabulary of development; inclusion is following hard on its heels. Though practice has lagged behind rhetoric, more and more social groups have been identified as marginal or excluded, and their participation and inclusion seen as priorities. So it has been with women, poor people, ethnic and religious minorities, refugees, the disabled, and the very old. While this has been happening, many have seen children as a different sort of category. Children's health, nutrition and education have long been on the agenda but not their active participation as partners in development.

In part this has reflected the views adults and teachers commonly hold of children and of the young. They are seen as ignorant – to be taught; irresponsible – to be disciplined; immature – to be 'brought up'; incapable – to be protected; a nuisance – 'to be seen and not heard'; or a resource – to be made use of. The pervasive powerlessness of children sustains and reinforces these views; female children or those from low social groups are especially disadvantaged and looked down upon.

With the authority of experience, this book turns these views on their heads. Many old beliefs and attitudes about children cannot survive the evidence presented here: again and again, in different cultures and in whatever context – school, communities or the family, whether as pupils, street children, child labourers or refugees – children are shown to be social actors, with evidence that their capabilities have been underestimated and their realities undervalued.

Appreciating the potentials of children's participation has taken time. An example is the evolution of PRA (participatory rural appraisal) over the past decade. At first, children and younger people were little noticed, even a nuisance. Sometimes they were neutralized by being given something to do –

fetching leaves of different trees, or different grasses, or drawing with chalks or pens – to make them useful, keep them quiet or simply for fun. But soon they demonstrated that they could do more than adults supposed. Like older people, they too could make maps, matrices and diagrams. Moreover these showed that their knowledge, realities, preferences and priorities were valid, and differed from those of women and men. Like other 'lowers' they, too, could be empowered to express and analyse their realities and present them to 'uppers'.

Stepping Forward brings together many other illustrations. The experiences described open up a new and wonderful world in which adults facilitate more than teach, and children show that they can do much more than adults thought they could. So we have here children's participation not just in their own social groups but in conferences, councils and community meetings; children's planning and analysis using techniques of mapping, diagramming and matrix scoring; children as researchers; children taking photographs and videos to document their lives; and children designing and performing their own drama, radio broadcasts and television programmes.

For many of us adults, this is more than an ordinary book. It is an invitation to see and relate to children in new ways. The change of view can be compared with becoming aware of gendered roles and attitudes. It demonstrates how much our mindsets about children, like those about gender roles, are socially constructed and reproduced through power relations.

There is, though, a difference. With gender-awareness there have been many adults, mostly women, able and willing to speak out for themselves and others. For children, in contrast, this is rarely possible. In cultures of adult power it is difficult for them to assert themselves, being as they are at once smaller, weaker, more dependent, less articulate, and less able to meet and organize.

For their reality to be recognized and to count they have then to rely on sensitive insight and enabling by adults. These qualities in adults, though still not common, are shown in full measure by the contributors to this book. Working separately in 30 countries spread through five continents, they have explored similar terrain and made similar discoveries. They have faced similar ethical issues in facilitating children's participation. Coming together in the workshop which gave rise to this book, their experiences generated synergy and an infectious excitement. These are now shared in a measured and balanced manner with a wider audience. Richly diverse in culture and context, the findings converge on striking conclusions: that children across the world can do more, and be more creative, than most adults believe; that children's knowledge, perceptions and priorities often differ from what adults suppose them to be; and that giving children space and encouragement to act and express themselves is doubly fulfilling, with rewards for children and adults alike. So this is a book not just about the participation of children and young people. It is also about new forms of fulfilment for adults, the rewards of sharing power and of enabling those who are younger to discover and express more of their potential.

Let me hope that when our children look back from later in the 21st century, they will see this book as part of a watershed in adult understanding and behaviour towards the young. There is perhaps no more powerful way of transforming human society than changing how the adults of today relate to children, the adults of tomorrow. By sharing their explorations and experiences with children and young people, the contributors and editors of *Stepping Forward* have done good service. Their new understandings of children will make many other adults want to change. Their contributions invite us to join them on a steep learning curve. For this, their insights give us a flying start, for they show us how we can enable children to participate and be included more as partners in development; how we can see, relate to and empower them in new ways; and how we can help them discover for themselves more of their remarkable potentials. The message I take from this book is that if we adults can only change our views and behaviour, children will astonish us with what they can do, be and become, and how in time they can make our world a better place.

What would it take to eliminate poverty in the world?

In August 2005 at the inaugural conference of the International Poverty Centre in Brasilia some of us were challenged on arrival to come up with a two-pager on What would it take to eliminate poverty in the world? As provocations go, this was outrageous. There was little time to think. How could we possibly eliminate poverty? But, provoked, I banged out a note. Here it is, omissions, warts and all. Before you read it, let me challenge you – to write your own list. Then you will see what I missed, and what I may have had that you did not. And what does this say about my mindset and orientation? And what does it say about yours? And where then does this take us, in thinking through what needs to be done, by whom and how? To transform our world.

What do you think it would take to eliminate poverty in the world?

Here then is your blank sheet:

What would it take to eliminate poverty in the world?

'If somebody's well-being is based on the ill-being of someone else it is not a true well-being'. (A poor man in the Kyrgyz Republic)

This question above that I was asked to address is huge. It is unanswerable in the sense that a world without any of the dimensions of human deprivation is inconceivable. But we can make the question less unanswerable by interpreting it as: how can we, humankind, make mega transformations in reducing deprivations and bad experiences of life and enhancing well-being and good experiences of life. Here is a personal view.

'High-level' policy:

- A level playing field: end of agricultural subsidies in the North, trade regimes to favour and protect poorer countries and people
- Elimination of debt
- Improved quality of aid
- Tobin tax
- Tax on airline fuels
- Kyoto plus
- A transformation in political leadership, especially in the USA, UK and other countries, radical reform of funding political parties, etc.
- Progressive taxation and redistributions of wealth
- Peace
- Social justice
- Much stronger, independently funded, UN

... and so on, and so on, and all those nice words – empowerment, partnership, ownership, transparency, accountability, participation, good governance... and all stations to nirvana, not to mention all sorts of imaginative ideas about guaranteed minimum incomes and the like...

Heard it before? The question becomes: what could make these and other good changes come about. The usual answers are that we need policy changes and political will. But these have had time to happen and have not happened, bar marginal shifts and nudges. Will we be saying the same, and asking the same questions, in ten, twenty, a hundred years' time?

Are we missing something?

We focus on 'them', poor people. We see commonalities in deprivation and well-being, but also immense diversity of priorities and needs. Simplifying to only five deprivations – material lack, physical weakness, bad social relations, insecurity, and powerlessness – and their opposites – enough for a good life, physical well-being, security, good social relations, and freedom of choice and action – people's priorities and needs differ so much – by person, gender, family, age, social group, livelihood, location...We have at least made progress in recognizing this diversity and the multidimensionality of poverty.

But should we not also, and even more, focus on 'us', the non-poor, the better off, the wealthy, the powerful? Can we discuss multi-dimensional poverty without multi-dimensional wealth and power? Are they not related? Can poverty be transformed without redistributions of wealth and power? Can policy and practice change without other radical changes? And are key changes professional, institutional, personal and methodological?

The *professional* changes implied are paradigmatic, shifting from the dominant paradigm of things (top-down, standardized, planned, controlled...) more to the paradigm of people (bottom-up, diverse, participatory, autonomous...). This implies radical changes in teaching and learning, in university and other curricula, and in textbooks, and continuous unlearning and new learning among active professionals.

The *institutional* changes implied are many including power and relationships in organizations, with procedures and incentives which empower and foster creative diversity.

The *personal* changes implied are the key to all the others. It is through people, especially those with wealth and those with power, acting differently, that all or any of these changes could be made to happen – the changes in policy, in professionalism, and in institutions. The new focus on power and relationships in development points us towards the personal, towards what sorts of people we are, our behaviours, attitudes and relationships, and what we do and do not do. It also points towards those with the most power and most wealth. It implies complementing rights-based approaches with obligations-based approaches. It opens scope for responsible well-being to be a win–win.

The *methodological* changes relate to all these. The question is whether we need now to shift emphasis and focus, finding new things to do and new ways to do them. Evolving methodologies is a starting point in going to scale. Here is my list of methodologies for development. What is yours?

Methodologies we now need. To learn and spread how to:

A. *Power and wealth*
   • Be better off with less wealth
   • Find fulfilment empowering others
   • Think through the effects of actions and non-actions and take responsibility
B. *Social relations*
   • Bring up children better
   • Improve gender relations
   • Find good expression for the energy of young males
C. *Personal*
   • Conduct immersions, and learn and change
   • Be reflexive, with self-insight into learning and unlearning (not taking oneself too seriously)
   • Combine empathy, insight, commitment and action

So let me lay down a challenge to the International Poverty Centre. One of Brazil's greatest sons gave us *Pedagogy of the Oppressed* (Freire, 1970). Could you now give us Pedagogy for the Non-Oppressed, Pedagogy for the Powerful?

For without such pedagogy, and without the transformations to which it could lead, is there any prospect at all of a world without poverty, a world of well-being for all?

References

Abah, O.S. (2004) 'Voices aloud: making communication and change together', *Participatory Learning and Action* 50: 45–52

Abbott, J., Chambers R., Dunn, C., Harris, T., de Merode, E., Porter, G., Townsend, J. and Werner, D. (1998) 'Participatory GIS: opportunity or oxymoron', *PLA Notes* 23: 27–34

Abebe, D., Catley A., Admassu, B. and Bekele, G. (2009) 'Using participatory impact assessment (PIA) to inform policy: lessons from Ethiopia', in I. Scoones and J. Thompson (eds), *Farmer First Revisited*, pp. 296–300, Practical Action Publishing, Rugby

Abeyasekera, S. (2001) 'Analysis approaches in participatory work involving ranks or scores', Statistical Services Centre, University of Reading, UK

ActionAid (2001) *Transforming Power: Participatory Methodologies Forum*, available from: http://www.asksource.info/pdf/37268_transformingpower_2001.pdf [accessed 5 April 2011]. For a copy of the full report *Transforming Power* please write to David Archer, davida@actionaid.org.uk or ActionAid UK

ActionAid International (2005) *Rights to End Poverty: ActionAid International Strategy 2005/2010*, Johannesburg: AAI, available from: http://216.219.73.118/assets/pdf%5CPolicy_StrategicPlan2005-2010.pdf [accessed 5 April 2011]

ActionAid International (2011) *Immersions: Making Poverty Personal*, available from: www.actionaid.org.uk/100588/immersions.html [accessed 30 March 2011]

Africare, Oxfam America, WWF-ICRISAT Project (2010) 'More rice for people, more water for the planet', WWF-ICRISAT Project, Hyderabad, India

Alfini, N. and Chambers, R. (2007) 'Words count: taking a count of the changing language of British aid', *Development in Practice* 17: 4–5, 492–504

Archer, D. and Newman, K. (compilers) (2003) *Communication and Power: Reflect Practical Resource Materials*, available from: www.reflect-action.org [accessed 25 July 2011]

Attwood, H. and May, J. (1998) 'Kicking down doors and lighting fires: the South African PPA', in J. Holland with J. Blackburn (eds), *Whose Voice? Participatory research and policy change*, pp. 119–130, Practical Action Publishing, Rugby

Australia Indonesia Partnership (2010) 'Indonesia reality check main study findings: listening to poor people's realities about basic education', Australia-Indonesia Basic Education Program, available from: http://www.ausaid.gov.au/publications/pdf/aibep-reality-check-report.pdf [accessed 5 April 2011]

Barahona, C. and Levy, S. (2003) 'How to generate statistics and influence policy using participatory methods in research: reflections on work in Malawi 1999–2002', IDS Working Paper 212, Institute of Development Studies, Brighton, available from: http://www.utoronto.ca/mcis/q2/papers/IV_Barahona_Levy.pdf [accessed 5 April 2011]

Barahona, C. and Levy, S. (2007) 'The best of both worlds: producing national statistics using participatory methods', *World Development* 35, 2: 326–41, available from: http://www.sciencedirect.com/science/article/B6VC6-4MT59F2-2/2/4a8e43345da3c60149e4fbf0b7290c14 [accessed 5 April 2011]

Berger, P. L. (1977) *Pyramids of Sacrifice: Political ethics and social change*, Penguin Books Harmondsworth, UK

Bird, B. and Kakande, M. (2001) *The Uganda Participatory Poverty Assessment Process* in Norton with others *A Rough Guide to PPAs*, Overseas Development Institute, London

Bongartz, P. and Chambers, R. with Kar, K. (2009) 'Beyond subsidies – triggering a revolution in rural sanitation', *IDS In Focus Policy Briefing*, Issue 10, Institute of Development Studies, Brighton

Boudreau, T. (2009) 'Livelihoods impact analysis and seasonality in Ethiopia', paper to IDS conference, July, Brighton, UK

Broad, R. (2007) 'Knowledge management': a case study of the World Bank's research department', *Development in Practice* 17: 4–5, pp. 700–708

Brock, K. (1999) 'It's not only wealth that matters – it's peace of mind too': a review of participatory work on poverty and illbeing, consultations with the poor, prepared for Global Synthesis Workshop September 22–23, 1999, Poverty Group, PREM, World Bank, Washington DC

Brock, K. and Pettit, J. (eds) (2007) *Springs of participation: Creating and evolving methods for participatory development*, Practical Action Publishing, Rugby

Burn, R.W. (2000) *Quantifying and Combining Causal Diagrams*, Statistical Services Centre, University of Reading, UK

Capra, F. (1996) *The Web of Being: A New Synthesis of Mind and Matter,* Harper Collins, London

Catley, A. (2009) 'From marginal to normative: institutionalizing participatory epidemiology', in I. Scoones and J. Thompson (eds), *Farmer First Revisited*, pp. 247–254, Practical Action Publishing, Rugby

Catley, A., Burns, J., Abebe, D. and Suji, S. (2008) *Participatory Impact Assessment: A guide for practitioners*, Feinstein International Center, Tufts University, USA

Chambers, R. (1979) 'Simple is sophisticated', *Development Forum* 6

Chambers, R. (1983) *Rural Development: Putting the last first*, Longman Scientific and Technical, Harlow

Chambers, R. (1995a) 'Professionals and the powerless: whose reality counts?' *Choices: The Human Development Magazine* 4(1): 14–15, UNDP, New York

Chambers, R. (1995b) 'Editorial: responsible well-being: a personal agenda for development', *World Development* 25(11): 1743–54

Chambers, R. (1997) *Whose Reality Counts? Putting the First Last*, Earthscan, London

Chambers, R. (2001) 'The World Development Report: concepts, content and a chapter 12', *Journal of International Development* 13: 299–306

Chambers, R. (2002) *Participatory Workshops: a sourcebook of 21 sets of ideas and activities*, Earthscan, London and Sterling VA

Chambers, R. (2005) *Ideas for Development*, Earthscan, London and Sterling VA

Chambers, R. (2006a) 'Poverty unperceived: traps, biases and agenda', *IDS Working Paper* 270, Institute of Development Studies, Brighton

Chambers, R. (2006b) 'Transforming power: from zero-sum to win–win?', in Eyben et al. (eds) *Power: Exploring power for change*, IDS Bulletin 37(6): 99–110, Institute of Development Studies, Brighton

Chambers, R. (2007) 'Who counts? The quiet revolution of participation and numbers', *IDS Working Paper* 296, Institute of Development Studies,

Brighton, available from: http://www.ntd.co.uk/idsbookshop/details. asp?id=1006 [accessed 5 April 2011]

Chambers, R. (2008) *Revolutions in Development Inquiry*, Earthscan, London and Sterling VA

Chambers, R. (2010) 'Paradigms, poverty and adaptive pluralism', *IDS Working Paper* 334, Institute of Development Studies, Brighton, available from: http://www.ibcperu.org/doc/isis/12789.pdf [accessed 5 April 2011]

Chambers, R., Longhurst, R. and Pacey, A. (eds) (1981) *Seasonal Dimensions to Rural Poverty*, Frances Pinter, London

Chambers, R., Saxena, N.C. and Shah, T. (1989) *To the Hands of the Poor: Water and Trees*, Oxford IBH Publishers, New Delhi, and Intermediate Technology Publishers, London

Chapman, J. and Mancini, A. (eds) (2005) *Critical Webs of Power and Change: Resource Pack for Planning, Reflection and Learning in People-centred Advocacy*, ActionAid International, Johannesburg

Coleman, H. (ed.) (2007) 'Words, power and the personal in development', *Language and Development: Africa and Beyond*, British Council, Addis Ababa

Collier, P. (2007) *The Bottom Billion: Why the Poorest Countries Are Failing and What Can Be Done About It*, Oxford University Press, Oxford

Cooke, B. and Kothari, U. (eds) (2001) *Participation: The New Tyranny?* Zed Books, London and New York

Cornwall, A. (2007) 'Buzzwords and fuzzwords: deconstructing development discourse', *Development in Practice* 17(4–5): 471–484

Cornwall, A. and Eade, D. (eds) (2010) *Deconstructing Development Discourse: Buzzwords and Fuzzwords*, Practical Action Publishing, Rugby, UK in association with Oxfam GB

Cornwall, A. and Welbourn, A. (eds) (2002) *Realising Rights: Transforming approaches to sexual and reproductive well-being*, Zed Books, London

Cornwall, A. and White, S.C. (eds) (2000) 'Men, masculinities and development: politics, policies and practice', *IDS Bulletin* 31.2, Institute of Development Studies, Brighton

Cox, S., Currie, D., Frederick, K., Jarvis, D., Lawes, S., Millner, E., Nudd, K., Robinson-Pant, A., Stubbs, I., Taylor, T. and White, D. (2006) *Children Decide: Power, Participation and Purpose in the Primary Classroom*, School of Education and Lifelong Learning, University of East Anglia, Norwich

CPRC (2005) *Chronic Poverty Report 2004–05*, Chronic Poverty Research Centre, Institute for Development Policy and Management, University of Manchester, Manchester

Cromwell, E., Kambewa, P., Mwanza, R. and Chirwa, R. with KWERA Development Centre (2001) 'Impact assessment using participatory approaches: "starter pack" and sustainable agriculture in Malawi', *Network Paper No 112*, Agricultural Research and Extension Network, Overseas Development Institute, London

DAC (2005) *Paris Declaration on Aid Effectiveness: ownership, harmonisation, alignment, results and mutual accountability*, Development Advisory Committee of the OECD, Paris, available from: http://www.adb.org/media/ articles/2005/7033_international_community_aid/paris_declaration.pdf [accessed 5 April 2011] de Boinod, A.J. (2005) *The Meaning of Tingo and Other Extraordinary Words from Around the World*, Penguin Books, London

Devereux, S., Longhurst R. and Sabates-Wheeler, R. (eds) (forthcoming) *Seasonality, Rural Livelihoods and Development*, Earthscan, London and Sterling VA

Devereux, S., Vaitla, B. and Swan, S.H. (2008) *Seasons of Hunger: fighting cycles of quiet starvation among the world's rural poor*, Pluto Press, London

Dogbe, Tony (1998) 'The one who rides the donkey does not know the ground is hot: CEDEP's involvement in the Ghana PPA', in J. Holland with J. Blackburn (eds) *Whose Voice? Participatory research and policy change*, pp. 97–102, Practical Action Publishers, Rugby

Eade, D. (2007) 'Editorial', *Development in Practice* 17(4–5): pp. 467–470

Eyben, R. (2004) 'Immersions for personal and policy change', *IDS Policy Briefing* Issue 22, Institute of Development Studies, Brighton

Eyben, R. (ed.) (2006) *Relationships for Aid*, Earthscan, London and Sterling, VA

Eyben, R. and Moncrieffe, J. (2006) 'The power of labelling in development practice', *IDS Policy Briefing*, Issue 28, Institute of Development Studies, Brighton

Eyben, R., Harris, C. and Pettit, J. (2006) 'Power: exploring power for change', *IDS Bulletin* 37 Number 6, Institute of Development Studies, Brighton

Fox, K. (2005) *Watching the English: the Hidden Rules of English Behaviour*, Hodder and Stoughton, London

Freire, P. (1970) *Pedagogy of the Oppressed*, The Seabury Press, New York

Freud, S. (1901) *The Psychopathology of Everyday Life*, English translation published in Pelican Books, Harmondsworth, UK

Gaventa, J. (2006) 'Finding the spaces for changes: a power analysis', in Eyben et al. (eds) *Power: Exploring power for change*, IDS Bulletin 37, Number 6, pp. 23–33, Institute of Development Studies, Brighton

George, R. (2008) *The Big Necessity: Adventures in the world of human waste*, Portobello Books, London

Gill, G. (1998) 'Using PRA for agricultural policy analysis in Nepal: the Tarai research network foodgrain study', in J. Holland with J. Blackburn (eds), *Whose Voice? Participatory research and policy change*, pp. 11–27, Practical Action Publishing, Rugby

Gill, G.J. (1991) *Seasonality and Agriculture in the Developing World: a problem of the poor and powerless*, Cambridge University Press, Cambridge

Gomucio-Dagron, A. and Tufte, T. (eds) (2006) *Communication for Social Change: Anthology and Contemporary Readings*, Communication for Social Change Consortium, New Jersey, USA

Groves, L. (2005) *UNHCR's Age and Gender Mainstreaming Pilot Project 2004: Synthesis Report*, Geneva: United Nations High Commissioners for Refugees Evaluation and Policy Analysis Unit, available from: www.unhcr.org/epau [accessed 23 June 2006]

Groves, L. and Hinton, R. (2004) *Inclusive Aid: Changing Power and Relationships in International Development*, Earthscan, London

Guijt, I. (ed.) (2007) *Negotiated Learning: Collaborative Monitoring in Resource Management*, Resources for the Future, Washington DC

Guijt, I. and Shah, M.K. (1998) *The Myth of Community: Gender issues in participatory development*, ITDG Publishing, London (now Practical Action Publishing, Rugby)

Hadley, S. (2010) *Seasonality and Access to Education: the case of primary education in sub-Saharan Africa*, Consortium for Research on Educational Access, Transitions and Equity, Create Pathways to Access Research Monograph 31, Centre for International Education, University of Sussex, Brighton

Harrell-Bond, B. (1986) *Imposing Aid: Emergency Assistance to Refugees*, Oxford University Press, Oxford, New York, Nairobi

Harris, C. (2006) 'Doing development with men: some reflections on a case study from Mali', in Eyben et al. (eds), 'The power of labelling in development practice', *IDS Policy Briefing*, Issue 28, pp. 47–56, Institute of Development Studies, Brighton

Hartmann, B. and Boyce, J. (1983) *Quiet Violence: View from a Bangladesh Village*, Zed Press, London

Haswell, M. (1975) *The Nature of Poverty: a case-history of the first quarter-century after World War II*, Macmillan, London and Basingstoke

Hickey, S. and Giles, M. (eds) (2004) *Participation: From Tyranny to Transformation? Exploring New Approaches to Participation in Development*, Zed Books, London and New York

Holland, J. with Blackburn, J. (eds) (1998) *Whose Voice? Participatory research and policy change*, Intermediate Technology Publications, (now Practical Action Publishing, Rugby)

Humphrey, J. (2009) 'Child undernutrition, tropical enteropathy, toilets, and handwashing', *The Lancet* 374 (9694): 1032–1035, 19 September

International HIV/AIDS Alliance (2003) *Developing HIV/AIDS Work with Drug Users: a guide to participatory assessment and response*, available from: http://www.aidsalliance.org/publicationsdetails.aspx?id=88 [accessed 19 December 2010]

Irvine, R., Chambers, R. and Eyben, R. (2006) 'Relations with people living in poverty: learning from immersions', in Eyben, R. (ed.) *Relationships for Aid*, pp. 63–79, Earthscan, London

Jackson, C. and Palmer-Jones, R. (1999) 'Rethinking gendered poverty and work', *Development and Change* 30(3): 557–583

Jennings, S. and McGrath, J. (2009) 'Whatever happened to the seasons?', paper for the Future Agricultures Consortium International Conference on Seasonality, IDS Sussex, July

Jodha, N.S. (1988) 'Poverty debate in India: a minority view', *Economic and Political Weekly* Special Number: 2421–28, November

Johansson, L. (1995) 'Reforming donor driven projects and state bureaucracies through PRA', *Forests, Trees and People Newsletter* 26/27: 62–3

Johnson, V., Ivan-Smith, E., Gordon, G., Pridmore, P. and Scott, P. (eds) (1998) *Stepping Forward: Children and Young People's Participation in Development*, Intermediate Technology Publications, London (now Practical Action Publishing, Rugby)

Jolly, S. (2006) 'Sexuality and Development', *IDS Policy Briefing* 29, Institute of Development Studies, Brighton, available from: http://www.ids.ac.uk/index.cfm?objectid=FA0BA902-5056-8171-7B9CCFC1C9FBC076 [accessed 5 April 2011]

Jung, C.G. (1916) *On the Psychology of the Unconscious*, Moffat, Yard and Co., New York

Jupp, D. (2003) 'Views of the poor: the perspectives of rural poor in Tanzania as recounted through their stories and pictures', Swiss Agency for Development and Cooperation, Berne

Jupp, D. (2004) 'Views of the poor: some thoughts on how to involve your own staff to conduct quick, low cost but insightful research into poor people's perspectives, based on the experience of SDC Tanzania in Morogoro in 2002', available on request from the author djupp@btinternet.com

Jupp, D. and Sohel Ibn Ali with contributions from C.E. Barahona (2010) *Measuring Empowerment? Ask Them: quantifying qualitative outcomes from people's own analysis – insights for results-based management from the experience of a social movement in Bangladesh,* Sida, Stockholm, available from: http://www. powercube.net/wp-content/uploads/2010/07/measuring-empowerment_ -ask-them.pdf [accessed 5 April 2011]

Kanbur, R. (2007) 'Basrabai, Meeraiben, and the master of Mohadi', *Participatory Learning and Action* 57(1): pp. 15–16

Kane, E., Bruce, L. and O'Reilly de Brun, M. (1997) 'Designing the future together: PRA and education policy in The Gambia', in J. Holland with J. Blackburn (eds), *Whose Voice? Participatory research and policy change*, pp. 31–43, Practical Action Publishing, Rugby

Kaner, S., Lind, L., Toldi, C., Fisk, S. and Berger, D. (1996) *Facilitator's Guide to Participatory Decision-Making*, Gabriola Island, BC, New Society Publishers, Canada

Kar, K. (2003) *Subsidy or Self-Respect? Participatory Total Sanitation in Bangladesh,* Workjing Paper 184, Institute of Development Studies, Brighton

Kar, K. and Bongartz, P. (2006) 'Latest update to subsidy or self-respect. Update to IDS working paper 257', Institute of Development Studies, Brighton, available from: http://www.communityledtotalsanitation.org/ resource/latest-update-subsidy-or-self-respect-update-ids-working-paper-257 [accessed 5 April 2011]

Kar, K. with Chambers, R. (2008) *Handbook of Community Led Total Sanitation,* Institute of Development Studies, Brighton and Plan UK, London

Kar, K. and Pasteur, K. (2005) 'Subsidy or self-respect? Community Led Total Sanitation. An update on recent developments', *IDS Working Paper* 257, Institute of Development Studies, Brighton

Khaila, S. et al. (1999) 'Malawi: consultations with the poor', prepared for the Global Synthesis Workshop, September 22–23, 1999, Poverty Group, PREM, World Bank, Washington DC

Krishna, A. (2007) 'The stages-of-progress methodology and results from five countries', in Moser (ed.), pp. 62–79, *Reducing Global Poverty*, Brookings, Washington DC

Krishna, A. (2010) *One Illness Away: why people become poor and how they escape poverty*, Oxford University Press, Oxford

Kumar, S. (1996) 'ABC of PRA report on the South-South workshop on PRA: attitudes and behaviour, Bangalore and Madurai', PRAXIS, New Delhi, India

Lawson, D., Hulme, D., Matin, I. and Moore, K. (eds) 2010 *What Works for the Poorest? Poverty reduction programmes for the world's extreme poor*, Practical Action Publishing, Rugby

Levy, S. (2003) 'Are we targeting the poor? Lessons from Malawi', *PLA Notes* 47:19–24

Levy, S. (ed.) (2005) *Starter Pack: a Strategy to Fight Hunger in Developing Countries?*, CABI Publishing, Wallingford, UK

Levy, S. (2007) 'Using numerical data from participatory research to support the Millennium Development Goals: The case for locally owned information systems', in K. Brock and J. Pettit (eds), pp. 137–149, *Springs of Participation*, Practical Action Publishing, Rugby

Lipton, M. (1977) *Why Poor People Stay Poor: a study of urban bias in world development*, Temple Smith, London

Lipton, M. (1986) 'Seasonality and ultrapoverty', in R. Longhurst (ed.), *Seasonality and Poverty, IDS Bulletin* 17(3): 4–8

Longhurst, R. (ed.) (1986) *Seasonality and Poverty*, IDS Bulletin 17(3), Institute of Development Studies, Brighton

Lunch, N. and Lunch, C. (2006) *Insights into Participatory Video: A Handbook for the Field*, Insight, Oxford

May, J. with Attwood, H., Ewang, P., Lund, F., Norton, A. and Wentzal, W. (1998) 'Experience and perceptions of poverty in South Africa, final report', Praxis Publishing, Durban

Mayoux, L. and Chambers, R. (2005) 'Reversing the paradigm: quantification, participatory methods and pro-poor impact assessment', *Journal of International Development* 17: 271–298, Wiley InterScience, available from: www.interscience.wiley.com [accessed 5 April 2011]

McCarthy, J. with Galvao, K. (2004) *Enacting Participatory Development: Theatre-Based Techniques*, Earthscan, London and Sterling VA

Mehta, L. and Movik, S. (eds) (2011) *Shit Matters*, Practical Action Publishing, Rugby

Milimo, J., Norton, A. and Owen, D. (1998) 'The impact of PRA approaches and methods on policy and practice: the Zambia PPA', in J. Holland with J. Blackburn (eds), *Whose Voice? Participatory research and policy change*, pp. 103–111, Practical Action Publishing, Rugby

Moser, C. and Holland, J. (1998) 'Can policy-focused research be participatory? Research on poverty and violence in Jamaica using PRA methods', in J. Holland with J. Blackburn (eds), *Whose Voice? Participatory research and policy change*, pp. 44–56, Practical Action Publishing, Rugby

Moser, C. and McIlwaine, C. (2004) *Encounters with Violence in Latin America: Urban poor perceptions from Colombia and Guatemala*, Routledge, New York and London

Nagasundari, S. (2007) 'Evolution of the internal learning system: a case study of the New Entity for Social Action', in K. Brock and J. Pettit (eds), *Springs of Participation: Creating and evolving methods for participatory development*, pp. 81–91, Practical Action Publishing, Rugby

Narayan, D., Chambers, R., Shah, M. and Petesch, P. (1999) 'Global synthesis, consultations with the poor, summary', prepared for the Global Synthesis Workshop, September 22–23, 1999, Poverty Group, PREM, World Bank, Washington DC

Narayan, D. with Patel, R., Schafft, K., Rademacher, A. and Koch-Schulte, S. (2000a) *Voices of the poor: Can Anyone Hear Us?*, Oxford University Press for the World Bank

Narayan, D., Chambers, R., Shah, M. and Petesch, P. (2000b) *Voices of the poor: Crying Out for Change*, Oxford University Press for the World Bank

Narendranath, D. (2007) 'Steering the boat of life with the Internal Learning System: the oar of learning', in K. Brock and J. Pettit (eds), *Springs of Participation: Creating and evolving methods for participatory development*, pp. 67–79, Practical Action Publishing, Rugby

Noponen, H. (2007) 'It's not just about the pictures! It's also about principle, process and power: tensions in the development of the Internal Learning System', in K. Brock and J. Pettit (eds), *Springs of Participation: Creating and evolving methods for participatory development*, pp. 53–65, Practical Action Publishing, Rugby

Norton, A. with Bird, B., Brock, K., Kakande, M. and Turk, C. (2001) *A Rough Guide to PPAs: Participatory Poverty Assessment: an introduction to the theory and practice*, Overseas Development Institute, London

OECD (2005) *Paris Declaration on Aid Effectiveness: ownership, harmonisation, alignment, results and mutual accountability*, High Level Forum, 28 February–2 March, Development Assistance Committee of the OECD, Paris

Orwell, G. (1945) *Animal Farm*, Martin Secker and Warburg, London

Parasuraman, S., Gomathy, Raj, K. and Fernandez, B. (2003) *Listening to People Living in Poverty*, Books for Change, Bangalore

Patt, A. (2005) 'Effects of seasonal climate forecasts and participatory workshops among subsistence farmers in Zimbabwe', *Proceedings of the National Academy of Sciences of the United States of America* 102(35): 12,623–12,628

Pettit, J. (2006) 'Power and pedagogy: learning for reflective development practice', *Exploring Power for Change*, IDS Bulletin 37(6): 69–78

PLA (2005) 'Tools for Influencing Power and Policy', *Participatory Learning and Action*, Issue 53

PLA (2006) 'Mapping for change: practice, technologies and communication', *Participatory Learning and Action*, Issue 54, available from: http://www.planotes.org/pla_backissues/54.html [accessed 5 January 2011]

PLA (2007) 'Immersions: learning about poverty face-to-face', *Participatory Learning and Action*, Issue 57, available from: http://pubs.iied.org/pdfs/14558IIED.pdf [accessed 20 March 2011]

Potter, R.B., Binns, T., Elliott, J.A. and David Smith, D. (2008) *Geographies of Development: an introduction to development studies*, 3rd edn, Pearson Education, Harlow, UK

Praxis (1999) 'Consultations with the poor: India 1999, country synthesis report', Consultations with the Poor, prepared for Global Synthesis Workshop, September 22–23, 1999, Poverty Group, PREM, World Bank, Washington, DC

Praxis (2007) *Participatory Poverty Assessments: a guide for critical practitioners*, PRAXIS – Institute for Participatory Practices, New Delhi

Prüss-Üstün, A. and Corvalán, C. (2006) *Preventing Disease through Healthy Environments*, WHO, Geneva

Rambaldi, G., Chambers, R., McCall, M. and Fox, J. (2006) 'Practical ethics for PGIS practitioners, facilitators, technology intermediaries and researchers', *Participatory Learning and Action* 54: 106–13

Reining, C. (1966) *The Zande Scheme: an anthropological case study of economic development in Africa*, Northwestern University Press

Robb, C.M. (2002) *Can the Poor Influence Policy? Participatory Poverty Assessments in the Developing World*, 2nd edn, International Monetary Fund and the World Bank, Washington DC

ROK (2010) 'The Proposed Constitution of Kenya', Government Printer, Republic of Kenya, 6 May

Sachs, J. (2005) *The End of Poverty: how we can make it happen in our lifetime*, Penguin Books, London

Sahn, D.E. (ed.) (1989) *Seasonal Variability in Third World Agriculture: the consequences for food security*, The Johns Hopkins Press, Baltimore

Scarry, E. (1985) *The Body in Pain: The making and unmaking of the world*, Oxford University Press, New York

Schofield, S. (1974) 'Seasonal factors affecting nutrition in different age groups, and especially preschool children', *Journal of Development Studies* 11(1): 22–40

Schoonmaker Freudenberger, K. (1998) 'The use of PRA to inform policy: tenure issues in Madagascar and Guinea', in J. Holland with J. Blackburn (eds), *Whose Voice? Participatory research and policy change*, pp. 67–84, Practical Action Publishing, Rugby

Scoones, I. and Thompson, J. (2009) (eds) *Farmer First Revisited: Innovation for Agricultural Research and Development*, Practical Action Publishing, Rugby

SDC (2003) *Views of the Poor: the perspectives of Rural and Urban Poor in Tanzania as recounted through their stories and pictures*, Swiss Agency for Development and Cooperation, Bern

Shah, A. (2007) 'Reality check: accountability, learning, and practice with the people who matter', *Participatory Learning and Action* 57: 107–116

Shah, M.K., Kambou, S.D., and Monihan B. (1999) *Embracing Participation in Development: Worldwide experience from CARE's reproductive health programs with a step-by-step field guide to participatory tools and techniques*, CARE, Atlanta

Sida (2008, 2009, 2010) *Reality Check Bangladesh 2007, 2008 and 2009* (respectively) *Listening to Poor People's Realities about Primary Healthcare and Primary Education*, Sida and GRM International, available from: www.sida.se [accessed on 5 April 2011]

Smita (2008) 'Distress seasonal migration and its impact on children's education', *Create Pathways to Access Research Monograph No.28*, Centre for International Education, University of Sussex and National University of Educational Planning and Administration, New Delhi

Spicker, P. (2007) *The Idea of Poverty*, The Policy Press, University of Bristol, Bristol

Spicker, P., Leguizamon, S.A. and Gordon, D. (eds) (2007) *Poverty: an international glossary*, 2nd edn, Zed Books, London

Sumner, A. (2010a) 'Global poverty and the new bottom billion: three-quarters of the world's poor live in middle-income countries', *IDS Working Paper* 349, Institute of Development Studies, Brighton

Sumner, A. (2010b) 'The new bottom billion and the MDGs – a plan of action', *IDS in Focus Policy Briefing*, Institute of Development Studies, Brighton

Thaler, R.H. and Sunstein, C.R. (2008) *Nudge: Improving Decisions About Health, Wealth, and Happiness*, Yale University Press, New Haven and London

Townsend, P. (1993) *The International Analysis of Poverty*, Harvester Wheatsheaf, New York and London

UNDP, Bangladesh (1996) 'UNDP's 1996 report on human development in Bangladesh, vol 3 poor people's perspectives', UNDP Dhaka

UNHCR (2006) *Facilitator's Guide for the Workshop on Participatory Assessment in Operations: Age, Gender and Diversity Analysis*, United Nations High Commissioner for Refugees, Geneva

Vallely, P. (2006) 'Bono: The Missionary', *The Independent*, London

VeneKlasen, L. and Miller, V. (2002) *A New Weave of Power, People and Politics: The Action Guide for Advocacy and Citizen Participation*, World Neighbours, Oklahoma City

Vermeulen, S. (2005) 'Power tools for participatory learning and action', *Participatory Learning and Action* 53: 9–15

Wallace, T. with Bornstein, L. and Chapman, C. (2006) *The Aid Chain: Coercion and Commitment in Development NGOs*, ITDG Publishing, London (now Practical Action Publishing, Rugby

Welbourn, A. (1991) 'RRA and the analysis of difference', *RRA Notes* 14: 14–23

Welbourn, A. (2002) 'Gender, sex and HIV: How to address issues that no one wants to hear about', in A. Cornwall and A. Welbourn (eds), pp. 99–112, *Realising Rights*, ZED Books, London

White, S. and Pettit, J. (2004) 'Participatory methods and the measurement of well-being', *Participatory Learning and Action* 50: 88–96

WHO/UNICEF (2010) 'Progress on sanitation and drinking-water: 2010 update', WHO/UNICEF Joint Monitoring Programme for Water Supply and Sanitation, WHO Geneva

Wilkinson, R. and Pickett, K. (2009) *The Spirit Level: why more equal societies almost always do better*, Allen Lane published by the Penguin Group, London

Wilks, A. and Lefrançois, F. (2002) *Blinding with Science or Encouraging Debate? How World Bank Analysis Determines PRSP [Poverty Reduction Strategy Papers] Policies*, (Bretton Woods Project), World Vision International, London

World Bank (1988) 'Rural development: World Bank experience 1965–86', Operations Evaluation Department, World Bank

World Bank (1994) *The World Bank and Participation*, Operations Policy Department, World Bank, Washington DC

World Bank (1996) *The World Bank Participation Sourcebook*, World Bank, Washington DC

World Bank (1999) *Consultations with the Poor: Process Guide for the 20 Country Study for the World Development Report 2000/01*, Poverty Group, PREM Network, The World Bank, Washington, DC

World Bank (2000) *World Development Report 2000–2001: Attacking Poverty*, Oxford University Press, New York and Oxford

World Bank (2008) *Environmental Health and Child Survival: Epidemiology, Economics, Experiences*, The World Bank, Washington DC

World Bank Counterpart Consortium Kyrgyzstan (1999) *Consultations with the Poor, Participatory Poverty Assessment in the Kyrgyz Republic, National Synthesis Report*, Bishkek, Kyrgyz Republic,and World Bank, Washington, DC

World Bank Operations Evaluation Department (2005) *The Effectiveness of World Bank Support for Community-Based and -Driven Development*. World Bank Operations Evaluation Department, Washington DC

A few useful websites

Note: it is sometimes faster to use an internet search engine for particular documents

www.eldis.org is 'a gateway to global development information on international development issues'

www.ids.ac.uk/go/bookshop for publications of the Institute of Development Studies, Brighton, UK

www.pnet.ids.ac.uk/ gives access to an online searchable database of over 5,000 documents on participatory approaches to development, including topics like rights, governance and citizenship

www.ppgis.net for an open forum (English, French, Spanish, Portuguese) on Participatory GIS

www.iapad.org for information and sources on community mapping, PGIS, and P3DM

www.powercube.net for the Power Cube and understanding power for social change

www.policy-powertools.org for 26 techniques, tactics and tips for policy influence in natural resource management

www.iied.org and http://pubs.iied.org for publications of the International Institute for Environment and Development

http://sri.ciifad.cornell.edu/ for the System of Rice Intensification. For India, www.sri-india.net/. For the System of Crop Intensification http://sri.ciifad.cornell.edu/aboutsri/othercrops/index.html

www.communityledtotalsanitation.org for Community-Led Total Sanitation including the Handbook in eight languages, many other materials, and information about CLTS in over 40 countries, and the international glossary of shit.

www.reflect-action.org for Reflect, an innovative approach to adult learning and social change.

www.actionaid.org.uk/100588/immersions.html and www.exposure-dialog.de and http://pubs.iied.org/pdfs/14558IIED.pdf for immersions

www.aidsalliance.org/publicationsdetails.aspx?id=88 for publications on HIV/AIDS, including participatory approaches

www.planotes.org/pla_backissues/54.html for back issues of RRA Notes, PLA Notes, and PLA (Participatory Learning and Action)

www.ewb.ca/en/whoweare/accountable/failure.html for Engineers Without Borders annual failure reports 2008. Also www.admittingfailures.com

Index